Foundations of Information Ethics

Foundations of Information Ethics

Edited by John T. F. Burgess
and Emily J. M. Knox

Foreword by Robert Hauptman

ALA
Neal-Schuman

CHICAGO :: 2019

Extensive effort has gone into ensuring the reliability of the information in this book; however, the publisher makes no warranty, express or implied, with respect to the material contained herein.

ISBNs
978-0-8389-1722-0 (paper)
978-0-8389-1850-0 (PDF)
978-0-8389-1849-4 (ePub)
978-0-8389-1851-7 (Kindle)

Library of Congress Cataloging-in-Publication Data
Names: Burgess, John T. F., editor. | Knox, Emily, 1976- editor.
Title: Foundations of information ethics / edited by John T.F. Burgess and Emily J.M. Knox ;
    foreword by Robert Hauptman.
Description: Chicago : ALA Neal-Schuman, 2019. | Includes bibliographical references.
Identifiers: LCCN 2018053595 | ISBN 9780838917220 (paper: alk. paper) | ISBN 9780838918494 (epub) |
    ISBN 9780838918500 (pdf) | ISBN 9780838918517 (Kindle)
Subjects: LCSH: Information technology—Moral and ethical aspects. | Information science—
    Moral and ethical aspects.
Classification: LCC QA76.9.M65 F68 2019 | DDC 175—dc23 LC record available at
    https://lccn.loc.gov/2018053595

Cover design by Kim Thornton. Cover image ©Will/Adobe Stock.
Book design and composition by Karen Sheets de Gracia in the Cardea and Acumin Pro typefaces.

♾ This paper meets the requirements of ANSI/NISO Z39.48–1992 (Permanence of Paper).

Printed in the United States of America
23 22 21 20 19   5 4 3 2 1

CONTENTS

FOREWORD

Robert Hauptman

Things have changed dramatically since I first used the term information ethics (IE) thirty years ago and subsequently founded the *Journal of Information Ethics.* The concept caught on slowly, first in library and information science and then in other disciplines. A few of us massaged and propagated it at conferences and workshops and in publications. And I scrupulously followed its development and evolution by monitoring journals and citation indices. Quite early, Martha Montague Smith decided to return to school to earn a second doctorate; she wrote the first dissertation on IE (at the University of North Carolina) and I served as the outside reader. One might say that eventually things exploded and IE could be found almost everywhere. A Google search for the precise term *information ethics* brings up 202,0000 hits and, amazingly, there are 620 YouTube videos available on the subject. This is all to the good, I think, because an ethical attitude to the production, dissemination, storage, access, and retrieval of information and data is beneficial and necessary to a well-functioning information society; this is affirmed by crisis after crisis concerning false news, fake facts, social media privacy invasions, and everything else.

Scholars have written about IE at great length, but surprisingly there have been very few monographic treatments (and some books that include the phrase in their titles may not home in precisely on the topic). Even my own recent study will not appear until 2019. Therefore, it is a wonderful occasion to celebrate the publication of *Foundations of Information Ethics,* which offers twelve chapters, some conceptual in nature (see Burgess, chapter 1) and others with a more practical emphasis (see Henderson, chapter 7) on privacy, cybersecurity, or human rights, for example, that are subsets of information ethics.

In chapter 1, John T. F. Burgess delineates guiding principles and concepts in a unique and enticing narrative framework, makes a case for argumentation, rightly insists that "information ethics may . . . provide normative, or morally guiding, principles," and presents an extremely useful, concise contextual overview of four ethical systems: deontology, consequentialism, character ethics, and contractual ethics. His chapter is an exemplary introduction to the means by which information professionals and others can proceed ethically in trying informational times. Kathrine Andrews Henderson (chapter 7) discusses intellectual property ethics, which is a difficult concept because property rights are based in law, and law and ethical commitment sometimes clash. It is difficult to strike a balance between different rights holders. She presciently notes that "The natural right of private property is one way of examining the ethics of the laws protecting the various types of intellectual property. However, another approach might also be applied—justice as fairness." Amelia Gibson's chapter 12 lays out an array of emerging issues so diverse and so pressing that one reels in fear: ethical problems with algorithmic bias, social media, marketing, fake news, open data, 3-D printing, AI, and health data ownership.

In other chapters, we learn that "increasingly, a central aspect of human rights is information," and that "it is more accurate to say that there is not a digital divide but many digital divides along economic, geographic, technical infrastructure, skills, gender, race, income, and other lines of separation." (Big) data presents innumerable, sometimes insurmountable ethical problems, but "at the same time, researchers in cybersecurity lack agreement upon common ethical principles and some remain unconvinced of the possibility of establishing a universal framework that can address the realm of cybersecurity at all." Cognitive justice insists that "different forms of knowledge . . . [are] equal to other forms of knowledge . . . [and have] the right to exist," and therefore "all forms of knowledge are valid and should co-exist in a dialogic relationship to each other." And we learn many other things.

A similar structure in many of the chapters lends an additional layer of continuity. Sections present continuing issues and concerns, case studies, primary source materials, and further reading, and may supplement the lists of references.

The extreme diversity of these chapters offers the reader an opportunity to survey the entire IE field and come away with a replete understanding of where we stand and where we must go to avoid the pitfalls that currently stalk us, whether we reside in the US, Western Europe, Russia, China, or Botswana. The global informational world is unbounded. We are all part of a single whole and should act with responsible ethical commitment to avoid censorious, disinformational, invasive, demagogic, or totalitarian control.

PREFACE

In January 2016, at the annual meeting of the Association for Library and Information Science Education, the Information Ethics Special Interest Group celebrated the tenth anniversary of the special interest group's (SIG's) formation. The occasion was marked by a session convened by the editors of this volume as an opportunity to reflect on the SIG's 2007 Position Statement on Information Ethics in LIS Education and to look forward to the next decade of SIG activities. Out of that meeting came a broad consensus among those who taught information ethics coursework that there was a need for a work to supplement existing professional ethics texts by articulating the intellectual underpinnings of the information ethics discipline. This volume was conceived as a direct response to that consensus.

Beyond the information ethics education community, there is also a need for greater understanding of the ethical dimensions of information systems and technologies. News broadcasts, social network posts, and everyday conversation increasingly turn to questions that are relevant to information ethics researchers: Are healthy discourses possible online? What is expertise and which experts should we trust? How much privacy should we be expected to give up in exchange for access to services? What are the appropriate limits when protecting intellectual property? And so on. All too often, public discussions of these topics come down to expressions of personal preferences or are subject to argument through identification. This is when, upon learning what position a group with whom one identifies holds, one begins to uphold and defend that group's position. Questions prompted by emerging information technologies, and the uses of those technologies, are often complex, nuanced, and difficult to resolve satisfactorily through reductive arguments, leaving the market to decide what is permissible instead of reasoned consensus. These chapters were selected to provide the terminology, frameworks, and principles needed to participate in these important conversations in deliberate and constructive ways.

The chapter authors have all previously contributed to the field of information ethics through research, teaching, and/or service. This collection of original chapters was written to address ethical precursors to or core concepts of information ethics. Although chapter presentations vary slightly, each is divided into a conceptual introduction that provides the reader with central ideas and key terminology, an intellectual history that discusses how the concept developed over time, an overview of major thinkers who have contributed to the concept, continuing issues that will be relevant to emerging research, and additional reading lists for further study. When appropriate, one or more case studies are also included to illustrate and concretize principles documented in the chapter.

The chapters can be divided into a few clusters that center on different aspects of information ethics. The first cluster presents a general overview of information ethics as a concept including its history and relationship to human flourishing. The first chapter, by editor John T. F. Burgess, provides an overview of major Western ethical frameworks, and discusses their relevance to information ethics practitioners. Chapter 2, written by Paul T. Jaeger, Ursula Gorham, and Natalie Greene Taylor, is an examination of the concept of human rights and its distinctions from and relationships with the information ethics discipline. Chapter 3, again by John T. F. Burgess, is a review of the professional ethical precursors that provide lessons in applied ethics and suggest a need for an information ethics distinct from those precursors.

The next cluster of chapters cover specific topics in information ethics. Emily J. M. Knox summarizes the theme of information access in pre- and post-enlightenment modes in chapter 4. Chapter 5, written by Michael Zimmer, covers the principles and intellectual history of privacy. The ethics of discourse is the subject of John M. Budd's chapter 6, including a discussion of conversational analysis ethics. Kathrine Andrews. Henderson contributes chapter 7 on intellectual property ethics, history, and law. Chapter 8, written by Peter Darch, covers data ethics and the emerging topic of big data and data activities. Chapter 9, by Jane Blanken-Webb, Imani Palmer, Roy H. Campbell, Nicholas C. Burbules, and Masooda Bashir, examines cybersecurity ethics, including a look at the influence of hacker culture.

Global and intercultural information ethics are discussed in the final cluster of chapters. Chapter 10, written by Rachel Fischer and Erin Klazar, covers the topics of cognitive justice and intercultural communication ethics, including epistemicide and indigenous knowledge. Margaret Zimmerman's chapter 11 on global digital citizenship takes the concept of global citizenship and considers the implications of networked online communities.

The concluding chapter, written by Amelia Gibson, stands alone. It covers a wide range of emerging issues, from algorithmic bias and AI decision-making to 3-D printing and regulated items.

Taken together, the chapters in this volume serve as a key to understanding the major topics of information ethics and as an invitation for the reader to participate in ongoing discussions as researchers, practitioners, students, and citizens.

John T. F. Burgess
Emily J. M. Knox

CHAPTER 1

Principles and Concepts in Information Ethics

John T. F. Burgess

I f, figuratively speaking, ethics is the story of what it means to be good and all the ways humans remain bad, then *information ethics* is the story of the good that can be accomplished with information, and all the ways it may be used to harm. It is a complex story, and as with any complex story, knowing the plot, themes, and characters can take what at first seems impenetrable and make it engaging. The story of information ethics plays out within individuals, among persons, in communities, and even between people and their creations, from social institutions to artificially intelligent machines. Each of us participate in telling this story with actions and with expectations. We turn to social networking sites to learn what happened while we were asleep, we share news articles that we may or may not have read, shop online for things we may or may not need, stream media we may not own even a digital copy of, and message loved ones or people we want to know better. These acts carry expectations about privacy and surveillance, intellectual freedom and social norms, and access to information and intellectual property. Such mundane actions have consequences in aggregate, and even those who reject creating an online presence are still affected by the social, political, and economic choices of those who do.

It is one of the underlying assumptions of this chapter that, rather than leave decisions about the beneficial and harmful applications of information systems to these kinds of aggregate decisions, it is important to reflect on them in a reasoned way. This assumption should not seem out of place to information professionals who have long been invested in the idea that, properly used, information systems provide a transformative public good, which when misused can harm many. The following serves as an introduction to the key elements of the story of information ethics, such as concepts and frameworks information ethicists use to conduct their research that will make information ethics research more engaging. A subsequent chapter deals with the history of information ethics as a discipline. Between these two, the reader should have a foundation for engaging with the remaining chapters of this volume, and more broadly, with information ethics research.

MORAL PHILOSOPHY

Although the terms *morals* and *ethics* are often used interchangeably even by moral philosophers, looking at their etymology over time reveals a useful distinction. The origins of the words overlap, as the Latin word *moralis* means proper social behavior, and the Greek ēthikós means practicing moral character. However, in Middle French the words began to diverge: *ethiques* is used to refer to the classical works of moral philosophy and their characteristics, while in post-classical Latin the word *mores* retained the sense of customs. It is with this distinction in mind that one may use *morals* to mean held beliefs and *ethics* to mean a systematic treatment of a moral principle. As an example of this distinction, the limits of one's moral duty (a held belief) to keep a promise are defined by one's preferred ethical framework (a systematic treatment) (*Oxford English Dictionary Online:* s.v. "ethics"; s.v. "moral"). It is not a simple thing to determine what actions are moral. Philosophical research requires a skill set unlike those of other forms of research. Generally speaking, in much experimental research the strength of the research depends on the number of subjects, the control over the experimental environment, and validity and reliability in the design, as well as statistically significant results. In philosophical research methods the primary instrument for generating new understanding is rigorous argumentation supported by logical analysis, models, examples, and thought experiments, among other things. Arguments are not made for the sake of the art of argumentation but are instead applied to achieve deeper, more nuanced understandings of the topic being argued. Experimentation has long since superseded argumentation as a way to know reliably how the natural world functions, yet one only has to look at the comments section of a social media post to know that this has not stopped people from using argumentation to engage with complex problems. Philosophies of empiricism from David Hume's *An Enquiry into Human Understanding* (Hume 1999) to Thomas Kuhn's *The Structure of Scientific Revolutions* (Kuhn and Hacking 2012) have also made it clear that argumentation is an integral part of interpreting experimental significance. Factual evidence alone is not enough to be sufficiently persuasive on issues of the physical world, much less on questions of what moral obligations we hold to one another. Learning to use argumentation more effectively can be an exercise in digital citizenship, the capacity to act responsibly in an online environment (Mossberger, Tolbert, and McNeal 2007, 1). Engaging with rigorous argumentation as a research method will reinforce the abilities to think critically about the substance of arguments, to discredit poor or bad faith arguments, to clarify and refine strong ones, and to increase the likelihood of good outcomes for projects implemented from them. For example, the Association of College and Research Libraries' Framework for Information Literacy is the outcome of a vigorous argument on how information literacy instruction should be performed (Beilin 2015).

Philosophy is a research method, but it is also a scholarly discipline that is divided into countless subdisciplines. Some of these are based on a desire to understand a concept better; these include *metaphysics,* the philosophical study of reality; *epistemology,* the philosophical study of truth; and *aesthetics,* the philosophical study of beauty. Information ethics resides within the subdiscipline of *moral philosophy.* Moral philosophy is concerned with the philosophical study of the good. In other words, what makes conduct good or bad, right or wrong? The "what makes" portion of that definition is important, because moral philosophers often focus their work on finding justified beliefs or *principles* that can be generalized enabling us make better, more moral decisions. Generations of moral philosophers have developed iterative arguments about what gives moral authority to principles, dividing moral philosophy into a variety of explanatory frameworks, each with a genealogy of supporters. A later portion of this chapter is devoted to familiarizing the reader with the four most prominent kinds of moral authority conceived in these frameworks.

INFORMATION ETHICS

An effective way to define information ethics is to encircle it and gain a sense of the territory it covers. If moral philosophy may be called a systematic exploration of the concept of goodness, then information ethics is that exploration dedicated to the domain of information. This is comparable to the way bioethics explores goodness as confined to the domain of living things. Both life and information concern broad conceptual territories, and both require careful definition in order to clarify where those boundaries lie. There are many definitions of information, each with its own merits. For the current task, recognizing that many distinctions may be made in how information is defined is more important than unpacking the meanings of those definitions. The distinction process begins with Claude Shannon's expression of information as signal fidelity rather than semantic, or meaningful, fidelity (Shannon 1948, 623). Marcia J. Bates effectively reviews the range of distinctions typologically as "Communicatory or semiotic, Activity-based (i.e., information as event), Propositional, Structural, Social, Multitype, and Deconstructionist" (Bates 2009, 2347-48). The philosophy of information (PI) is its own subdiscipline within philosophy, examining the metaphysical nature of information (Floridi 2002; 2011). Awareness of the breadth and complexity of the concept of information should encourage readers of information ethics to take the time to unpack how authors are using that concept, both in terms of which definitions they include and which they exclude.

The conceptual breadth of information is one of the boundary-setting challenges in establishing information ethics' domain. Another challenge is that information ethics addresses moral issues that arise from the implementation of new information and communication technologies (ICTs), and innovation in ICTs can be broadly disruptive. For example, principles towards privacy worked out to address the social, political, and economic ramifications of the manual printing press and the postal system are insufficient to deal with an environment where, once posted online, sensitive items may persist indefinitely, decentralized outside of the direct control of any authority (Rosen 2011). By the time a principle has been established, innovation may require revision. This makes information ethics an applied ethics, one that is concerned less with timeless truths and more with unpacking implications and guiding implementations of information systems.

A final boundary-setting challenge is that globally networked information systems are not the territory of any one nation, religion, or culture, and therefore promote cosmopolitanism, the belief that although we are all connected, differences between people are real, legitimate on their own terms, and should be respected (Beck and Sznaider 2006). Information ethical solutions should reflect the fact that as a result of pluralism and generational shifts, there is not likely to be one set of answers to what constitutes morally permissible uses of information. For this reason, not only is the definition of information broad, but the range of ethical standards to consider must be equally broad in order to arrive at useful principles. Despite this, information ethics may still provide *normative,* or morally guiding, principles. These should be responsive to innovations and receptive to the importance of decentralizing philosophy to remain relevant and resistant to a rise in nativist or nationalistic thinking (Narayan and Harding 2000).

With these three parameters in place, it is possible to see information ethics as an applied ethics, dedicated to negotiating the moral terrain between emerging information and communication technologies, the pervasive information systems supported by those technologies, and the deeply interconnected world that is dependent on the information provided by those systems.

INTELLECTUAL HISTORY

This intellectual history briefly summarizes four Western ethical frameworks: *deontology, consequentialism, character ethics,* and *contractual ethics.* It does so in a way that presents each framework as a moral lens, a way to interpret the world if a certain set of ethical principles are true. Such a lens is called a *hermeneutic.* Viewing a problem with a new hermeneutical lens may aid in creative analysis and facilitate discovery of fresh insights, so it is beneficial to have a range of hermeneutics available beyond one's own personal moral preferences. Ethical frameworks are non-rivalrous in the sense that one does not owe personal allegiance to a system of ethics the way one might to a religious tradition or even a political movement. Nor should these frameworks be seen as a comprehensive list in any way. These four frameworks are encountered widely in information ethics literature but represent only a fraction of global moral and wisdom traditions. Significant contributions to information ethics from African, Asian, and South American traditions are introduced in subsequent chapters, where they can be explored more fully. The decision to present European ethical traditions first should not be interpreted as evidence of their quality or sophistication relative to other traditions. Instead it is a legacy of colonialism that Western ideas have dominated the available ways to discuss the relationship among information, technology, and the needs of people. By necessity even these four traditions are given broad treatments. Suggested readings in this and subsequent chapters will provide guidance to primary source documents.

Deontology

Into early modern European history, living a good life meant being religiously pious. After the Protestant reformation, the question of which interpretation of piety was correct became a pressing concern and the answer often had more to do with political rather than moral authority. Enlightenment-era philosophers, inspired by the way that empiricism enabled understanding of nature, began to wonder if reasoned inquiry could also lead to understanding the moral order. One of the most influential attempts to create a rational foundation for ethics is *deontology.* The word deontology comes from the Greek and means the study of what is necessary, in the sense that something ought to be done rather than the sense of being required. This focus on necessary action results in deontology being known as the ethics of *duty* or of *rules.* The towering figure of the Enlightenment, German philosopher Immanuel Kant (1724–1804) argued that these rules could be discovered in an *a priori* way, that is before or without experience, in the same way that we know mathematical or logical truths. A rule that is said to be universally true is known as a *maxim.* Moral rules that could be reduced to practical concerns, needs born of circumstance, were not maxims and could not be considered good in and of themselves. Maxims function in a similar way to religious commandments, setting the boundaries of moral acceptability.

In this framework, a rule may be called moral if it can be applied universally: what is moral for a king is moral for a pauper, in every circumstance. Additionally, one must treat people as ends instead of means to achieve an end. Finally, for a rule to be moral, it must leave room for the agency of others, because rather than be obedient to rules, the person should be guided by a well-developed moral *conscience* or *goodwill* towards doing what is right. These standards form the basis of deontological moral authority, what Kant called the *categorical imperative*. Deontology then is a *normative* form of ethics, meaning that it seeks to define which actions are right and which are wrong. The identification of maxims, justified by the categorical imperative means that even those who do not develop a conscience may be judged for carrying out wrong action. Observance of moral rules, such as "it is wrong to kill, steal, or lie," then becomes the objective marker that one can use to evaluate the behavior of others.

Applying Deontology

To the modern mind, the idea of a reductive moral order that existed in a pure way outside of context may be difficult to accept. For Kant's contemporaries, this justified a strongly held belief that moral values were absolute, and anything that was not absolute could not be moral. Even if this idea is based on assumptions we no longer hold, the legacy of Kantian ethics is still with us in the idea that ethics can be applied universally. It can be seen in the idea of universal human rights and other natural rights arguments (Freeman 2017, 27). It is also present in the form of professional codes of ethics. Even without using exclusively a priori proof of ethical principles, codes of ethics are presented in a way that is meant to create a universal standard for conduct (L'Etang 1992, 738). Information professionals who view privacy, access to information, and intellectual freedom as universal human rights and see it as their duty to protect them are operating in a deontological ethical framework. Refusing to treat their patrons as means instead of ends and respecting their agency and autonomy is also a legacy of deontological thinking. The objective and shared nature of rules make deontology well-suited to serve as the basis for professional codes of ethics. This is particularly true for those professions without the centralized authority to enforce ethical behavior because those who believe that their professional ethics are universal and promote dignity may be more likely to defend them than those who feel they are arbitrary or even situational.

Limitations of Deontology

At times, two or more maxims will conflict with each other, which calls into question the assumption of a moral order. An *ethical dilemma* occurs when multiple maxims ought to be applied universally but are contradictory. This is distinct from a moral crisis or quandary, when it is difficult to apply a single maxim in a satisfactory way. Reconciling a dilemma requires either proving that the rules involved do not actually contradict or introducing the possibility that some criteria beyond reason is necessary in making moral evaluations, establishing a need for other ethical frameworks. Few modern deontologists are Kantian absolutists, and modern forms of deontology add elements to make it possible to determine which rule is given priority in terms of value, importance, or some other standard, such as consistency (Marcus 1980, 135).

A more difficult limitation to accommodate is the so-called *moral disaster.* If a maxim is universally moral then breaking it, even to avoid a disastrous outcome, must be considered immoral. One of the reasons to employ an ethical framework is to guide people to do the right thing, so it seems counterintuitive to call a decision moral if the outcome of that act leads to great suffering. This may make sense if there are theological consequences to acting immorally, but otherwise it seems to place the moral conscience of one person over the well-being of many others. Contemporary deontologists have proposed solutions for these limitations, such as Frances Kamm's *Principle of Permissible Harm* (Kamm 2007, 5). In the context of this chapter, knowing potential resolutions is less important than knowing what spurred the development of additional ethical frameworks, and the presence of moral dilemmas, the immunity of morality from consequences, and the focus on individual morality did so for deontology.

Major Thinkers

Immanuel Kant (1724–1804). German founder of rules-based deontology and leading figure of the Enlightenment. One of the most influential ethicists and philosophers of the past four centuries.

John Locke (1632–1704). English philosopher and empiricist who articulated deontology from a rights-based approach, positing that a creator had fashioned natural laws from which human beings could not be alienated.

Thomas Nagel (1937–). American philosopher of mind who laid out a distinction between what are now known as *agent-relative* and *agent-neutral* reasons. Something is considered agent-neutral if it would be good for all persons, substituting for the universality requirement. Something is agent-relative if circumstances might change our evaluation of an otherwise universally moral or immoral decision (Nagel 1978, 120). This addresses the moral disaster problem by recasting how reason is used to identify rules.

Frances Kamm. American applied ethicist, active in the twentieth and twenty-first centuries, who developed the Principle of Permissible Harm, a refinement of deontology. This is the argument that principles can be constructed from an aggregate of case-based judgments, creating a normative rule from experience rather than from an *a priori* judgment. This is done is a way that uses the substitution of persons in a conflict to minimize individual preferences (Kamm 2007, 4–5).

Consequentialism

The second ethical framework to consider is *consequentialism,* which in many ways should be seen as a response to the limitations of deontology raised above. A *consequence* is something that results from a deliberate action or choice. Consequentialism, then, is the ethical framework that bases the determination of what is moral on the consequences of choices. For example, it may or may not be immoral to tell a lie, depending on the outcomes of that lie. The moral weight does not reside in the act, but in the consequences of the act. There are many forms of consequentialism, but under *act consequentialism,* a core version, judgment occurs entirely after the fact, rather than before. In deontology the morality of a decision is known before the results of an action by applying moral maxims, but under act consequentialism morality is known using evidential proof. It requires no *a priori* judgments, instead taking the circumstances of decisions into account.

What distinguishes consequentialism from *casuistry,* the ethical evaluation of cases by circumstance and precedent alone, is the existence of a consistent measure for evaluating acts. Originally the moral measure of an act was determined by its *utility* or capacity to do the greatest good for the greatest number. A measurable indicator of utility is *hedonism* or maximizing pleasure and minimizing pain. The value of hedonism is that it is a natural function of living beings, in some way harkening back to natural law as proof of its validity. It is also seen as an *intrinsic good,* or something that is good in and of itself. Those who promoted maximizing utility were known as *utilitarians,* including English social reformer Jeremy Bentham (1748–1832), English empiricist John Stuart Mill (1806–1873), and English moral philosopher Henry Sidgwick (1838–1900). Setting hedonism as the standard measure for utility was controversial from the beginning due to distaste for the idea of a life spent pursuing pleasures and resulting in discussions over whether quantity of pleasure was all that mattered, or if some measures of quality could be included. Over the decades many ideas for measures of intrinsic good have been introduced, including human welfare (Sen 1979, 471) and expanding human capabilities (Nussbaum 2001). Some versions of consequentialism feature multiple ideas for the good, which may come in one of multiple forms including lists of moral values or even sets of rules. The one idea that connects all forms of consequentialism is that regardless of how measures occur, evaluation of morality takes place after the act, not before.

Applying Consequentialism

Consequentialist arguments do not depend on belief in an underlying, metaphysical moral order. Nor is it necessary to determine a set of moral norms before actions can be taken with confidence. As long as one has a clear standard for measuring the outcomes of a decision, even if that standard is simply to minimize harm while maximizing the number of happy people, judging outcomes is possible. This gives consequentialism two attractive characteristics: assessability and flexibility. In an environment where change is a near-constant, a framework of predetermined principles may be difficult to apply to unforeseen circumstances, for example, being able to respond to new technologies like facial detection software that have both desirable and troubling applications. A framework that can be objectively assessed can be evaluated without all parties having to share the same moral outlook on the world, which is useful in a pluralistic society. Consequentialist dilemmas involve choosing between multiple good or multiple bad outcomes, which are not paradoxical unlike deontological dilemmas. Likewise, moral catastrophes are also of no concern because the disastrous outcome would be the evidence that a decision was immoral.

Information professionals who use consequentialism may identify intrinsic goods against which to measure utility. This might be something akin to Melvil Dewey's *library faith,* the belief that access to high-quality reading material is intrinsically good and will have positive effects on individual patrons and on society (Wiegand 1999, 4). Assumptions about what constitutes the best reading and the positive effects of reading are culturally biased and flawed, but the library faith is still echoed in established values such as intellectual freedom and access to information as ideas that have utility and should be maximized. These ideas of the good would still be evaluated circumstantially. For example, even if intellectual freedom is intrinsically desirable, allowing internet filters to be installed on public computers may be necessary in order to maintain access to US federal E-Rate funding (Dresang 2006, 180). If loss of funding would result in massive service cutbacks or even closures, which would be the moral course of action? Consequentialist thinking would allow practitioners the autonomy to apply professional values rationally in a given circumstance while maintaining a moral obligation seek the best outcome.

Limitations of Consequentialism

Consequentialism is susceptible to the argument that it is an ethics of calculation and relativism. Additionally, it is worthwhile to recognize that sometimes the means are important, not just the ends, because part of moral identity is aspirational. Then there is the problem of judging consequences. One cannot know consequences until after the act has already occurred, and because it is impossible to know all of the remote consequences, judgment is necessarily incomplete. In recognition of this, a consequentialist does not attempt to forecast all of the consequences of an action before making a decision. Instead, these decisions are made using experience from the outcomes of prior decisions and using moral intuition to choose what seems like the right thing to do. The first mitigates consequentialism's advantage in novel situations, whereas moral intuition is inherently subjective, thus qualifying the benefits of objectivity.

Additional limitations arise from the idea of an intrinsic good because the idea of goodness is culturally and generationally dependent. For example, who decides if sensual pleasure is an intrinsic good or if refined, epicurean pleasure is better? What about the library faith? This is another mark against consequentialism's objectivity. As mentioned above, there are many forms of consequentialism with titles such as *actual consequentialism, total consequentialism,* and *universal consequentialism.* One of the factors leading to the development of new forms was the need to accommodate instances when an intrinsic good, or when measuring the good, turned out to be problematical. If the good and the standard for measuring it are both arbitrary, it becomes even harder to repel objections of relativism. A further limitation is that seeking to maximize a good may lead to difficulties in itself. Even if a good is intrinsic, there is no strong justification that it will still be good if maximized. The appropriately named "Transplant Problem" provides one example of why this may not be the best approach. The transplant problem is a thought experiment where a doctor chooses to save the lives of several patients by transplanting the vital organs of a healthy person into them (Thomson 1985, 1410). Maximization may require consequentialist observers to judge this act as moral even though most observers would consider it abhorrent. Consequentialists have developed approaches to compensate for this thought experiment, but ultimately neither deontology nor consequentialism are simple to adopt as a single lens since both means and consequences carry moral weight.

Major Thinkers

Jeremy Bentham (1748-1832). English early proponent of secular utilitarian thought. Social reformer. Published texts applying utilitarian principles to penal law and the principles of good governance.

John Stuart Mill (1806-1873). English philosopher and empiricist who expanded Bentham's ideas of hedonism to include qualitative distinctions. Brought utilitarian thought to the economic, social, and political values of classical liberalism.

Bernard Williams (1929-2003). English moral philosopher who was one of the most influential critics of consequentialism. Introduced a critique on the basis of *negative responsibilities,* the principle that one might be responsible for what one does not do as well as what one does. He also raised the issue of the importance of agent integrity in the moral process and the damage caused in reducing moral decision-making to a calculation.

Peter Singer (1946-). Australian moral philosopher who in his "Drowning Child" thought experiment explored the implications of negative responsibilities for society. If one has the moral responsibility to save a drowning child who is in front of us, might that not mean that through an expanding circle of responsibility we also are responsible for the welfare of all those who we could save?

Character Ethics

Character ethics is both older and newer than the first two ethical frameworks presented above. It is older because many of the ideas in this framework come from classical Greek philosophers such as Aristotle and Plato. However, it fell out of wide practice during the Enlightenment in favor of the search for an objective moral order, only to be revived in the mid-twentieth century by British analytic philosopher and ethicist Elizabeth Anscombe (1919-2001) and British virtue and meta-ethicist Philippa Foot (1920-2010), among others. The reintroduction provided a third way to think about moral philosophy, breaking the gridlock between deontologists and consequentialists that was prevalent at the time. *Character* is a set of stable but not immutable qualities, often related to a person's moral faculties or disposition. In this framework, one considers what a person of good character would do in a given situation and seeks to emulate that person. This may seem arbitrary, but it recognizes the social dimension of morality, particularly the influence of family and community (Blum 1998, 164). Certain values are held up as being laudable in one's culture, and to be a trusted member of that culture requires the ability to act according to certain norms. There is no moral obligation to adopt them, but rejecting the values of one's community may make life more difficult.

The traditional form of character ethics is *virtue ethics.* In virtue ethics one cultivates a good character by practicing the *virtues* while minimizing corresponding *vices.* The Greek word for virtue, *arete,* means excellence, so practicing virtue suggests pursuing excellence rather than seeking an intrinsic good. Many forms of character ethics identify *flourishing* as the indicator of a well-lived life, not moment to moment, but in totality. To flourish means to grow and thrive in the way that one might describe a healthy farm or a community as flourishing. The Greek word for flourishing is *eudaimonia,* and forms of character ethics that promote flourishing are called *eudaimonic ethics.* For character ethics it is not the dutiful person but the *prudent* person who is good. Prudence is a form of self-control guided by practical wisdom. The prudent person pursues the *golden mean,* or middle ground between two moral extremes. For example, on a continuum between caution and bravery, an excess of caution may lead to the inability to act at a critical moment and an excess of bravery may lead to taking foolhardy risks. Building a habit of prudence is an essential part of developing good character. Virtue ethics is summarily to emulate those people one considers laudable and develop a prudent character by habituating the moral virtue, to better the odds of flourishing over the course of a lifetime.

Applying Character Ethics

Character ethics shares characteristics with both deontology and consequentialism. In character ethics, the virtues provide a standard for ethical decision-making that is more comparable to the way rules work in deontology than to the function of intrinsic good of consequentialism. Both rules and virtues are explicitly meant to provide guidance during the decision-making process. Flourishing, on the other hand, provides an objective to maximize similar to the one provided by the intrinsic good in consequentialism. Practitioners of deontology and virtue ethics both seek to develop a stable, guiding disposition: moral conscience for deontology and prudent character for virtue and other character ethics. Like consequentialism, eudaimonic character ethics does take into account the moral consequences of actions, in particular are they more or less likely to promote flourishing, but having a good character is the moral good, and flourishing is only the desired outcome, so although one cannot ensure flourishing, one can still seek to always be a person of good character.

The information professional employing a virtue ethics lens is likely to look to exemplars of virtue in the profession and emulate their approaches. Here, the profession as a whole may serve as the community, providing both virtuous exemplars and expectations to follow. In this way, there is a social element that is not emphasized in the previous two frameworks. This has implications for professional education because this places a premium on modeling ethical behaviors as well as providing functional instruction. Beyond this, the idea of the golden mean can inform the performance of ethical duties. For example, seeing social responsibility and neutrality as two virtues to be balanced may lead to adopting prudential, rather than competing, strategies (Burgess 2016). Finally, the idea that continued flourishing should not be seen as a direct goal to pursue, but rather is a condition one invites through acting virtuously and prudentially, provides a further justification for placing those virtues ahead of other immediate concerns. For example, protecting privacy, providing access to information, and defending intellectual freedom, rather than being the moral goals themselves, may be virtues to pursue because doing so helps to define an essential professional character, and developing that character is what gives the profession the best chance to flourish (Burgess 2013).

Limitations of Character Ethics

There are potential limitations associated with a normative ethical framework that lacks specific moral principles. The distinction between moral rules and the virtues is that breaking a moral rule is a *transgression.* To transgress is to go beyond a set boundary, in other words, to do something unacceptable or, in this case, immoral. It is a wrong action, and doing a wrong action carries a negative moral judgment, including any accompanying sense of guilt or shame. Pursuing a vice instead of a virtue is not transgressive; instead, it is considered *akratic,* acting against one's self-interests in an undisciplined way. It is a missed opportunity to build character and invite flourishing. An approach such as virtue ethics that does not set hard behavioral boundaries frees the moral agent to think about the overall goal of becoming a person of good character.

This leaves virtue ethics open to charges of *egoism,* or excessive focus on the moral trajectory of the individual, instead of developing principles or ideas of the good that can be used by everyone. The *ethics of care,* a feminist approach to character ethics, emphasizes the importance of relationships rather than individual flourishing as a response to this limitation (Held 2006, 19). The second and related limitation is that flourishing is a personal goal, and if no particular actions are purely transgressive, then one may be tempted to act in ways that an external observer might consider immoral in order to pursue one's idea of flourishing. Although originally character was developed in a tightly knit community where that community could keep a person in line with social norms, modern society is more anonymous. A final limitation is that even if one lives a virtuous and habitually prudent life, flourishing is often a result of circumstances and is not guaranteed, leaving a strong disconnect between moral behavior and reward. The deontologist's reward is a clear conscience, the utilitarian's is the pursuit of pleasure, while the virtue ethicist's may only be a life of disciplined moderation.

Major Thinkers

Aristotle (384–322 BCE). Greek philosopher whose work framed much of pre-Enlightenment Western philosophy and established many of the concepts and domains of study that are core to Western philosophical inquiry.

G. E. M. Anscombe (1919–2001). British analytic philosopher and ethicist. Through her 1958 essay "Modern Moral Philosophy," she spoke of the shortcomings of moral philosophy in the first half of the twentieth century and made the case for an ethical foundation that relies on something beyond appeals to morally normative assertions in ways that have more in common with religious obligations that Aristotle's ideas of virtue.

Philippa Foot (1920–2010). British virtue and meta-ethicist who promoted virtue ethics as a normative alternative to consequentialism and deontology.

Rosalind Hursthouse (1943–). New Zealander moral philosopher who has popularized virtue ethics, as well as developed applied theories of virtue ethics, while giving special attention to issues of abortion and moral motivation.

Alasdair MacIntyre (1929–). Scottish moral philosopher whose influential 1981 book *After Virtue* applied Aristotelian ethics to critique both the Enlightenment era conception of human nature and individualist ethics.

Robert Louden (1935–). American ethical theorist who illustrated that virtue ethics is an egoistic form of ethics, which is effective in outlining how individuals may develop moral qualities but is insufficient to resolve moral quandaries in society.

Contractual Ethics

The final major Western ethical framework to be considered in this chapter begins with the idea that it is possible for members of a society to agree on a standard of moral behavior without having to derive the authority to do so from anything except mutual self-interest. In this framework, members of a society collectively agree on what is moral, which requires the belief that it is rational for people to agree that shared morals are beneficial. The value of this approach is particularly clear in pluralistic societies where many different cultures hold standards of right and wrong behavior. The political philosophical framework for this line of thinking is called the *social contract*. Classical social contract theory proceeds from the idea that legitimate rule relies on the consent of the governed, rather than divine right, to form a stable civil society. English political philosopher Thomas Hobbes (1588–1679) argued in his work *Leviathan* that consent should be given because the alternative is an anarchic war of all against all, which is even less tolerable than being ruled by a monarch. It can be considered rational to give up certain freedoms in exchange for protection of person and property.

The moral philosophical version of this idea is called *contractual ethics,* which consists of both *contractarianism* and *contractualism*. In contractarianism one's theory of human nature is based on rational self-interest, as per Hobbes, and it is considered worth giving up certain freedoms in exchange for shared moral protections. In contractualism, one's theory of human nature is based on the dignity of persons to accept a persuasive moral argument, as with American moral philosopher T. M. Scanlon (1940–) (1982, 128). One of the most prominent examples of something that is both a moral protection and a persuasive moral argument is the principle of *justice as fairness,* articulated as an overlapping consensus of philosophical and religious positions by American moral philosopher John Rawls (1921–2002) (1985, 225–26). Versions of moral contract theory promoted by Enlightenment era thinkers like political philosopher Jean-Jacques Rousseau (1712–1778) focused on this idea of consent as a binding process where people are born free but exchange that freedom for services (Rousseau 2012, 157). However, modern contractual ethics focuses not on ways that people may bind themselves to one another, but instead on finding those principles that all parties would agree to uphold.

Applying Contractual Ethics

Under contractual ethics, reason aids in identifying upholdable principles, rather than finding rules a person must commit to and obey. The goal is to better understand rational positions that could be agreed upon, rather than demonstrating actual agreement. As mentioned above, Thomas Hobbes's contractarian argument that civil society is rational because it is in everyone's interest to stave off a war of all against all is an example of *rational self-interest*. This is a libertarian idea that acting in accord with one's self interest is enough to deem a decision rational. Designing a moral contract where all pursued their self-interests might lead to a system being seen as moral as long as it preserved individual liberties and staved off a more undesirable condition. Compare this to the most influential example of a contractualist model, Rawls's *original position*. In the original position, Rawls argues that if we were re-creating society and all knowledge of a person's living conditions were hidden behind the *veil of ignorance,* then everyone would choose to create a state that would provide basic living needs for everyone rather than risk being impoverished and powerless (Rawls 1999). In this way, most arguments from contractual forms of ethics rely on either making a reasoned argument that everyone would agree with or on showing that through self-interest alone one would choose to create a system of morality.

The information professional employing a contractarian lens is likely to look for how professional values could be justified by arguments of rational self-interest alone. Michael Harris's account of the founding of the public library movement as an exercise of rational self-interest by cultural elites would be one example of a contractarian approach (Harris 1972). An information professional using a contractualist lens might try to craft a reasoned model for professional practice to which everyone would be able to agree. For instance, it might be rational for everyone to agree to a principle protecting intellectual freedom because doing so creates a moral environment where we are free to explore ideas without fear of censure. A contractarian version of the same principle might be that in order to protect one's own ability to speak freely, one would give up the right to censor other people's ideas. In general, the benefit of employing a contractual ethics lens is that it removes the potential for hypocrisy from the contingent nature of ethical frameworks. It emphasizes how greatly ethical frameworks rely on agreement, and how it is possible to revise moral contracts collaboratively. This extends both to the services provided by information professionals and the social responsibilities for which they advocate.

Limitations of Contractual Ethics

In contractual ethics, there are no actual contracts involved, so nothing is binding, and nothing exists to assent to. These frameworks may be seen as a form of ethical thought experiment, designed to help those reflecting on why one would agree to the things one already has. Contractual ethics, like consequentialism, is not designed to help one make moral decisions in the moment. The arguments used to make a case tend to be hypothetical, often applying models removed not just from direct experience, like a thought experiment, but also from even the possibility of experience. Consider Rawls's original position, which requires everyone to be ignorant of his or her own circumstances in order to reach agreement. This is called the *standard indictment:* hypothetical contracts cannot lead to real, binding agreements (Stark 2000, 314). They are also prone to confirming that the things that one already believes to be moral are moral, making it difficult to challenge preconceptions. For example, if one is already persuaded that rational self-interest makes sense, then moral contracts based on self-interest will be judged valid. The same holds true for welfarist moral contracts.

Major Thinkers

Thomas Hobbes (1588-1679). English political philosopher whose book *Leviathan* is the foundation of political social contract theory. In this theory, a strong civil society is needed to save human beings from dwelling in a combative state of nature.

Jean-Jacques Rousseau (1712-1778). Genovese Swiss political philosopher who contributed to the idea of premoral natural rights and the relationship among those rights, social contracts, and human endeavors.

John Rawls (1921–2002). American moral philosopher best known for developing justice as fairness as a contractualist principle, securing a politically liberal argument for a welfarist position.

T. M. Scanlon (1940–). American moral philosopher who articulated the contractualist position and how it can be distinguished from the contractarian position.

David Gauthier (1932–). Canadian-American contractarian philosopher whose work rekindled interest in contractual ethics in the twentieth century. Promoted the idea of the *initial bargaining position* as an alternative to the Enlightenment era state of nature (Gauthier 1986, 130).

CONTINUING ISSUES AND CONCERNS

As will be evident in subsequent chapters in this volume, no single ethical framework will be sufficient to address the variety of issues raised in information ethics research and practice. This is because ethical frameworks are an abstraction from the world as lived experience, resigned to explain one or more facets of the story of what it means to be good. This insufficiency does not mean that coming to know more about these ethical frameworks is without merit. Each raises issues about how it is possible to label one act moral and another immoral, one beneficial and the other detrimental. By presenting these Western ethical frameworks in a non-rivalrous way, they may be used as required, overlapping to fulfill a given need. If assistance in decision-making is essential, understanding deontological tests of means or virtue ethics' emphasis on prudence may provide guidance. When assumptions about the underlying morality of an aspect of society needs to be called into question, the language of moral contracts will be available. When concepts are presented as intrinsic goods, one should be as skeptical of them as consequentialists critiquing each other's expressions of the good. Moral philosophy cannot provide absolute answers, but it can facilitate asking more sophisticated questions. Having these four hermeneutical lenses in place to interrogate ethical arguments will facilitate engaging both with the information ethics concepts presented in the remainder of this work and in wider practice.

REFERENCES

Bates, Marcia J. 2009. "Information." *Encyclopedia of Library and Information Sciences.* Boca Raton, FL: CRC Press. https://www-taylorfrancis-com.libdata.lib.ua.edu/books/e/9780849397110.

Beck, Ulrich, and Natan Sznaider. 2006. "Unpacking Cosmopolitanism for the Social Sciences: A Research Agenda." *The British Journal of Sociology* 57 (1): 1-23.

Beilin, Ian. 2015. "Beyond the Threshold: Conformity, Resistance, and the ACRL Information Literacy Framework for Higher Education." *In the Library with the Lead Pipe* (blog). February 25, 2015. www.inthelibrarywiththeleadpipe.org/2015/beyond-the-threshold-conformity-resistance-and-the-aclr-information-literacy-framework-for-higher-education/.

Blum, Lawrence. 1998. "Community and Virtue." In *How Should One Live?: Essays on the Virtues,* edited by Roger Crisp, 163-78. Oxford, UK: Clarendon Press.

Burgess, John T. F. 2013. "Virtue Ethics and the Narrative Identity of American Librarianship 1876 to Present." PhD diss., Tuscaloosa, AL: University of Alabama Libraries.

_____. 2016. "Reconciling Social Responsibility and Neutrality in LIS Professional Ethics: A Virtue Ethics Approach." In *Information Cultures in the Digital Age: A Festschrift in Honor of Rafael Capurro,* edited by Jared Bielby and Matt Kelly, 161-72.

Dresang, Eliza T. 2006. "Intellectual Freedom and Libraries: Complexity and Chance in the Twenty-First-Century Digital Environment." *Library Quarterly,* 169-92.

Floridi, Luciano. 2002. "What Is the Philosophy of Information?" *Metaphilosophy* 33 (1-2): 123-45.

_____. 2011. *The Philosophy of Information.* Oxford ; New York: Oxford University Press. www.blackwell publishing.com/pci/downloads/introduction.pdf.

Freeman, Michael. 2017. *Human Rights.* Cambridge, UK: Polity Press Cambridge.

Gauthier, David. 1986. *Morals by Agreement.* Oxford: Clarendon Press.

Harris, Michael H. 1972. "The Purpose of the American Public Library in Historical Perspective: A Revisionist Interpretation." Washington, DC: ERIC Clearinghouse on Library and Information Sciences. www.eric.ed.gov/ERICWebPortal/contentdelivery/servlet/ERICServlet?accno =ED071668.

Held, Virginia. 2006. *The Ethics of Care: Personal, Political, and Global.* Oxford ; New York: Oxford University Press, USA.

Hume, David. 1999. *An Enquiry Concerning Human Understanding,* edited by Tom L. Beauchamp. Oxford; New York: Oxford University Press.

Kamm, Frances Myrna. 2007. *Intricate Ethics: Rights, Responsibilities, and Permissible Harm.* Oxford; New York: Oxford University Press.

Kuhn, Thomas S., and Ian Hacking. 2012. *The Structure of Scientific Revolutions: 50th Anniversary Edition.* 4th ed. Chicago ; London: University of Chicago Press.

L'Etang, Jacquie. 1992. "A Kantian Approach to Codes of Ethics." *Journal of Business Ethics* 11 (10): 737-44. https://doi.org/10.1007/BF00872305.

Marcus, Ruth Barcan. 1980. "Moral Dilemmas and Consistency." *The Journal of Philosophy* 77 (3): 121-36. https://doi.org/10.2307/2025665.

Mossberger, Karen, Caroline J. Tolbert, and Ramona S. McNeal. 2007. *Digital Citizenship: The Internet, Society, and Participation.* Cambridge, MA: MIT Press.

Nagel, Thomas. 1978. *The Possibility of Altruism.* Princeton, NJ: Princeton University Press.

Narayan, Uma, and Sandra Harding. 2000. "Introduction." In *Decentering the Center: Philosophy for a Multicultural, Postcolonial, and Feminist World,* vii-xvi. Bloomington, IN: Indiana University Press.

Nussbaum, Martha C. 2001. *Women and Human Development: The Capabilities Approach.* Cambridge, UK: Cambridge University Press.

Oxford English Dictionary Online. s.v. "ethics (*n.*)." www.oed.com/view/Entry/355823?.

_____. s.v. "moral (*n.*)." www.oed.com/view/Entry/122085.

Rawls, John. 1985. "Justice as Fairness: Political Not Metaphysical." *Philosophy and Public Affairs,* 223-51.

_____. 1999. *A Theory of Justice.* Revised ed. Cambridge, MA: Belknap Press of Harvard University.

Rosen, Jeffrey. 2011. "Free Speech, Privacy, and the Web That Never Forgets." *Journal on Telecommunications and High Technology Law* 9 (2): 345.

Rousseau, Jean-Jacques. 2012. *Rousseau: The Basic Political Writings: Discourse on the Sciences and the Arts, Discourse on the Origin of Inequality, Discourse on Political Economy, . . . Contract, The State of War.* Edited by David Wootton. Translated by Donald A. Cress. 2nd ed. Indianapolis, IN: Cambridge: Hackett Publishing Company, Inc.

Scanlon, T. M. 1982. "Contractualism and Utilitarianism." In *Utilitarianism and Beyond,* edited by Amartya Sen and Bernard Williams, 103-28. Cambridge: Cambridge University Press. http://sites.google.com .libdata.lib.ua.edu/site/philosophy450/home/ContractualismandUtilitarianism.pdf.

Sen, Amartya. 1979. "Utilitarianism and Welfarism." *The Journal of Philosophy* 76 (9): 463-89. https://doi.org/10.2307/2025934.

Shannon, C. E. 1948. "A Mathematical Theory of Communication." *Bell System Technical Journal* 27 (4): 623–56. https://doi.org/10.1002/j.1538-7305.1948.tb00917.x.

Stark, Cynthia A. 2000. "Hypothetical Consent and Justification." *The Journal of Philosophy* 97 (6): 313–34. https: //doi.org/10.2307/2678406.

Thomson, Judith Jarvis. 1985. "The Trolley Problem." *The Yale Law Journal* 94 (6): 1395–1415. https: //doi.org/10.2307/796133.

Wiegand, Wayne A. 1999. "Tunnel Vision and Blind Spots: What the Past Tells Us About the Present; Reflections on the Twentieth-Century History of American Librarianship." *The Library Quarterly* 69 (1): 1–32.

ADDITIONAL RESOURCES

Anscombe, G. E. M. 1958. "Modern Moral Philosophy." *Philosophy* 33 (124): 1–19.

Aristotle. 1999. *Nicomachean Ethics.* Translated by Terence Irwin. Indianapolis, IN: Hackett Publishing.

Bentham, Jeremy. 1907. *An Introduction to the Principles of Morals and Legislation.* Oxford, UK: Clarendon Press.

Hobbes, Thomas. 1998. *Leviathan.* Oxford, UK: Oxford University Press.

Hursthouse, Rosalind. 1999. *On Virtue Ethics.* Oxford , UK: Oxford University Press.

Kant, Immanuel. 2012. *Groundwork of the Metaphysics of Morals,* translated by Mary J. Gregor and Jens Timmermann. Cambridge, UK: Cambridge University Press.

MacIntyre, Alasdair C. 2007. *After Virtue: A Study in Moral Theory.* 3rd ed. Notre Dame, IN: University of Notre Dame Press.

Mill, John Stuart. 2010. *Utilitarianism.* Oxford, UK: Oxford University Press.

Parfit, Derek. 1984. *Reasons and Persons.* Oxford, UK: Clarendon Press.

Sidgwick, Henry. 1981. *The Methods of Ethics.* Indianapolis, IN; Cambridge: Hackett Publishing.

CHAPTER 2

Human Rights and Information Ethics

Paul T. Jaeger, Ursula Gorham, and Natalie Greene Taylor

This chapter introduces the ways in which the concept of human rights influences and supports the goals of information ethics. This chapter will present an overview of the concept of human rights, its development, its unique connections to information and information technologies, its relationships to information ethics, and different interpretations of and responses to human rights within different approaches to information ethics.

Human rights is the belief that all individuals deserve certain equal rights as members of a community or a society. The implementation of human rights is dependent on the creation of specific legal and policy mechanisms that promote this equality. Human rights scholar Anthony Woodiwiss offers a very practical definition of human rights: "a legally enforceable set of expectations as to how others, most obviously the state, should behave toward the rights bearers" (2005, xi).

The language of human rights is generally employed to express the need for fairness, equality, respect, and equity (Sensoy and DiAngelo 2012). The achievement of equality, however, requires more than finding a way to accomplish equitable distribution of resources or opportunities, as different needs and social contexts may require greater interventions for certain groups to achieve equality (Cramme and Diamond 2009; Nieto 2010). Significantly, the lack of human rights is linked to "low life expectancy, social exclusion, ill health, illiteracy, dependency, and effective enslavement" (Pogge 2005, 1).

Increasingly, a central aspect of human rights is information. As information and related technologies have become increasingly essential to education, employment, social interaction, and civic participation, greater focus has been placed on the idea that information can be seen as a necessary human right. Information intersects with human rights in several major ways, including

- the wide range of social, cultural, economic, legal, and political forces shaping information and rights;
- impacts of rights on information professions, practices, standards, and cultural institutions; and
- considerations of rights in the information behavior of different populations (Jaeger, Gorham, and Taylor 2015).

In short, human rights can serve as an ethical framework, providing moral, and often legal, weight (Mathiesen 2012).

INTELLECTUAL HISTORY AND MAJOR THINKERS

The term *human rights* was a creation of the twentieth century, but the origins of the underlying principles of human rights are much older. The first clear statement of a set of tangible human rights—which she identifies as "birthrights"—may have been Mary Wollstonecraft's 1790 antipoverty treatise *A Vindication of the Rights of Man,* which attacked the wrongs of social hierarchies, poverty, economic inequality, and state oppression in England (Blau and Moncada 2006). In terms of philosophical arguments, the idea of human rights has long been a part of debates between those who believe that people are born with natural rights, most notably natural law theorist John Locke. Others believe rights only exist if allowed and protected by larger community and social structures, such as logical positivist philosopher Jeremy Bentham. The Declaration of Independence of the United States (discussed below) evidences clear adherence to the former rather than the latter.

The foundations for modern conceptualizations of human rights were articulated and developed during the Enlightenment and first expressed in governance through the American and French revolutions (Sellars 2002). The Magna Carta in the United Kingdom and the Declaration of Independence and Constitution of the United States include many rights that were initially intended for the moneyed and male classes of those nations.

Moreover, the founding documents of the United States contain broad—and ambiguous—rights, such as the pursuit of happiness, as well as more specific rights to activities like assembly and expression. By no means were these documents written to create universal rights, as evidenced by the Constitution's original limitations on political participation and the inclusion of the right to keep certain types of other people as property. Despite these limitations in the founding documents, the international structures of human rights rely heavily on the Declaration of Independence in creating the notion of the state as the protector of individual rights (Calhoun 2007).

Discussions of human rights also reflect perceptions not just of the meaning of "rights," but of the meaning of "human" as well. Some believe that human rights reflect the best of human nature, arguing that human rights "cannot be distinguished from the origins of humans" and they are what "distinguishes mankind from other animals" (Blau and Moncada 2006, 12). Such statements are focusing on the positive side of human rights—society offering legal guarantees of equity and equality. On the other hand, some conceive of human rights as protections from the continual inequality, violence, and chaos that so often define human interactions. Focusing on the darker side of human rights, this point of view characterizes them as "profound and disturbing" because "they tend to strike at our very core and make us confront difficult and discomforting issues" (Lauren 2011, 5).

The first major proposals for what we would now think of as an international human rights structure began circulating in the 1920s as a reaction to the First World War. The modern idea of universal human rights, and what such rights might be, derives heavily from the welfare programs and social protections articulated in the United States during President Franklin Delano Roosevelt's administration (Woodiwiss 2005). The new social programs to protect the disadvantaged and ensure that basic needs were met, together with the broader ideals expressed as goals of the president, created a nascent human rights program within the United States. A speech that Roosevelt gave in 1941 advocating for an international social contract of "Four Freedoms"—to speech and expression, to religion, from want, and from fear—was a key inspiration for the development of human rights structures (Woodiwiss 2005).

In his 1944 State of the Union address, Roosevelt used the fact that the Second World War was winding down to expand the idea of the Four Freedoms into what he hoped to be a centerpiece of his post-war legislative agenda—what he dubbed "a Second Bill of Rights" (Sunstein 2004). Proposals for an international human rights structure began circulating during and in the aftermath of World War II, such as the Conference of Evian in 1938, the Catholic Association for International Peace in 1941, and the American Law Institute's Statement of Essential Human Rights from 1946 that was directly based on Roosevelt's Four Freedoms speech (Whelan 2010, Wronka, 1998).

The creation and adoption of the *Universal Declaration of Human Rights* (UDHR) represent the symbolic arrival of rights to the world stage in 1948 (Ignatieff 2005; Raphael 1967). The UDHR and its two later accompanying covenants—the International Covenant on Civil and Political Rights and the International Covenant on Economic, Social, and Cultural Rights—are known as the International Bill of Human Rights. The UDHR is now seen as customary international law (Sellars 2002; Wronka 1998) and internationally accepted human rights contained therein "include freedom of expression, freedom of association, freedom from fear and persecution, freedom of religion, as well as a right to shelter, education, health and work" (Halpin, Hick, and Hoskins 2000, 5).

The UDHR situates people as the agents of their own rights rather than the objects of rights bestowed by the nation-state (Blau and Moncada 2006). Unlike the US Constitution, which focuses on sovereignty and personal autonomy, the UDHR links individual rights with rights of community, focusing on society. The UDHR contains twenty-four specific rights. Eighteen of these rights are civil and political rights, such as expression, cultural heritage, and mobility. The remaining six are economic rights, focusing on concepts of property, employment, and social services. The United Nations (UN) now views these articulated human rights as being "indivisible, interdependent, and interrelated"—though none of these terms are in the UDHR—meaning that the rights must be provided and protected as a complete set (Whelan 2010).

The UN has engaged in many further steps to encourage the adoption, as well as to elaborate on, the International Bill of Human Rights. As one example, the 1993 Vienna World Conference on Human Rights reaffirmed the intentional commitment to UDHR and the subsequent conventions. Other organizations have held meetings to focus on the role of international human rights in specific areas. The 2003 and 2005 World Summits on the Information Society, for instance, yielded assertions of the importance of technology for rights to exist in the age of the internet. However, in spite of these UN proclamations, resolutions, and summits—as well as the establishment of global and regional human rights advocates and agencies—the protection of human rights has been left primarily to national governments, local community agencies, and non-governmental organizations (NGOs).

CONTINUING ISSUES AND CONCERNS

At the tail end of the last millennium, Kofi Annan, the Seventh Secretary General of the United Nations, stated, "People lack many things: jobs, shelter, food, healthcare, and drinkable water. Today, being cut off from basic telecommunications services is a hardship almost as acute as these other deprivations, which may indeed reduce the chances of finding remedies to them" (1999). Twenty years later, the observation still holds true. In the intervening years, the ability to access, use, and understand information and communication technologies (ICTs) has become far more important to education, employment, social inclusion, civic engagement, and much more than could have been imagined in 1999. Now, guarantees of human rights are dependent on information and the ability to use information is its own issue of rights.

To see how information is an issue of growing significance over time, an examination of the UDHR is instructive. Although antecedents of current information technologies were still fairly new when the UN issued the UDHR in 1948, the idea of human rights has been evolving and adapting to social, cultural, and technological change. Though the desktop computer, the internet, and mobile devices were developed long after the UDHR was originally drafted, many of the principles articulated in the UDHR are directly related to information, communication, and technology; many more rely on information, communication, and technology to support the principles.

Most items directly stated as rights are now either entirely dependent on or greatly enabled by information access and digital literacy, including such major activities as education, employment, and civic participation. As examples, freedom of speech, press, assembly, and expression are far more practicable when involving a literate populace with access to information technologies. Human rights to education and development are possible without access to and use of information technologies, but they are much more effective with the technologies.

Article 19 of the UDHR most explicitly deals with issues of information, enshrining rights to "freedom of opinion and expression" and to "seek, receive and impart information and ideas through any media," as well as freedom from "interference" in seeking and exchanging information and ideas. Based on this Article and many other parts of the UDHR, the ability to access and use the internet for purposes of education and expression has been identified as a human right in many quarters. Not long after use of the World Wide Web became commonplace, scholars of law, information, technology, and education began making arguments in favor of universal internet access as a necessary part of human rights (e.g., Brophy and Halpin 1999; Lievrouw and Farb 2003; Mart 2003; McIver, Birdsall, and Rasmussen 2003; Willingham 2008). As internet-enabled technologies have become more mobile and omnipresent—and vital to education, employment, civic engagement, communication, and entertainment—these arguments have matured into assertions that the abilities to successfully access and use the internet are both human rights (e.g., Jaeger 2013; Koepfler, Mascaro, and Jaeger 2014; Lyons 2011; Sturges and Gastinger 2010; Thompson, Jaeger, Taylor, Subramaniam, and Bertot 2014).

The American Library Association (ALA), the International Federation of Library Associations and Institutions (IFLA), the United Nations Education, Scientific and Cultural Organization (UNESCO), and other information professional and governmental organizations have adopted Article 19 and the principles of information access as a human right into their bylaws and policies. The Progressive Librarians Guild (PLG) in particular has advocated on human rights issues for several decades. Even the Internet Society, an organization that bills itself as "the world's trusted independent source of leadership for Internet policy, technology standards, and future development," declared the ability to use the internet to be a human right in 2011.

Also in 2011, a UN report explicitly discussed internet access as being central to supporting Article 19 of the UDHR and enabling many other aspects of the UDHR (Human

Rights Council 2011). Although the report never explicitly labels internet access to be a human right, many media outlets interpreted the report as doing so (e.g., Olivarez-Giles 2011). The IFLA-led Lyons Declaration on Access to Information and Development (2014) called upon the UN to make information literacy and digital inclusion central to their human rights and development agendas, building upon the assertions made in the 2006 Alexandria Proclamation for the UN and individual nations to make information literacy a central part of their goals (UNESCO, IFLA, and National Forum on Information Literacy [NFIL] 2006). Such statements reflect the ideas that have come to be known as information and communications technologies for development (ICT4D), which encourages the use of ICTs to promote community development and the growth of education, health care, and general welfare (Zelenika and Pearce 2013).

As technologies, related laws, and societal expectations related to information continue to evolve, key issues that will impact and reshape the intersection of human rights and information ethics include:

- Will information be viewed as a primary human right (one that stands on its own) or is it a derived human right (dependent on other rights)? Will the centrality of information to so many rights lead to it being considered a "lynchpin" right on which all others depend (Mathiesen 2012)?
- Will rights to information become more standardized under the law? Currently, the laws of most nations—including the United States—do not provide for an overall right to information, instead having laws that grant certain rights, such as privacy (Kelmor 2016).
- How will increasingly conflicting values about information—what is correct information, what is a reputable source, what constitutes information literacy, who should have access to certain types of information—shape rights and ethics related to information?
- Are human rights the most effective framework on which to establish information ethics? Nonlegal articulations of rights, such as the ethics of care, emphasize community responsibilities and provide alternative ways for ensuring rights (Caswell, Cifor, and Ramirez 2016).

There are also questions about this intersection that are important to the future of the information professions.

In recent years, as more attention has been paid to the role of information in human rights, many clear articulations have been made for the central role of educational and cultural heritage institutions—including libraries, archives, and museums—in ensuring human rights related to information in an age so dependent on information and technology (e.g., Duffy 2001; Hoffman 2001; McCook and Phenix 2006; Phenix and McCook 2005; Stinnett 2009; Suárez 2007; Thompson, Jaeger, Taylor, Subramaniam, and Bertot 2014). Libraries, archives, museums, and other educational and cultural heritage institutions are engaged in many activities at the intersection of human rights and information ethics, and often are finding new ways to foster and promote rights to information in the communities that they serve (Gorham, Taylor, and Jaeger 2016). Further, given their unique understanding of information issues, the information professions have the potential to be a societal leader in areas such as privacy, intellectual property, and other key topics at this intersection of human rights and information ethics (Mathiesen 2015). Ultimately, for information professionals, a primary question for the future of the profession is the extent to which supporting and advocating for human rights related to information will be central to the ethics of the information profession.

CASE STUDIES

1. According to the ALA's statement on Prisoners' Right to Read,

   > Participation in a democratic society requires unfettered access to current social, political, economic, cultural, scientific, and religious information. Information and ideas available outside the prison are essential to prisoners for a successful transition to freedom. Learning to be free requires access to a wide range of knowledge, and suppression of ideas does not prepare the incarcerated of any age for life in a free society. Even those individuals that a lawful society chooses to imprison permanently deserve access to information, to literature, and to a window on the world.

   In the case of *Bounds v. Smith,* the US Supreme Court established that prisoners have a constitutional right to access to the courts; however, in a later case—*Lewis v. Casey*—the Court held that prisoners do not have "an abstract, freestanding right to a law library or legal assistance." Could it be argued that this failure to provide prisoners with legal information is a violation of human rights, particularly if this restricts access to information in certain formats (e.g., books or the internet)?

2. With the "Homeless Hotspots" project, homeless residents of Austin, Texas, were paid to serve as Wi-Fi hotspots for visitors to the South by Southwest Festival. Critics of the project argued that this blurring of the lines between people and technology dehumanized the participants. Does the UDHR provide sufficient guidance with respect to the ethical issues raised here?

3. Do government policies that mandate the filtering of the content that can be accessed through library computers amount to a violation of human rights?

REFERENCES

Annan, Kofi. 1999. Comments at Telecom 99 + Interactive 99. www.un.org/press/en/1999/19991011 .sgsm7164.doc.html.

Blau, Judith R., and Alberto Moncada. 2006. *Justice in the United States: Human Rights and the US Constitution.* Lanham, MD: Rowman and Littlefield.

Brophy, Peter, and Edward Halpin. 1999. "Through the Net to Freedom: Information, the Internet and Human Rights." *Journal of Information Science* 25 (5): 351–64.

Calhoun, Craig. 2007. *Nations Matter: Culture, History and the Cosmopolitan Dream.* London: Routledge.

Caswell, Michelle, Marika Cifor, and Mario H. Ramirez. 2016. "'To Suddenly Discover Yourself Existing': Uncovering the Impact of Community Archives." *The American Archivist* 79 (1): 56–81.

Cramme, Olaf, and Patrick Diamond. 2009. "Rethinking Social Justice in the Global Age." In *Social Justice in the Global Age,* edited by Olaf Cramme and Patrick Diamond, 3-20. Cambridge, UK: Polity.

Duffy, Terence M. "Museums of 'human suffering' and the struggle for human rights." *Museum International* 53, no. 1 (2001): 10-16.

Gorham, Ursula, Natalie Greene Taylor, and Paul T. Jaeger, eds. 2016. *Perspectives on Libraries as Institutions of Human Rights and Social Justice.* London: Emerald.

Halpin, Edward, Steven Hick, and Eric Hoskins, 2000. "Introduction." In *Human Rights and the Internet,* edited by Steven Hick, Edward Halpin, and Eric Hoskins, 3-15. New York: St. Martin's Press.

Hoffman, Marci. 2001. "Developing an Electronic Collection: The University of Minnesota Human Rights Library." *Legal Reference Services Quarterly* 19 (3-4): 143-55.

Human Rights Council. 2011. *Report of the Special Rapporteur on the Promotion and Protection of the Right to Freedom of Opinion and Expression, Frank La Rue.* United Nations.www2.ohchr.org/english/bodies/hrcouncil/docs/17session/A.HRC.17.27_en.pdf.

Ignatieff, Michael. 2005. "Introduction: American Exceptionalism and Human Rights." In *American Exceptionalism and Human Rights,* edited by Michael Ignatieff, 1-26. Princeton, NJ: Princeton University Press.

Jaeger, Paul T. 2013. "Internet Justice: Reconceptualizing the Legal Rights of Persons with Disabilities to Promote Equal Access in the Age of Rapid Technological Change." *Review of Disability Studies* 9 (1): 39-59.

Jaeger, Paul T., and Taylor, Natalie Greene. 2019. *Foundations of Information Policy.* Chicago: ALA Editions.

Jaeger, Paul T., Natalie Greene Taylor, and Ursula Gorham. 2015. *Libraries, Human Rights, and Social Justice: Enabling Access and Promoting Inclusion.* Lanham, MD: Rowman and Littlefield.

Kelmor, Kimberli M. 2016. "Legal Formulations of a Human Right to Information." *Journal of Information Ethics* 25 (1): 101-13.

Koepfler, Jes A., Christopher Mascaro, and Paul T. Jaeger. 2014. "Homelessness, Wirelessness, and (In)Visibility: Critical Reflections on the Homeless Hotspots Project and the Ensuing Online Discourse." *First Monday* 19 (3).

Lauren, Paul Gordon. 2011. *The Evolution of International Human Rights: Visions Seen,* 3rd edition. Philadelphia: University of Pennsylvania Press.

Lievrouw, Leah A., and Sharon E. Farb. 2003. "Information and Equity." *Annual Review of Information Science and Technology* 37 (1): 499-540.

Lyons, Lucy Eleonore. 2011. "Human Rights: A Universal Declaration." *College and Research Libraries News* 72 (5): 290-93.

Mart, Susan Nevelow. 2003. "The Right to Receive Information." *Law Library Journal* 95: 175-89.

Mathiesen, Kay. 2012. "The Human Right to Internet Access: A Philosophical Defense." *International Review of Information Ethics* 18 (December): 9-22.

_____. 2015. "Human Rights as a Topic and Guide for LIS Research and Practice." *Journal of the Association for Information Science and Technology* 66 (7): 1305-22.

McCook, Kathleen de la Peña, and Katharine J. Phenix. 2006. "Public Libraries and Human Rights." *Public Library Quarterly* 25 (1-2): 57-73.

McIver, William, William Birdsall, and Merrilee Rasmussen. 2003. "The Internet and the Right to Communicate." *First Monday* 8 (12).

Nieto, Sonia. 2010. "Forward." In *Social Justice Pedagogy across the Curriculum: The Practice of Freedom,* edited by Thandeka K. Chapman and Nikola Hobbel, ix-x. New York: Routledge.

Olivarez-Giles, Nathan. 2011. United Nations Report: Internet Access Is a Human Right. *Los Angeles Times,* June 3, 2017. www.latimes.com/business/technology.

Phenix, Katharine J., and Kathleen de la Peña McCook. 2005. "Human Rights and lLbrarians." *Reference and User Services Quarterly* 45 (1): 23-26.

Pogge, Thomas. 2005. "World Poverty and Human Rghts." *Ethics and International Affairs* 19, (1): 1-7.

Raphael, David Daiches. 1967. *Political Theory and the Rights of Man.* London: Macmillan.

Sellars, Kirsten. 2002. *The Rise and Rise of Human Rights.* Stroud, UK: Sutton.

Sensoy, Ozlem, and Robin DiAngelo. 2012. *Is Everyone Really Equal?: An Introduction to Key Concepts in Social Justice Education.* New York: Teachers College.

Stinnett, Graham. 2009. "Archival Landscape: Archives and Human Rights." *Progressive Librarian* 32: 10.

Sturges, Paul, and Almuth Gastinger. 2010. "Information Literacy as a Human Right." *Libri* 60 (3): 195-202.

Suárez, David. 2007. "Education Professionals and the Construction of Human Rights Education." *Comparative Education Review* 51 (1): 48-70.

Sunstein, C. R. 2004. We Need to Reclaim the Second Bill of Rights. *Chronicle of Higher Education* 50 (40).

Thompson, Kim, Paul T. Jaeger, Natalie Greene Taylor, Mega Subramaniam, and John Carlo Bertot. 2014. *Digital Literacy and Digital Inclusion: Information Policy and the Public Library.* Lanham, MD: Rowman and Littlefield.

United Nations Education, Scientific and Cultural Organization, International Federation of Library Associations and Institutions, and National Forum on Information Literacy. 2006. *Beacons of the Information Society: The Alexandria Proclamation on Information Literacy and Lifelong Learning.* http://portal.unesco.org.

Whelan, Daniel, J. 2010. *Indivisible Human Rights: A History.* Philadelphia: University of Pennsylvania Press.

Willingham, Taylor L. 2008. "Libraries as Civic Agents." *Public Library Quarterly* 27 (2): 97-110.

Woodiwiss, Anthony. 2005. *Human Rights.* New York: Routledge.

Wronka, Joseph. 1998. *Human Rights and Social Policy in the 21st Century.* Lanham, MD: University Press of America.

Zelenika, Ivana, and Joshua M. Pearce. 2013. "The Internet and Other ICTs as Tools and Catalysts for Sustainable Development: Innovation for 21st Century." *Information Development* 29 (3): 217-32.

ADDITIONAL RESOURCES

Gorham, Ursula, Natalie Greene Taylor, and Paul T. Jaeger, eds. 2016. *Perspectives on Libraries as Institutions of Human Rights and Social Justice.* London: Emerald.

Jaeger, Paul T., Natalie Greene Taylor, and Ursula Gorham. 2015. *Libraries, Human Rights, and Social Justice: Enabling Access and Promoting Inclusion.* Lanham, MD: Rowman and Littlefield.

Mathiesen, Kay. 2012. "The Human Right to Internet Access: A Philosophical Defense." *International Review of Information Ethics* 18: 9-22.

Whelan, Daniel, J. 2010. *Indivisible Human Rights: A History.* Philadelphia: University of Pennsylvania Press.

Woodiwiss, Anthony. 2005. *Human Rights.* New York: Routledge.

PRIMARY SOURCE MATERIALS

Universal Declaration of Human Rights. www.un.org/en/universal-declaration-human-rights/.

CHAPTER 3

History of Ethics in the Information Professions

John T. F. Burgess

T his chapter is a review of the historical precursors to information ethics. It includes an introduction to the major themes and contributions of precursor disciplines, a list of significant figures associated with information ethics, and continuing issues and concerns. It functions as a conceptual primer, providing context and perspective for further study and does not seek to be comprehensive or to provide a chronology. Excellent examples of those already exist and are listed in the additional readings list at the end of this chapter.

Information ethics is a young discipline, and as is sometimes true with young disciplines, the boundaries of information ethics are still being drawn. Reviewing the terrain covered by historical precursors, such as the codes of ethics of information professions and trades, may provide better understanding of those boundaries. Codes represent the most significant applied ethical questions that emerged from these information practices and the resulting ethical guidance given to their members. By looking at the similarities and differences among the concerns of these codes of ethics, it is also possible to extrapolate the need for an ethics that focuses on information rather than practice as its domain. Before reviewing historical precursors, it will be useful to have a taxonomy of themes to sort similarities in topics across professional interests.

MAJOR THEMES

In her 2001 essay "Information Ethics," Martha M. Smith identified five major themes in information ethics literature: access, ownership, privacy, security, and community (M. Smith 2001, 33). These themes are addressed in more detail in subsequent chapters, but brief introductions are necessary here before attempting to show common historical concerns among information professions. Although these do not represent all of the themes that are common in information ethics research, they do highlight issues that have arisen repeatedly throughout the history of information work.

Access—Moral implications of limiting and providing access to information, information systems, and information technologies. Questions concerning access to information may explore such topics as whether limits on the ability to gain information are appropriate, the moral foundations of those limits, ways of prioritizing competing values and obligations with respect to access, and related topics. See chapter 4 for further discussion on access.

Ownership—Moral concerns related to the concept of property, frequently intellectual property, and increasingly digital intellectual property. Questions concerning ownership may explore the relative merits for society of privileging intellectual property rights holders versus the merits of extending the public domain. For example, who should benefit from innovations created through funding by tax-supported research, and how long should the descendants of artists profit from their work? See chapter 7 for a discussion on intellectual property.

Privacy and confidentiality—Questions about privacy, an expectation of reasonable anonymity and freedom from unwanted surveillance, and confidentiality, an expectation that communication is reasonably exclusive to its intended recipients, are frequent topics of information ethics research. One of the key moral issues considered by information ethicists is the value of privacy and confidentiality to a democratic society and how to balance those goods with the needs of law enforcement and defense. See chapter 5 for an overview of privacy and confidentiality.

Security—The expectation that one's person and property are protected from deliberate harm. In a highly networked society, the information systems and technologies that people interact with on a daily basis provide unprecedented access to personal information. One ethical consideration is what obligations governments have to protect their citizens, or companies their clients, and individuals to protect themselves and others against malicious or exploitative actors? Another concerns physical safety, and the ways that insecure information systems may compromise that. Many of the other issues of privacy, ownership, and access are complicated by issues of security. See chapter 9 for a discussion of cybersecurity ethics.

Community—Communication is an essential part of maintaining real-world and online communities. Questions arise about the moral obligations groups of people owe one another in a shared society and which ethical practices can best foster harmonious relations. For example, what does it mean to be a good digital citizen? How can information use promote or detract from the public good? How do information and communication technologies amplify existing social challenges or create new ones? See chapters 2, 6, 10, and 11 for aspects of community.

Each of these five themes is presented in terms of questions about obligations or expected norms. They may also be presented more proactively. For example, in what ways can information, its systems, and its technologies best provide opportunities and conditions for security, ownership, access, and so on? Regardless of the ethical framework from which one argues, these are all instances of applied ethics, a form of ethics devoted to resolving dilemmas. These themes represent real-world situations that can be made better or worse by the decisions we make.

PRECURSORS TO INFORMATION ETHICS

Before the formation of information ethics as a sub-discipline within ethics, people needed answers to the questions raised in the themes discussed above. Often, the people in search of these answers were information laborers, workers in trades and professions who oversaw the creation, storage, retrieval, dissemination, and monetization of information and information systems. Thomas Froehlich identified the fields engaged in precursor work as "media, journalism, library and information science, computer ethics (including cyberethics), management information systems, business and the internet" (Froehlich 2004, para.

1). In order to better understand contemporary information ethics research and practice, it is useful to look briefly at the contributions to applied ethics made by the members of these concerned groups who have produced professional codes of ethics. These codes serve as records of the kinds of ethical issues with which each typically deals, as well as current stances of those issues.

Journalism and Media Ethics

Journalism ethics are the applied professional ethics of reporters, editors, publishers, and other media producers. Applied ethics derived from journalistic practices can inform information ethicists about how to handle conflicts related to information gathering, distribution, and monetization. Although formal codes of journalistic ethics date back to the 1920s, Stephen Ward locates the origins of journalism ethics in the West to the English press in the seventeenth century, when an informal system of norms was developed by editors. One of these norms was the pledge of impartiality, which Ward points out was not so much an appeal to the idea of objective fact is it was a means of protecting journalists when publishing in authoritarian regimes while still cultivating the trust of the readership (Ward 2004, 126–27). This problem of how to remain financially viable while establishing and maintaining trust is an example of an applied ethical question and is one that persists, necessitating reflection and research. In his survey of information ethics, Paul Sturges points out the emphasis on access to information at the heart of the Code of Ethics of the Society of Professional Journalists, including familiar ideas such as "accuracy, balance, citing sources (when possible), avoidance of plagiarism, representation of minority and marginalized views, and encouraging open government" (Sturges 2009, 242). These strongly touch on the theme of access mentioned above but also speak to themes of ownership, confidentiality, security, and community. He also points out that the American Society of Newspaper Editors promotes ethics of "freedom, responsibility, independence, truthfulness, impartiality and fairness of the press" (Sturges 2009, 242). These could be seen as more of a core values-style or virtue-based normative approach to ethical dilemmas, demonstrating a range of means of addressing ethical challenges. Although the development of these codes of ethics suggest responses to specific crises arising from practice, they fit into the broader project of information ethics.

Computer Ethics

Computer ethics is a domain of ethical research focusing on the moral issues related to computation and the development of computing machines. As its own domain, it may be considered a sibling discipline as well as a precursor to information ethics. The history of the development of computer ethics is covered in more detail in chapter 9 of this volume. This section emphasizes computer ethics as it is currently applied in ethical codes by leading societies of engineers and programmers. Applied computer ethics considers questions of every phase of information labor, from creation and storage to dissemination and monetization, with a specific focus on the obligations of those creating information systems.

The Institute of Electrical and Electronics Engineers (IEEE) is the leading professional body of electrical engineers. The Code of Ethics of the IEEE features a list of obligations engineers owe one another, their institutions, and society, a number of which involve the appropriate use of information. These include issues of security that arise from the implementation of engineered systems, the need for honesty in truth claims, and the importance of avoiding harming others through false statements (Institute of Electrical and Electronics Engineers 2017). Part of the same initiative that led to the revision of the IEEE Code of Ethics in 2017, also brought about the launch of the information system specific efforts found in the IEEE Global Initiative on Ethics of Autonomous and Intelligent Systems. This group is working to develop standards outlined in the document *Ethically Aligned Design* (EAD) with goals of the promotion of human rights, well-being, accountability, transparency, and awareness of misuse (IEEE Global Initiative on Ethics of Autonomous and Intelligent Systems 2017, 6). The use of classical ethics is one of the foundations of this development process (IEEE Global Initiative on Ethics of Autonomous and Intelligent Systems 2017, 8).

The Association for Computing Machinery (ACM) is the world's largest computing society, encompassing researchers, educators, and practitioners. The ACM Code of Ethics and Professional Conduct was released in 2018 and consists of a preamble, collection of general ethical principles, specific professional responsibilities, professional leadership principles, and directions for responding to code violations (Association for Computing Machinery 2018). The preamble establishes the social responsibility of computing professionals and frames the need for those professionals to consider the public good. The general ethical principles discussed in the code that are of interest to information ethicists include honesty (1.3), respect for intellectual property and prior innovation (1.5), privacy (1.6), and confidentiality (1.7). The included guidance on professional responsibilities addresses security concerns involving computing systems (2.5, 2.7) and makes appeals to the public good when implementing systems (2.8). Under the leadership principles section, there is again an emphasis on community and the public good (3.1, 3.7).

Library and Information Science Ethics

Library and information science (LIS) professionals, such as librarians, archivists, and curators, have made significant contributions to the scope of information ethics. LIS professionals are charged with being stewards of institutions of memory and discovery. This institutional focus means that for every information practice being considered, there are multiple interested parties to consider: the individual user of an information system, the institution providing access to that system, LIS professionals, and the societies and cultures that those practices impact. This is even before considering obligations to the collections being managed, which also have ethical dimensions.

The American Library Association (ALA) is the oldest professional organization for librarians in the world, as well as the largest. Its major codes of ethics include the Code of Ethics of the American Library Association, the Library Bill of Rights, the Freedom to Read Statement, and the Core Values of Librarianship. The Code of Ethics was revised in 2008 and is a list of eight responsibilities for librarians and other library workers. Of interest to information ethicists are item II, which protects intellectual freedom; item III, which affirms the value of privacy and confidentiality; item IV, which addresses the value of a balanced approach to intellectual property; and item VII, which is meant to curb individual biases that might affect providing access to information sources (ALA 2008). The Library Bill of Rights was last updated in 1996 and includes six guides for policy. These are of interest to information ethicists because they seek to settle questions of how best to provide access to information resources, including the use of library spaces, in a pluralistic society. Most take a liberal position that what is most important is to allow individuals to evaluate information on their own without obstacles or bias. Of these guides, item IV may have the farthest-reaching implications for information access, as it instructs librarians to adopt a proactive stance and "cooperate with all persons and groups concerned with resisting abridgment of free expression and free access to ideas." (ALA 1996a, sec. IV) The Freedom to Read Statement was revised most recently in 2004 and is a collection of seven propositions. If the Library Bill of Rights was meant to address questions about library resources, the Freedom to Read Statement addresses questions of the value to society of diversity of opinion, taste, or inquiry. Information ethicists may turn to it to for a summary of arguments against censorship and for fostering tolerant communities and governments. Item six is particularly clear on the normative nature of this matter, stating that it is librarians' responsibility to "contest encroachments upon that freedom by individuals or groups seeking to impose their own standards or tastes upon the community at large; and by the government whenever it seeks to reduce or deny public access to public information" (ALA and AAP 2004, sec. 6) The Core Values of Librarianship document was adopted in 2004 and is a collection of eleven ideas that are meant to "define, inform, and guide" professional practice for librarians and library workers (ALA 2004, para. 1). In addition to reinforcing the guidance provided in the prior ALA ethics statements, the Core Values of Librarianship makes a new contribution by expressly aligning the library profession with particular political and economic theories. Specifically, with democracy and with the idea of the public good, particularly in the sense that public libraries and their services should not be replaced by for-profit companies (ALA 2004, paras. 5, 9).

The International Federation of Library Associations (IFLA) is a global organization made up of institutional and individual members, representing librarians and library users. The IFLA Code of Ethics for Librarians and Other Information Workers was last revised in 2016, and consists of a preamble and six principles, many of which address the themes of information ethics previously discussed in ways that are more sensitive to international concerns. The preamble does add a new consideration for information ethicists when it expressly aligns the international library community with the *United Nations Universal Declaration of Human Rights* (United Nations 1948). The relationship between human rights and information ethics is discussed in detail in chapter 2 of this volume. One concept that is made explicit in item five of the Code is that of being "strictly committed to neutrality," with a goal of creating balance in the collection and in access to other information services (IFLA Committee on Freedom of Access to Information and Freedom of Expression 2012, sec. 5) This is significant because espousing balance as its own desired outcome beyond the autonomy of patrons and publishers may been seen to set a more prescriptive goal for how information should be collected, with strict neutrality possibly outweighing other considerations. For instance, prioritizing neutrality may be in opposition to efforts to build collections in ways that oppose systemic racism. (Gibson et al. 2017, 752). In this example, we see how codes of ethics may also serve to point out areas of practice where established principles conflict, and where information ethical research may be of benefit (Burgess 2016, 162).

The Society of American Archivists (SAA) is North America's leading professional organization for archivists. In addition to the complexities of being institutionally based, shared with libraries, the information contained in archives may take the form of primary source documents and cultural objects. The ethics of SAA reflect the additional questions raised through practice as a result. Its Core Values of Archivists statement was approved in 2011, and its Code of Ethics of Archivists was most recently revised in 2012. Along with familiar concerns about access, diversity, service, and social responsibility, the Core Values also contains guidance on preservation, responsible custody, and history and memory (Society of American Archivists 2011, paras. 10, 11, 13). History and memory have an implied subject, the history and memory of real people and real cultures and the power that comes with being able to define history and shape public memory for others (Schwartz and Cook 2002, 2). This emphasis on the moral responsibility to specific people, particularly people who have been historically marginalized and exploited, is one reason for a shift towards the principles of community archiving. Community archiving happens when archivists yield custodial power to work to empower community members to choose what to archive and to share their professional expertise with that community (Cook 2013, 115). This applied ethical solution to an issue of memory and power may inform other information ethics questions of access, intellectual property, privacy, and community.

The International Council of Museums (ICOM) is a non-governmental organization representing museums and museum professionals. Its Code of Ethics of Museums was last updated in 2004 and consists of a preamble, eight principles, and the detailed operationalization of those principles. In addition to the obligations of librarians and archivists, museum curators have the public promotion of the contents of their collection as an ethical concern. Although significant portions of museum collections are stored for preservation, other portions are selected for public display. Professional expertise goes into deciding how to lay out the collection into classified categories, group items and arrange items within displays, and provide labels and other metadata content to inform visitors. Particularly pressing decisions come when culturally sensitive items or those of religious significance are selected, and when displaying human remains or the depictions of ancestors of members of extant cultures.

If one of the fundamental information ethical questions posed by archival practice is what the moral obligations are to preserve memory, the corresponding question for curators is what are the moral obligations inherent in representing knowledge about the natural world and human activities in it. The Code of Ethics of Museums describes this kind of moral obligation as being the public trust, and many of the specific behavioral guidelines outlined in the Code relate to meeting that obligation (International Council of Museums 2017, 8–10). Concern in the public trust is an expression of accountability that represents a pivot in emphasis in museum ethics, making museum users the primary obligation instead of the collection (Besterman 2011, 435). This prompts the question of who is the user, the visitor or society as a whole? In critical and comparative museology, the study of museums and museum professionals, care is exercised to unpack the legacy assumptions of colonialism on how the natural and human worlds should be represented, by seeking to incorporate indigenous understandings into decisions and practices (Kreps 2011, 458–59). These applied ethical questions can be seen in questions of cognitive justice and intercultural communication ethics, discussed in chapter 10 of this volume, and global digital citizenship as discussed in chapter 11.

Journalism ethics, computer ethics, and library and information science ethics are only three of the many fields identified by Froehlich as precursors to information ethics. However, in these three it is possible to note how often the themes of information ethics arise in the practice of information work. Professional ethical codes are examples of applied ethics in action, providing guidance and seeking to resolve conflicts. Through this analysis of the development of codes of information professionals it becomes clear that in addition to developing practice-specific ethical guidelines, there is a need for broader ethical principles that directly address what each of these professional organizations have in common: information.

INFORMATION AS SUBJECT OF A DOMAIN

If the majority of people using information ethics will be doing so from within the practice of a profession or trade, why is it beneficial to develop an ethical system that focuses on information in a more abstract way? One answer is that the nature of academic research and professional organizations tend to promote the siloing of their findings. The ethical innovations of programmers or archivists may never reach journalism or library ethicists, and vice versa, as a result of the tendency for researchers to read and discuss the work of their own peers. Another is that the inherently applied nature of professional ethics may skew ethical conversations towards norms that are highly situational: the right way to build a collection of information resources equitably, the right way to minimize bias in reporting, the right way to inform visitors about a culture that is not one's own, and so forth. Focusing instead directly on the more general questions of equity, bias, and representation may promote the articulation of more general principles that could be applied across profession or trade. Finally, the concept of information is used extensively in technical and specialist communication, lending it semantic weight. Philosophers of technology Norbert Wiener and Derek J. de Solla Price are two thinkers who are often credited with shaping the conversation about information production, control, and power (Wiener 1948; Price 1963). If industry leaders, professionals, and the general public use the word information in a way that gives it status, ethical inquiry into its nature and use is important as a means of unpacking where that power comes from, as a means of preventing its misuse.

In his series of essays on the history and domain of information ethics, Jared Bielby discusses information ethics as a phenomenological entity, one that arose out of the lived discourse of professionals but which is a distinct concept warranting philosophical inquiry (Bielby 2014, para. 12). Part of the philosophical inquiry process is definitional and must begin with a definition of information as the domain of information ethics. A full intellectual history of the concept of information is beyond the scope of this project. For that, see Rafael Capurro and Birger Hjørland's detailed summary of the etymological and multidisciplinary origins of information as concept. Although that essay was written as part of a project to consider the use of the term *information* as it relates to the LIS discipline, it outlines many of the ways the concept of information has been used across disciplines and over time. Their broad taxonomy of uses of the term information "breaks down to information as an object or a thing (e.g., number of bits) and information as a subjective concept, information as a sign, i.e., as depending on the interpretation of a cognitive agent" (Capurro and Hjørland 2003, sec. 5). Both of these broad definitions find expression in how major thinkers developed information ethics as described in the next section.

MAJOR THINKERS

Robert Hauptman (1941-). American academic librarian, library ethicist, and information ethicist. Credited by Martha Smith, Thomas Froehlich and others as the first to expound on information ethics as a domain in his influential 1988 monograph *Ethical Challenges in Librarianship* (M. Smith 2001, 30; Froehlich 2004, para. 2). He contributed to the growth of information ethics research by founding the *Journal of Information Ethics* in 1992. Hauptman writes extensively on themes of access, intellectual property, privacy, and confidentiality.

Rafael Capurro (1945-). Uruguayan philosopher of hermeneutics, information scientist, and information ethicist, active in Germany for much of his career. Reflected on the need for information ethics in practice, research, and teaching in an 1982 article review, and delivered lectures on the topic in 1985 (Bielby 2014, paras. 18, 24). Developed the angeletics theory of information, where information is conceived as natural messages in a way that resisted the kinds of reduction seen in other theories of information (Capurro 2009a, 80). The angeletics theory features an emphasis on context, and the theme of facilitating meaningful communication is extended through Capurro's writings on intercultural information ethics (Capurro 2009b). Capurro summarizes information ethics as having to do with "the problematization of behavioural rules about what is allowed or not to be communicated, by whom, and in which medium due to basic changes and challenges in the power structures of communication in a given society" (Capurro 2006, 177). He fostered the growth of information ethics research by founding the journal *International Review of Information Ethics* in 2004 as the publication arm of the International Center for Information Ethics, itself founded by Capurro in 1999. Capurro writes extensively on information theory, the information science discipline, and privacy.

Luciano Floridi (1964-). Italian analytical philosopher of information and digital ethicist. Floridi's core concept of information ethics extends from the idea of the infosphere, which in its conservative formulation is comprised of all existing "informational entities," which are digital and analog information bearing objects, broadly construed (Floridi 2014, 41). In an early work, when establishing that information ethics is a macroethic or framework for computer ethics, akin to virtue ethics, Floridi asserts a parallel between "life/ecosystem/pain" of the environmental ethicist and "information object/infosphere/entropy" for the information ethicist (Floridi and Sanders 2002, 1). In an extension of the harm principle, the ethical value of human actions towards the infosphere is measured in the degree to which those actions prevent or result in information entropy (Bielby 2014, para. 28). Floridi is the director of the Oxford Internet Institute's Digital Ethics Lab. He writes extensively on the philosophy of technology, logic, epistemology, and skepticism.

Martha M. Smith (1945-). American pastor and information ethicist. Smith was one of the first people in the United States to teach information ethics as distinct from library ethics. She developed an early synthesis of the writings on cyber and computer ethics and the philosophies of information and technology in a significant work of boundary-setting for information ethics that she calls global information ethics (M. Smith 1997, 39). She is also responsible for the influential taxonomy of information ethics themes used in this chapter. In her reflective essay on her early contributions to information ethics, using her experience in hospice care as a guide, Smith lays out the six fundamental dilemmas inherent in her taxonomy that deepens our understanding of the relationship among these themes. These dilemmas are access versus ownership, access versus privacy and confidentiality, ownership vs. security, community vs. access and privacy, community vs. ownership, and community vs. corporate and personal security (M. Smith 2011, 16). In that same essay, Smith documents the difficulties that came from being a pioneering woman in information ethics, which ultimately led to her leaving the academy, and gives advice to others who seek to make similar contributions in emerging fields (M. Smith 2011, 22).

CONTINUING ISSUES AND CONCERNS

In a chapter on the historical precursors and major themes of information ethics, the main continuing issue must be one of boundary-setting. Smith identified information ethics as a highly interdisciplinary field with a domain that is more abstract than those of its precursors. This means that those undertaking teaching, practice, and particularly research in information ethics must be prepared to continue the work of pioneering thinkers. Whether conceiving information ethics in one of the ways outlined above or not, like those thinkers one is likely to be called on to differentiate one's ideas from existing applied professional ethics while still being able to speak meaningfully to that professional audience. Although this can be a challenge, it is also an opportunity to make a distinctive contribution in a still-young discipline. In a time when questions about the right relationship among people, information, society, and cultures are both plentiful and urgent, there is room for new insights, new perspectives, and new disciplinary partnerships to further expand the boundaries of information ethics.

REFERENCES

American Library Association. 1996. Library Bill of Rights." www.ala.org/advocacy/intfreedom/librarybill.

———. 2004. "Core Values of Librarianship | Advocacy, Legislation and Issues." www.ala.org/advocacy/intfreedom/statementspols/corevalues.

———. 2008. Code of Ethics of the American Library Association. www.ala.org/advocacy/proethics/codeofethics/codeethics.

American Library Association and Association of American Publishers. 2004. *The Freedom to Read Statement.* www.ala.org/advocacy/intfreedom/statementspols/freedomreadstatement.

Association for Computing Machinery. 2018. ACM Code of Ethics and Professional Conduct. 2018. www.acm.org/code-of-ethics.

Besterman, Tristram. 2011. "Museum Ethics." In *A Companion to Museum Studies,* edited by Shannon MacDonald, 431–41. United Kingdom: Wiley-Blackwell.

Bielby, Jared. 2014. "Information Ethics I: Origins and Evolutions." Edmonton, Alberta: The University of Alberta. www.linkedin.com/pulse/20140625225908-299816747-information-ethics-i-origins-and-evolutions/.

Burgess, John T. F. 2016. "Reconciling Social Responsibility and Neutrality in LIS Professional Ethics: A Virtue Ethics Approach." In *Information Cultures in the Digital Age: A Festschrift in Honor of Rafael Capurro,* edited by Jared Bielby and Matt Kelly, 161–72. Wiesbaden: Springer VS.

Capurro, Rafael. 2006. "Towards an Ontological Foundation of Information Ethics." *Ethics and Information Technology* 8 (4): 175–86.

———. 2009a. "Angeletics—A Message Theory." *The Scientific Annals of "Alexandru Ioan Cuza" University of Iasi Communication Sciences* 2 (1).

_____. 2009b. "Intercultural Information Ethics." In *Case Studies in Library and Information Science Ethics,* edited by Elizabeth Buchanan and Katherine Henderson. Jefferson, NC: McFarland and Company.

Capurro, Rafael, and Birger Hjørland. 2003. "The Concept of Information." *Annual Review of Information Science and Technology* 37 (1): 343–411.

Cook, Terry. 2013. "Evidence, Memory, Identity, and Community: Four Shifting Archival Paradigms." *Archival Science* 13 (2–3): 95–120.

Floridi, Luciano. 2014. *The Fourth Revolution: How the Infosphere Is Reshaping Human Reality.* Oxford, UK: Oxford University Press.

Floridi, Luciano, and Jeff W. Sanders. 2002. "Mapping the Foundationalist Debate in Computer Ethics." *Ethics and Information Technology* 4 (1): 1–9.

Froehlich, Thomas J. 2004. "A Brief History of Information Ethics." *BiD: Textos Universitaris de Biblioteconomia i Documentació* 13 (December). http://bid.ub.edu/13froe12.htm.

Gibson, Amelia N., Renate L. Chancellor, Nicole A. Cooke, Sarah Park Dahlen, Shari A. Lee, and Yasmeen L. Shorish. 2017. "Libraries on the Frontlines: Neutrality and Social Justice." *Equality, Diversity and Inclusion: An International Journal* 36 (8): 751–66. https://doi.org/10.1108/EDI-11-2016-0100.

IFLA Committee on Freedom of Access to Information and Freedom of Expression. 2012. IFLA Code of Ethics for Librarians and Other Information Workers (Full Version.) www.ifla.org/news/ifla-code-of-ethics-for-librarians-and-other-information-workers-full-version.

Institute of Electrical and Electronics Engineers. 2017. IEEE Code of Ethics. www.ieee.org/about/corporate/governance/p7-8.html.

International Council of Museums. 2017. ICOM Code of Ethics for Museums. Paris: ICOM.

Kreps, Christina. 2011. "Non-Western Models of Museums and Curation in Cross-Cultural Perspective." In *A Companion to Museum Studies,* edited by Shannon MacDonald, 457–72. Malden, MA ; Oxford, UK: Wiley-Blackwell.

Price, Derek J. de Solla. 1963. *Little Science, Big Science.* New York: Columbia University Press.

Schwartz, Joan M., and Terry Cook. 2002. "Archives, Records, and Power: The Making of Modern Memory." *Archival Science* 2 (1–2): 1–19.

Smith, Martha. 1997. "Information Ethics." *Annual Review of Information Science and Technology (ARIST)* 32: 339–66.

_____. 2001. "Information Ethics." In *Advances in Librarianship,* edited by Frederick Lynden, 25: 29–66. Bingley, UK: Emerald Group Publishing Limited.

_____. 2011. "The Beginning of Information Ethics: Reflections on Memory and Meaning." *Journal of Information Ethics* 20 (2): 15–24.

Society of American Archivists. 2011. "SAA Core Values Statement and Code of Ethics." www2.archivists.org/statements/saa-core-values-statement-and-code-of-ethics.

Sturges, Paul. 2009. "Information Ethics in the Twenty First Century." *Australian Academic and Research Libraries* 40 (4): 241–51.

The IEEE Global Initiative on Ethics of Autonomous and Intelligent Systems. 2017. *Ethically Aligned Design: A Vision for Prioritizing Human Well-Being with Autonomous and Intelligent Systems, Version 2.* http://standards. ieee.org/develop/indconn/ec/autonomous_systems.html.

United Nations. 1948. *Universal Declaration of Human Rights.*

Ward, Stephen J. A. 2004. *The Invention of Journalism Ethics: The Path to Objectivity and Beyond.* McGill-Queen's Studies in the History of Ideas, no. 38. Montreal ; Ithaca: McGill-Queen's University Press.

Wiener, Norbert. 1948. *Cybernetics or Control and Communication in the Animal and the Machine.* Boston, MA: MIT Press.

ADDITIONAL RESOURCES

Alfino, Mark, and Linda Pierce. 1997. *Information Ethics for Librarians*. 1st Edition. Jefferson, NC: McFarland Publishing.

Besnoy, Amy, ed. 2009. *Ethics and Integrity in Libraries*. 1st edition. London; New York: Routledge.

Capurro, Rafael. 2006. "Towards an Ontological Foundation of Information Ethics." *Ethics and Information Technology* 8 (4): 175–86.

———. 2008. "Intercultural Information Ethics." In *The Handbook of Information and Computer Ethics*, edited by Kenneth Einar Himma and Herman T. Tavani, 639–65.

Carbo, Toni. 2008. "Ethics Education for Information Professionals." *Journal of Library Administration* 47 (3/4): 5–25. https://doi.org/10.1080/01930820802186324.

Fallis, Don. 2007. "Information Ethics for Twenty-First Century Library Professionals." Edited by Kenneth Einar Himma. *Library Hi Tech* 25 (1): 23–36. https://doi.org/10.1108/07378830710735830.

Floridi, L. 2006. "Information Ethics, Its Nature and Scope." *ACM SIGCAS Computers and Society* 36 (3): 21–36.

———. 2013. *The Ethics of Information*. Oxford University Press.

Froehlich, Thomas J. 2017. "A Not-So-Brief Account of Current Information Ethics: The Ethics of Ignorance, Missing Information, Misinformation, Disinformation and Other Forms of Deception or Incompetence." BiD: Textos Universitaris de Biblioteconomia i Documentació 39: 14.

———. 2004. "A Brief History of Information Ethics." BiD: Textos Universitaris de Biblioteconomia i Documentació 13 (December). http://bid.ub.edu/13froe12.htm.

Hauptman, Robert. 1976. "Professionalism or Culpability? An Experiment in Ethics." *Wilson Library Bulletin* 50 (8): 626–27.

———. 1988. *Ethical Challenges in Librarianship*. Phoenix, AZ: Oryx Press.

———. 2002. *Ethics and Librarianship*. Jefferson, NC: McFarland and Company.

Himma, Kenneth E., and Herman T. Tavani. 2008. *The Handbook of Information and Computer Ethics*. New York: John Wiley and Sons.

Kochen, Manfred. 1987. "Ethics and Information Science." *Journal of the American Society for Information Science* 38 (3): 206–10. https://doi.org/10.1002/(SICI)1097-4571(198705) 38: 3<206:AID-ASI9>3.0.CO;2-8.

Koehler, Wallace. 2015. *Ethics and Values in Librarianship: A History*. Lanham, MD: Rowman and Littlefield Publishers.

Kostrewski, B. J., and Charles Oppenheim. 1980. "Ethics in Information Science." *Journal of Information Science* 1 (5): 277–83. https://doi.org/10.1177/016555157900100505.

Mathiesen, Kay. 2004. "What Is Information Ethics?" *SIGCAS Computers and Society* 34 (1): 6.

Moore, Adam Daniel, ed. 2005. *Information Ethics: Privacy, Property, and Power*. Seattle, WA: University of Washington Press.

Preer, Jean L. 2008. *Library Ethics*. Westport, CT: Libraries Unlimited.

Samek, Toni. 2001. *Intellectual Freedom and Social Responsibility in American Librarianship, 1967–1974*. Jefferson, NC: McFarland and Co. Inc. Pub.

———. 2007. *Librarianship and Human Rights: A Twenty-First Century Guide*. Oxford, UK: Chandos.

Spinello, Richard A. 2012. "Information and Computer Ethics: A Brief History." *Journal of Information Ethics* 21 (2): 17–32. https://doi.org/10.3172/JIE.21.2.17.

Weckert, John, and Douglas Adeney. 1997. *Computer and Information Ethics*. Westport, CT: Greenwood Publishing Group Inc.

CHAPTER 4

Information Access

Emily J. M. Knox

I nformation access is the act of creating, disseminating, organizing, and preserving information for a given population. Providing access to information has long been considered the purpose for institutions and organizations such as libraries and museums (Preer 2008, 12). Information access is also related to the broader concepts of freedom of expression and the right to communicate. As Kay Mathiesen (2008, 574) notes, encouraging access to information allows for the realization of expressive acts and also provides for rich information cultures that lead to human dignity and autonomy. Information access is linked to concepts such as intellectual freedom, freedom of the press, and—in the context of government—freedom of information. Finally, information access is concerned with both accessibility as well as the moral obligations and principles of providing knowledge across many different dimensions.

DIMENSIONS OF ACCESS

Dimensions of information access can be most easily understood through the lens of the digital divide. The United Nations Educational, Scientific, and Cultural Organization (UNESCO) defines the digital divide as "the distinction between those who have internet access and are able to make use of new services offered on the World Wide Web, and those who are excluded from these services" (UNESCO 2016). It is more accurate to say that there is not a digital divide but many digital divides along economic, geographic, technical infrastructure, skills, gender, race, income, and other lines of separation. For example, there is an international digital divide, which describes how developed countries have greater access to ICTs and the internet than less-developed countries. There is also a skills gap where some people have the ability to use digital tools efficiently and meet their everyday needs and wants. All of these dimensions can also be applied to other types of information access more generally. For example, information access can describe the state of the freedom of the press in a given country or between countries. It can also refer to whether or not an individual person has the right to obtain and use a given piece of information. As noted, the ethics of information access is concerned with all of these dimensions though some theories are more strongly related to one dimension than another.

INTELLECTUAL HISTORY

Ethical theories of information access can also be classified along several dimensions. For example, in his article on freedom of expression, Kent Greenawalt (2005) notes that justifications for free expression can be divided among those that center on, for instance, society vs. the individual or speakers vs. audience. Like all ethical theories, justifications for information access can be divided into consequentialist and non-consequentialist. This section begins with a brief overview of ethical theories of information access including justifications for before the modern era.

Pre-Renaissance and the Enlightenment: Controlling Knowledge

The formal history of the ethics of information access is somewhat difficult to discern before John Stuart Mill's "On Liberty," which is discussed in more detail below. However, it is important to state that access to information and other forms of human expression has long been a source of concern for human societies. As Burke (2000) notes, there are many different types of knowledge and societies have grappled to determine which knowledges should become public. These types have been subject to regulatory schemes throughout history, even before the development of formal ethical arguments. For example, in monarchies, kings would legitimate certain information through the use of privilege (Lyons 2010).

Control over the ability to read and write is a method for controlling access to information. Often pre-Enlightenment arguments made for withholding literacy education from certain populations were consequentialist: "if this person is given access to this information or knowledge of reading, then harm will come to that person or society." Information has long been seen as a key to power within human societies and throughout history, humans have made ethical arguments concerning the controlling access to this power.

In Europe, the Enlightenment and the democratization of society led to more people having the ability to read and therefore the ability to access many different types of written information. During this time, individuals of influence began to offer new approaches to the democratization of information. For example, in 1621 King James I attempted to impose speech restrictions on the House of Commons who replied with a formal Protestation. In France, Diderot's published the *Encyclopédie,* an attempt to catalog the known universe of knowledge and give people ready access to it (Darnton 1979).

Post-Enlightenment: Truth, Rights, and Justice

In the post-Enlightenment Era, formal justifications for information access can be divided into three types: those that seek truth, those that are concerned with human rights, and those that are concerned with justice. No writer has been quite as influential in the area of information access than John Stuart Mill. Although it must be noted that his concern is more with freedom of expression than information access more broadly. First published in 1859, Mill's argument in "On Liberty" (Mill and Rappaport 1978) has long been employed as the basis for access to information in liberal democracies. The major theme of "On Liberty" can be stated as a question: "How can you know if what you believe is true if you do not hear the arguments of those who disagree with you?" Mill makes a consequentialist argument stating that self-protection from harm is the sole justification for interference with the right to free expression. Mill states that there are for freedom of expression: (1) silenced opinions may be true; (2) silenced opinion may contain some grain of truth even if it is held in error; (3) truth must be contested or it is simply prejudiced opinion; and (4) the meaning of truth must be held with conviction from reason and person.

Another important aspect of Mill's theory is his harm principle. One may only curb another's freedom of expression if it will cause harm. This "harm principle" is often contested especially regarding what constitutes harm and what should be done in response to harm. Also of importance is Mill's harm principle, which holds that preventing harm to others is the only good justification for curbing an individual's actions against her will. In the realm of information access this would mean that causing harm would be the only reason why information should be withheld from someone

According to Kent Greenawalt (2005, 282) what he calls the "truth-discovery justification" is often taken as an axiom in liberal society. He also notes that freedom of expression in service of truth is closely linked to the justification that seeks to both uncover and discourage abuses of power. As will be discussed below, this justification is strongly linked to laws that provide for access to government information or sunshine laws.

In the twentieth century, the *Universal Declaration of Human Rights* enshrined access to information as the right of every human being in 1948. Article 19 states, "Everyone has the right to freedom of opinion and expression; this right includes freedom to hold opinions without interference and to seek, receive and impart information and ideas through any media and regardless of frontiers." Kay Mathieson (2013) argues that this non-consequentialist argument is based on access to information as a linchpin right that secures access to other rights by preserving, remedying, and empowering information for all.

As noted, there is great concern over the harm that information access might cause. Ethical arguments are often rooted in social justice. The knowledge that there was foreign interference with the 2016 US and French federal executive elections has led to concern over how people access information and whether or not they have the skills to interpret the information they are given. There is also continuing concern regarding information bubbles and information literacy. In fact, much of this can be seen as response to a new medium for receiving information—the World Wide Web and the internet. This fairly new technology has shifted society in many ways and ethical responses are just beginning to emerge.

MAJOR THINKERS

John Stuart Mill (1806-1873). A Utilitarian, John Stuart Mill expanded the work of Jeremy Bentham and looked for the "best for the most" (or similar). As noted, his "On Liberty" is one of the defining works in the moral theory of freedom of expression and the arguments he made form the basis for information access in many liberal democracies. According to Elizabeth Rappaport the major influences on Mill include his partner, Harriet Taylor, and Alexis de Tocqueville, who argued that liberty could not be secured through the overthrow of tradition (Mill and Rappaport 1978).

Robert Hauptman (1941-). Hauptman (1976) famously requested information about bomb-making from thirteen libraries in 1976. He was appalled that he was not questioned by the reference librarians about this request. He wrote about this again in 1996 and noted that he was still concerned that librarians place information access above all other ethical considerations but was pleased that more normative work is being completed. In his book, *Ethics and Librarianship* (2002), Hauptman notes that he is especially concerned about the level of access that the internet provides. Although he praises the interaction that the internet affords, he writes that it does not live up to its promise: "The internet also allows scam artists, criminals, child abusers, and hatemongers easy access to their victims" (126). Hauptman argues that normative information ethics is a necessary palliative for the internet's information and communication excesses. Hauptman is also the founder and editor of the *Journal of Information Ethics*.

Elfreda Chatman (1943–2002). Although she was a social scientist and not an ethicist, Elfreda Chatman's theory of information poverty is important for understanding some aspects of information access. She notes "an impoverished information world is one in which a person is unwilling or unable to solve a critical worry or concern" (Chatman 1996, 197). This theory holds that some members of society are: (1) lacking sources; (2) this lack is associated with class; (3) they engage in self-protective behaviors; (4) these behaviors include secrecy and deception due to mistrust of outsiders; and (5) the negative consequences of not engaging with information sometimes outweigh the benefits. Chatman's theory is especially important for understanding the digital divide and how people operate within systemic information inequality.

CONTINUING ISSUES AND CONCERNS

Access to Information

Access to information (as opposed to information access) specifically refers to freedom of government information. As noted, Greenawalt (2005) argues that this conceptualization of information access is a subcomponent of freedom of expression that is intended to curb the abuse of government power. Access to information is part of the regulatory state and is ensured through the passage and implementation of what are variously called open records, sunshine, and freedom of information laws. In the United States, there are both state and federal freedom of information laws with varying degrees of strength and enforcement (Oltmann et al. 2015). Ethical concerns center on what sort of information should be made available and to whom. Although the laws are broadly written, in reality much government information is not available to the public. Over-classification (see, e.g., Aftergood 2017) as well as nonresponses to requests remain a continuing issue. The disclosures made by Edward Snowden in 2013 of warrantless surveillance by the US National Security Agency (Greenwald and MacAskill 2013) indicate that that governments are in fact abusing their power to surveil their citizens via technological means.

Intellectual Freedom

The American Library Association defines intellectual freedom as "the right of every individual to both seek and receive information from all points of view without restriction"

(Jones 2015). In information institutions, this right is often based in a liberal understanding of freedom of expression that can be found in Mill's "On Liberty." It has long been a core value of librarianship and other information professions that the outcome of the effects of new knowledge is unknown and therefore institutions can afford to include all points of view in their collections (Shera 1961; Knox 2014). However, this value has long been in tension with other values, such as justice and social responsibility. Toni Samek's (2001) monograph on intellectual freedom and social responsibility details this history within American librarianship. More recently, political shifts across the world have led some to question liberal intellectual freedom in the face of hate speech and other harms. The question of what an individual or group's response should be in the face of such changes is far from settled. The rights of employees to free speech and the status of whistleblowers continue to be issues of concern.

Digital Inclusion

As noted, the digital divide is the gap between the haves and the have-nots with regard to information communication technologies. Rather than working toward closing the digital divide, many groups and organizations focus on digital inclusion. Based in theories of social justice and the ethics of care, digital inclusion is "meant to signal a focus on a practical, policy-driven approach that addresses the needs of communities as a whole. In short, digital inclusion is a framework for assessing and considering the readiness of communities to provide access to opportunities in a digital age" (Digital Inclusion Survey n.d.). There are three aspects of digital inclusion according to the Digital Inclusion Survey: (1) *access,* which focuses on availability and affordability; (2) *adoption,* which focuses on digital literacy; and (3) *application,* or how ICTs are used in and for workforce development, education, healthcare, and civic engagement.

Information Literacy

After revelations that there was foreign interference in elections across the globe in 2016 and 2017, the issue of information literacy has come to the fore. So-called "fake news," information bubbles (Cooke 2018) and other threats have become ubiquitous. This seems to be the downside of information access. Referring to a *New York Times* editorial by Alexander Stille from 2001, Hauptmann noted that "discussants who agree reinforce each other's perspective, which then solidifies into a more extreme position; this results in fragmented communities" (2002, 126). The effects of this fragmentation have been felt in political processes and social movements across the world.

CASE STUDY 1

The library of a small-liberal arts college in Maryland has recently been contacted by the Chinese embassy. The Chinese government would like to pay for the linear feet of shelving to house 10,000 books that the government would donate to the library's collection. The payment is intended to ensure that the books are prominently displayed within the library building. The library's gift policy allows for acceptance of significant collections, but these are not usually made by foreign governments. The college has a large population of Chinese-national students as well as students who are interested in foreign service. The library's collection development budget for books has shrunk over the past five years.

Questions

1. Should the library accept the payment from the Chinese government? Why or why not?
2. What are the effects of shrinking budgets on information access? How should information institutions respond?

CASE STUDY 2

In 2017 the Environmental Protection Agency removed information from its website that discusses climate change. The United States has a system of depository libraries that offer free, public access to government information that is distributed to these libraries by the US Government Publishing Offices (GPO). In recent years, a large amount of government information has been published electronically rather than in print format.

Questions

1. Should federal agencies remove this kind of information from their websites?
2. Is removing this information an ethical issue? Why or why not?

Primary Source Materials

"On Liberty" (1859) [excerpts]

As noted, Mill's essay is a foundational text for justifications for freedom of expression.

> We have now recognized the necessity to the mental well-being of mankind (on which all their other well-being depends) of freedom of opinion, and freedom of the expression of opinion, on four distinct grounds; which we will now briefly recapitulate.
>
> First, if any opinion is compelled to silence, that opinion may, for aught we can certainly know, be true. To deny this is to assume our own infallibility.
>
> Secondly, though the silenced opinion be an error, it may, and very commonly does, contain a portion of truth; and since the general or prevailing opinion on any subject is rarely or never the whole truth, it is only by the collision of adverse opinions, that the remainder of the truth has any chance of being supplied.

Thirdly, even if the received opinion be not only true, but the whole truth; unless it is suffered to be, and actually is, vigorously and earnestly contested, it will, by most of those who receive it, be held in the manner of a prejudice, with little comprehension or feeling of its rational grounds.

And not only this, but, fourthly, the meaning of the doctrine itself will be in danger of being lost, or enfeebled, and deprived of its vital effect on the character and conduct: the dogma becoming a mere formal profession, inefficacious for good, but cumbering the ground, and preventing the growth of any real and heartfelt conviction, from reason or personal experience.

Before quitting the subject of freedom of opinion, it is fit to take some notice of those who say, that the free expression of all opinions should be permitted, on condition that the manner be temperate, and do not pass the bounds of fair discussion. Much might be said on the impossibility of fixing where these supposed bounds are to be placed; for if the test be offence to those whose opinion is attacked, I think experience testifies that this offence is given whenever the attack is telling and powerful, and that every opponent who pushes them hard, and whom they find it difficult to answer, appears to them, if he shows any strong feeling on the subject, an intemperate opponent. But this, though an important consideration in a practical point of view, merges in a more fundamental objection. Undoubtedly the manner of asserting an opinion, even though it be a true one, may be very objectionable, and may justly incur severe censure. But the principal offences of the kind are such as it is mostly impossible, unless by accidental self-betrayal, to bring home to conviction. The gravest of them is, to argue sophistically, to suppress facts or arguments, to misstate the elements of the case, or misrepresent the opposite opinion. But all this, even to the most aggravated degree, is so continually done in perfect good faith, by persons who are not considered, and in many other respects may not deserve to be considered, ignorant or incompetent, that it is rarely possible on adequate grounds conscientiously to stamp the misrepresentation as morally culpable; and still less could law presume to interfere with this kind of controversial misconduct.

With regard to what is commonly meant by intemperate discussion, namely invective, sarcasm, personality, and the like, the denunciation of these weapons would deserve more sympathy if it were ever proposed to interdict them equally to both sides; but it is only desired to restrain the employment of them against the prevailing opinion: against the unprevailing they may not only be used without general disapproval, but will be likely to obtain for him who uses them the praise of honest zeal and righteous indignation. Yet whatever mischief arises from their use, is greatest when they are employed against the comparatively defenseless; and whatever unfair advantage can be derived by any opinion from this mode of asserting it, accrues almost exclusively to received opinions. The worst offence of this kind which can be committed by a polemic, is to stigmatize those who hold the contrary opinion as bad and immoral men. To calumny of this sort, those who hold any unpopular opinion are peculiarly exposed, because they are in general few and uninfluential, and nobody but themselves feel much interest in seeing justice done them; but this weapon is, from the nature of the case, denied to those who attack a prevailing opinion: they can neither use it with safety to themselves, nor, if they could, would it do anything but recoil on their own cause. In general, opinions contrary to those commonly received can only obtain a hearing by studied moderation of language, and the most cautious avoidance of unnecessary offence, from which they hardly ever deviate even in a slight degree without losing ground: while unmeasured vituperation employed on the side of the prevailing opinion, really does deter people from professing contrary opinions, and from listening to those who profess them.

For the interest, therefore, of truth and justice, it is far more important to restrain this employment of vituperative language than the other; and, for example, if it were necessary to choose, there would be much more need to discourage offensive attacks on infidelity, than on religion. It is, however, obvious that law and authority have no business with restraining either, while opinion ought, in every instance, to determine its verdict by the circumstances of the individual case; condemning every one, on whichever side of the argument he places himself, in whose mode of advocacy either want of candor, or malignity, bigotry, or intolerance of feeling manifest themselves; but not inferring these vices from the side which a person takes, though it be the contrary side of the question to our own: and giving merited honor to everyone, whatever opinion he may hold, who has calmness to see and honesty to state what his opponents and their opinions really are, exaggerating nothing to their discredit, keeping nothing back which tells, or can be supposed to tell, in their favor. This is the real morality of public discussion; and if often violated, I am happy to think that there are many controversialists who to a great extent observe it, and a still greater number who conscientiously strive towards it.

The Universal Declaration of Human Rights (1948) [excerpts]

Ratified by the UN in 1948, there are five articles that relate to information access. Article 19 is the most direct, but the others have resonance with freedom of express, information literacy, and other rights related to communication.

Article 18.

Everyone has the right to freedom of thought, conscience and religion; this right includes freedom to change his religion or belief, and freedom, either alone or in community with others and in public or private, to manifest his religion or belief in teaching, practice, worship and observance.

Article 19.

Everyone has the right to freedom of opinion and expression; this right includes freedom to hold opinions without interference and to seek, receive and impart information and ideas through any media and regardless of frontiers.

Article 26.

(1) Everyone has the right to education. Education shall be free, at least in the elementary and fundamental stages. Elementary education shall be compulsory. Technical and professional education shall be made generally available and higher education shall be equally accessible to all on the basis of merit.

(2) Education shall be directed to the full development of the human personality and to the strengthening of respect for human rights and fundamental freedoms. It shall promote understanding, tolerance and friendship among all nations, racial or religious groups, and shall further the activities of the United Nations for the maintenance of peace.

(3) Parents have a prior right to choose the kind of education that shall be given to their children.

Article 27.

(1) Everyone has the right freely to participate in the cultural life of the community, to enjoy the arts and to share in scientific advancement and its benefits.

(2) Everyone has the right to the protection of the moral and material interests resulting from any scientific, literary or artistic production of which he is the author.

REFERENCES

Aftergood, Steven. 2017. "'Risk Avoidance' Leads to Over-Classification." Federation of American Scientists (blog), posted April 10, 2017. https://fas.org/blogs/secrecy/2017/04/risk-avoidance/.

Burke, Peter. 2000. *A Social History of Knowledge: From Gutenberg to Diderot, Based on the First Series of Vonhoff Lectures Given at the University of Groningen (Netherlands).* Malden, MA: Polity Press.

Chatman, E. A. 1996. "The Impoverished Life-World of Outsiders." *Journal of the American Society for Information Science* 47 (3): 193–206.

Cooke, Nicole A. 2018. *Fake News and Alternative Facts: Information Literacy in a Post-Truth Era.* Chicago, IL: American Library Association.

Digital Inclusion Survey. n.d. "What Is Digital Inclusion?" http://digitalinclusion.umd.edu/content/what-digital-inclusion.

Darnton, Robert. 1979. *The Business of Enlightenment: A Publishing History of the Encyclopédie, 1775–1800.* Cambridge, MA: Belknap Press.

Greenawalt, Kent. 2005. "Rationales for Freedom of Speech." In *Information Ethics: Privacy, Property, and Power,* edited by Adam D. Moore, 278–96. Seattle, WA: University of Washington Press.

Greenwald, Glenn, and Ewen MacAskill. 2013. "NSA Prism Program Taps in to User Data of Apple, Google and Others." *The Guardian,* June 7. www.theguardian.com/world/2013/jun/06/us-tech-giants-nsa-data.

Hauptman, Robert. 1976. "Professionalism or Culpability? An Experiment in Ethics." *Wilson Library Bulletin* 50 (8): 626–27.

_____. 2002. *Ethics and Librarianship.* Jefferson, NC: McFarland.

Jones, Barbara M. 2015. "What Is Intellectual Freedom?" *In Intellectual Freedom Manual,* edited by Trina J Magi and Martin Garnar, 3–13. Chicago, IL: American Library Association.

Knox, Emily J. M. 2014. "Intellectual Freedom and the Agnostic-Postmodern View of Reading Effects." *Library Trends* 63 (1): 11–26.

Lyons, Martyn. 2010. *A History of Reading and Writing in the Western World.* New York: Palgrave Macmillan.

Mathiesen, Kay. 2008. "Censorship and Access to Expression." *The Handbook of Information and Computer Ethics,* 573.

_____ . 2013. "The Human Right to a Public Library." *Journal of Information Ethics* 22 (1): 60–79. doi: 10.3172/JIE.22.1.60.

Mill, John Stuart, and Elizabeth Rappaport. 1978. "Editor's Introduction." In *On Liberty,* vii–xxi. Indianapolis, IN: Hackett Publications.

Oltmann, Shannon M., Emily J. M. Knox, Chris Peterson, and Shawn Musgrave. 2015. "Using Open Records Laws for Research Purposes." *Library and Information Science Research* 37 (4): 323–28. doi: 10.1016/j.lisr.2015.11.006.

Preer, Jean. 2008. *Library Ethics.* Westport, CT: Libraries Unlimited.

Samek, Toni. 2001. *Intellectual Freedom and Social Responsibility in American Librarianship: 1967–1974.* Jefferson, NC: McFarland.

Shera, J. 1961. "Social Epistemology, General Semantics, and Librarianship." *Wilson Library Bulletin* 35: 767–70.

UNESCO. 2016. "UNESCO-UNEVOC TVETipedia." www.unevoc.unesco.org/go.php?q=TVETipedia+Glossary+A-Z&term=Digital+divide.

ADDITIONAL RESOURCES

Greenawalt, Kent. 2005. "Rationales for Freedom of Speech." In *Information Ethics: Privacy, Property, and Power,* edited by Adam D Moore, 278–96. Seattle, WA: University of Washington Press.

Hauptman, Robert. 1976. "Professionalism or Culpability? An Experiment in Ethics." *Wilson Library Bulletin* 50 (8): 626–27.

Lor, Peter Johan, and Johannes Jacobus Britz. 2007. "Is a Knowledge Society Possible without Freedom of Access to Information?" *Journal of Information Science* 33 (4): 387–97. doi: 10.1177/0165551506075327.

Mathiesen, Kay. 2008. "Censorship and Access to Expression." *The Handbook of Information and Computer Ethics,* 573.

Preer, Jean. 2008. *Library Ethics.* Westport, CT: Libraries Unlimited.

CHAPTER 5

Privacy

Michael Zimmer

Privacy is a difficult concept to singularly define. Its meaning, value, and level of protection vary across cultures and have evolved continuously over time. Yet, from an information policy and ethics perspective, privacy has had a central role to play throughout history, sparking considerable debate, and often rising in importance alongside technological development.*

INTELLECTUAL HISTORY

While the concept of privacy has been central throughout history, its definition has evolved considerably since the eighteenth century. Initially, privacy was largely conceptualized in terms of freedom from physical intrusion into one's personal property or other private spaces, as famously articulated in prominent US jurists Warren and Brandeis's (1890) seminal essay "The Right to Privacy," in which they quote Judge Cooley's view of privacy as the right to be left alone. Later, in the wake of US Supreme Court decisions in *Griswold v. Connecticut* (1965) and *Roe v. Wade* (1973), privacy in US law became associated with freedom from interference into one's personal affairs, including having control over one's entire realm of intimate decisions, including those dealing with physical access to oneself; cognitive access to one's thoughts and one's intimate behaviors (Gavison 1980; Inness 1992). Most recently, building from Westin's (1970) early conception of privacy as the ability to control information about oneself, privacy has been closely identified with concerns affecting access to, and control of, one's personal information, including information about daily activities, personal lifestyle choices, medical history, finances, religious, or philosophical beliefs, distinctive physical descriptions, employment history, personal relationships, and sexual orientation, to name a few.

The vast legal and philosophical discourse on privacy has been summarized in various ways. Clarke (1997), for example, identifies four key dimensions of the concept of privacy in an attempt to reconcile this plurality of conceptualizations: (1) privacy of the person—concerned with the integrity of the individual's body; (2) privacy of personal behavior—relating to all aspects of behavior, but especially to sensitive matters, such as sexual preferences and habits, political and intellectual activities, and religious practices, both in private and in public places; (3) privacy of personal communications—the interest in being able to

---

* An earlier version of this text appeared in Zimmer, M. (2015). "Privacy Law and Policy." In P. Ang & R. Mansell (Eds.), *The International Encyclopedia of Digital Communication and Society.* Wiley-Blackwell.

communicate with other individuals, using various media, without routine monitoring of their communications by other persons or organizations; and (4) privacy of personal data—the claim that data about oneself should not be automatically available to other individuals and organizations, and that, even where data are possessed by another party, the individual must be able to exercise a substantial degree of control over that data and its use. Solove (2008) identifies six broad conceptualizations: (1) the right to be left alone-Warren and Brandeis's famous formulation; (2) limited access to the self—the ability to shield oneself from unwanted access by others; (3) secrecy—the concealment of certain matters from others; (4) control over personal information—the ability to exercise control over information about oneself; (5) personhood—the protection of one's personality, individuality, and dignity; and (6) intimacy—control over, or limited access to, one's intimate relationships or aspects of life. And Tavani (2009) reduces the philosophical discourse to four dimensions: (1) physical/accessibility privacy—freedom from unwarranted intrusion; (2) decisional privacy—freedom from interference in one's personal choices, plans, and decisions; (3) psychological/mental privacy—freedom from psychological interference and protecting one's intimate thoughts; and (4) informational privacy—having control over/limiting access to one's personal information.

In addition to the various conceptions of privacy presented above, there are further distinctions that are commonly used to help define privacy. The first is the distinction between descriptive and normative conceptions of privacy. A descriptive, or neutral, conception states what privacy *is* without incorporating into its meaning whether possessing privacy is a good thing or worth legal protection, such as Gavison's (1980) articulation of privacy as the measure of one's ability to control the access others have to oneself. A normative conception of privacy, by contrast, incorporates a presumption that privacy is something inherently worthwhile, valuable, and deserves protection. Here, privacy is defined not as something one simply has, but something one has a right to, such as the view of privacy as the right to be left alone.

Other distinctions focus on whether privacy is an intrinsic value—something desired for its own sake and necessary for human flourishing—or merely instrumental towards achieving higher-order values such as security or autonomy. And, although most conceptualizations of privacy focus on its importance for individuals, distinctions are also made on the social value of privacy (Regan 1995), maintaining that privacy serves not just individual interests but also common, public, and collective principles like freedom of speech, association, and religion. A growing perspective focuses the value of privacy (and, inversely, the level of concern over a privacy violation) on the practices and contexts that are involved in a particular information exchange. The need for privacy protection, in such a view, is not predetermined by overarching conceptualizations of the *de jure* value of privacy, but rather through a normative analysis of expectations of privacy in particular contexts (Nissenbaum 2009).

Solove's Taxonomy of Privacy Violations

Evidenced by the complex assemblage of conceptualizations and distinctions summarized above, a single authoritative definition of privacy remains elusive. Concerned that this lack of clarity impedes the ability to create law and policy to ensure appropriate privacy protections, Solove (2005) suggests a shift away from the vague term "privacy" and the attempts to articulate how such a right might exist, and instead moves us toward gaining a firmer grasp on the different kinds of activities that pose privacy violations. Such a framework can provide more concrete ways to understand and identify potential harms, and thus guide legislative and policy strategy.

Solove identifies four basic groups of activities that threaten to violate privacy, each with different related subcategories of activities: (1) information collection, (2) information processing, (3) information dissemination, and (4) invasion.

Examples of information collection include *surveillance,* the watching, listening to, or recording of an individual's activities, as well as *interrogation,* consisting of various forms of questioning or probing for information.

The second group of activities is information processing, the way information is stored, manipulated, and used after collection. Examples include *aggregation,* the combination of various pieces of data about a person; *identification,* the linking of information to particular individuals; *insecurity,* meaning any carelessness in protecting stored information from leaks and improper access; the *secondary use* of information collected for one purpose without the data subject's consent, and *exclusion,* concerning the failure to allow the data subject to know about the data that others have about her and participate in its handling and use.

Solove's third group of privacy-threatening activities identifies examples of information dissemination, which involve the spreading or transfer of personal data, or the threat to do so. *Breach of confidentiality* is breaking a promise to keep a person's information confidential. *Disclosure* involves the revelation of truthful information about a person that impacts the way others judge her character. *Exposure* involves revealing another's sensitive or personal activities, such as nudity, grief, or bodily functions. *Increased accessibility* refers to the amplification of the accessibility of information. *Blackmail* is the threat to disclose personal information. *Appropriation* involves the use of the data subject's identity to serve the aims and interests of another. And *distortion* consists of the dissemination of false or misleading information about individuals.

The fourth group in Solove's taxonomy involves the invasion into people's private affairs. Examples include *intrusion,* invasive acts that disturb one's tranquility or solitude, or *decisional interference,* the government's incursion into the data subject's decisions regarding her private affairs.

CONTINUING ISSUES AND CONCERNS

Privacy rights are inherently intertwined with information and communication technologies. Warren and Brandeis's argument for privacy as the "right to be let alone" was in direct response to threats posed by the latest technological developments of the late nineteenth century—the "snap camera" and "instantaneous photography"—which allowed people to take candid photographs in public places for the first time. Fast-forward 100 years and similar privacy concerns persist with cellphone cameras and online photo- and video-sharing websites.

In recent decades, digital communication technologies—including, but not limited to, cellphones, personal computers, the internet and World Wide Web, and the rise of social media—have generated powerful new infrastructures for the routine capture and flow of personal information. These flows take many forms and stem from various motivations. Cellphone providers track the geographic location of their customers to provide services and optimize network efficiency. Large-scale web advertising platforms and search engines use robust infrastructures to collect data about web browsing and search activities to provide relevant advertising. Users' consumption habits are captured by online service providers, such as Amazon and Netflix, fueling powerful recommendation systems meant to improve user satisfaction. Millions of people openly share personal information with friends and colleagues (and strangers) on social networking services, such as Facebook and LinkedIn, and their random thoughts and utterances with the world on platforms like Blogger, Tumblr, and Twitter. As evidenced by the rise of social networking and Web 2.0 platforms, the internet has become a platform for the open flow of personal information—flows that are largely voluntarily provided by users—and, as such, appears to have validated Sun Microsystems CEO Scott McNealy's infamous remark that "You have zero privacy anyway. . . . get over it" (Sprenger 1999).

Notwithstanding McNealy's view, privacy has remained a central concern amid the open information flows in our contemporary digital information society, including worries about the growing size and role of networked databases, the possibility of tracking and surveillance by internet service providers and Web search engines, privacy threats to digital rights management technologies, growing concerns about protecting the privacy of users of social networking sites and related Web 2.0 services, and threats of large-scale surveillance of online communication by law enforcement and other government agencies.

These privacy concerns have evolved far beyond what the framers of the Constitution, Warren and Brandeis, or Prosser (1960) could have envisioned. To focus our understanding—and to identify and address the legal and policy measures to address them—we can return to Solove's taxonomy of privacy violations as a means of organizing this panoply of privacy threats posed by digital information and communication technologies.

Information Collection

One common type of information collection that is currently the subject of public debate is using surveillance for the collection and processing of personal data, whether identifiable or not, for the purposes of influencing, managing, or protecting individuals. Surveillance, of course, has existed for centuries, and its methods have been continuously refined to broaden its reach and effectiveness. Clarke (1988) coined the term *dataveillance* —a portmanteau of "data" and "surveillance"—in recognition of the power of advanced digital information technologies and computer databases to facilitate the collection and exchange of information about individuals.

The role of digital information and communication technologies within infrastructures of dataveillance cannot be understated: store loyalty cards connect purchasing patterns to customer databases, intelligent transportation systems enable the tracking and recording of vehicles as they travel the highways, electronic key cards manage access to locations while creating a record of one's movements, and biometric technologies digitize one's intrinsic physical or behavioral traits for automated identification and authentication. More recently, the internet has emerged as not only a revolutionary technology for communication, commerce, and the distribution of information, but also as an ideal infrastructure of dataveillance, enabling the widespread monitoring and collection of personal and identifiable information about its millions of users. The privacy and surveillance concerns with various internet technologies have been well-documented and debated, ranging from the use of web cookies and tracking bugs, the emergence of spyware and digital rights management systems, workplace monitoring of electronic communications, the aggregation and data mining of personal information available online, and the widespread monitoring of internet traffic by law-enforcement agencies.

In the United States, limits on government surveillance and related information collection practices have been based on applications of the Fourth Amendment, most notably in *Katz v. United States* (1967), which made government wiretapping of communication subject to the Fourth Amendment's warrant requirements. With the emergence of new digital information and communication technologies, Congress revised wiretapping laws with the Electronic Communications Privacy Act (ECPA) in 1986, which restricted the interception of transmitted communications and the searching of stored communications. By specifying standards for law enforcement access to electronic communications and associated data, ECPA afforded important privacy protections to subscribers of emerging wireless and internet technologies. Although ECPA was a forward-looking statute when enacted in 1986, digital information and communication technology has advanced dramatically since its passage. It was enacted before web-based email became ubiquitous, before individuals began using cloud-based providers to store and share documents, and before individuals relied on social media platforms to share and archive personal histories, messages, and photos. Under ECPA, it is relatively easy for a governmental agency to demand service providers to hand over these types of personal information that has been stored on their servers. Efforts have increased in recent years to update ECPA to better reflect the contemporary digital information and communication environment.

Notably, US laws regulating information collection were considerably loosened with the passage of the USA PATRIOT Act (an acronym for the Uniting and Strengthening America by Providing Appropriate Tools Required to Intercept and Obstruct Terrorism Act of 2001) following the September 11, 2001, terrorist attacks. The PATRIOT Act effectively amended the ECPA, expanding the authorized use of wiretapping and electronic surveillance, ostensibly to intercept and obstruct terrorism. Provisions included expanding the definition of pen registers and trap and trace devices to apply to addressing information on emails and to IP addresses, allowing enforcement officials to read the addresses of all the emails that are sent from a computer and see all websites visited. The Act also provided for new justifications for delayed notice of search warrants, increasing the types of subscriber records that could be obtained from ISPs and communications providers, and expanding the application of the Foreign Intelligence Surveillance Act (FISA) to make gaining foreign intelligence the "significant" purpose of FISA-based surveillance, where previously it had been the "primary" purpose, thus loosening the standard for utilizing the secret approval process for engaging in surveillance actions. Although the PATRIOT Act has generated a great deal of controversy, it has withstood challenges and been reauthorized by the US Congress.

Other digital information collection methods have met some resistance, although it is often the presence of comprehensive global privacy laws that spark new privacy protections for users. The widespread use of web cookies by search engines, social media platforms, and advertising networks to track users' online activities has drawn considerable attention from privacy advocates and policymakers. While users in the United States have little legal protection from such threats to their online privacy by private companies, pressure from European regulators has resulted in improved privacy protections. For example, Google's practice of retaining personally identifiable information (e.g., IP addresses and cookie information) indefinitely came under fire by the Norwegian Data Inspectorate. Google relented and limited the length of time it would retain identifiable information on its users. Similarly, Facebook was investigated by Canada's Privacy Commissioner and was found to be in violation of Canadian privacy laws. In response, Facebook agreed to add significant new privacy safeguards. In both these cases, large multinational digital information companies were forced to respond to strong privacy laws from relatively small countries (in terms of their user base) in ways that benefited all users across the globe, irrespective of their provincial regulatory landscape.

Information Processing

The increase in information collection further exposes individuals to the privacy harms caused by new forms of information processing. New digital information processing technologies and techniques make aggregation more efficient and combining data and analyzing it certainly can be put to beneficial uses. Amazon.com, for example, uses aggregated data about a person's book-buying history to recommend other books that the person might find of interest. Credit reporting allows creditors to assess people's financial histories in a world where first-hand experience of the financial condition and trustworthiness of individuals is no longer possible.

Alongside these benefits, however, aggregation can cause privacy harms because of how it unsettles expectations. People expect certain limits on what is known about them and on what others will find out. Aggregation upsets these expectations because it involves the combination of data in new, potentially unanticipated ways to reveal facts about a person that are not readily known. From a law and policy perspective, the United States has done little to limit or regulate information processing in this way. The European Union's (EU's) Data Directive, however, has specific provisions intended to limit unwanted information processing. It mandates that personal data shall be obtained only for specified and lawful purposes and shall not be further processed in any manner incompatible with those purposes without specific consent. The EU's rules on information processing have impacted how companies like Facebook and Google handle and process personal information, forcing changes to features like automated tagging of faces in uploaded photos and the automated targeting of advertising based on user data.

One form of digital information processing receiving considerable attention from US regulators and lawmakers is online behavioral targeting. Behavioral targeting involves the collection of information about a consumers' online activities to deliver advertising targeted to their potential upcoming purchases. By observing the web activities of millions of consumers, advertising networks can closely match advertising to potential customers. Data collected includes what websites users visit, how long they stay there, what pages they view, and where they go next. The most well-known method for tagging consumers is with cookies, although methods such as web beacons and Flash cookies are actively used. Generally, the data that behavioral advertisers collect is not personally identifiable because it does not include the consumer's name, physical address, email address, or other personal identifiers that could translate directly to the offline world. Nonetheless, numerous threats to informational privacy persist. Online behavioral targeting results in the compilation and processing of a sizable array of potentially sensitive data about the consumers that exists outside their ability to protect, control, or monitor that data. By merely participating in the internet economy, consumers lose control over which details about their private lives are known, and they have little control over who gets to learn of these details after the data passes into a profiler's hands.

In response to these privacy concerns, the US Federal Trade Commission issued the report *Protecting Consumer Privacy in an Era of Rapid Change: Recommendations for Businesses and Policymakers* in 2010, which proposed a framework to balance the privacy interests of consumers with innovation that relies on consumer information to develop beneficial new products and services. The report also suggested the implementation of a "Do Not Track" mechanism—likely a persistent setting on consumers' browsers—so consumers can choose whether to allow the collection of data regarding their online searching and browsing activities. Some online advertising providers, such as Google and the Digital Advertising Alliance, a group of digital advertising trade organizations, have adjusted their behavioral targeting procedures as a result, offering consumers more transparency and access to information on how they are being profiled, and the ability to opt-out of tracking altogether.

Information Dissemination

Digital communication and information technologies have made information dissemination easier, faster, broader, and harder to reverse. The privacy harms that accompany disclosure and exposure are amplified when personal information can be disseminated via the internet and World Wide Web. With blogs and social networking sites, personal information is being posted online at a staggering rate, and given the ease at which information can be digitally recorded and spread, information previously contained within particular contexts or circles easily escapes out of one's control. Further, once personal information has been disseminated across digital networks, it is nearly impossible to recover or remove it. The proliferation of personal data on the internet can have significant effects on people's reputations, dignity, and privacy.

The fundamental premise behind most so-called Web 2.0 applications and services—characterized by popular websites, such as Flickr, Wikipedia, del.icio.us, Facebook, and YouTube, which feature user-generated content, opportunities for collaboration and harnessing collective intelligence, and relatively open platforms where anyone can participate, modify, or share content—is the open flow of personal information online. The wide-scale dissemination of personal information powered by Web 2.0 is further fueled by search engines that actively incorporate the information flows from Web 2.0 applications directly into searchable indexes. For example, a Google search for an individual's name routinely returns Facebook and LinkedIn profile pages, and Yahoo's purchase of Web 2.0 properties including Flickr and del.icio.us results in the possible integration of personal photos or bookmarks directly into its search engine results.

A similar privacy threat stems from the increased accessibility of archival information in a digital environment. Powerful web search engines can put pieces of information hidden in the most obscure websites at one's fingertips, information brokers provide detailed background checks and digital dossiers of personal information that are only a click away, and large databases of public records are increasingly placed online, removing any practical obscurity previously enjoyed by individuals who presumed only the most diligent researchers would find personal details of their lives hidden away in government archives.

Invasion

The privacy threats stemming from Solove's "invasion" category permeate many of the preceding examples. The collection of personal information through various digital surveillance technologies, web tracking cookies, or data mining algorithms all lead to a feeling of "digital intrusion" into our activities and lives—both online and off. New and innovative features of our digital landscape—such as Google's Street View cameras, Facebook's desire to track online purchases and automatically post such activities to a consumer's public profile, the ability for individuals to digitally record and process everything they "see" with the Google Glass wearable computer—present invasions to our personal spaces and activities in much the same way as the instant photography Warren and Brandeis fought in the late nineteenth century.

Perhaps the most potent example of digital invasion in the early twenty-first century is the discovery of, and reactions to, the US National Security Agency's robust globalized mass surveillance programs. Through a series of disclosures by Edward Snowden in 2013, the general public became aware of a variety of digital and electronic surveillance programs. The NSA's PRISM surveillance program, for example, combined many of the information collection, processing, and dissemination concerns outlined above through its massive aggregation of private electronic data belonging to users of major internet providers like Gmail, Facebook, AOL, Microsoft, and others. The NSA also reportedly routinely collected metadata on the phone records of more than 300 million Americans, and each day collects contacts from an estimated 500,000 buddy lists on live-chat services as well as from the inbox displays of web-based email accounts. Taken together, the data enables the NSA to draw detailed maps of people's lives based on their personal, professional, religious, and political connections.

The level of privacy invasions felt by these wide-scale digital surveillance programs and techniques has sparked considerable global concern and outrage. Various members of the US Congress have called for reform of existing surveillance laws and policies, and members of the European Parliament have proposed a measure that, if enacted, would require US companies to seek clearance from European officials before complying with US warrants seeking private data about European citizens. These reactions have met some resistance by those arguing for the need for advanced surveillance measures for national and global security, highlighting the ever-present tension between security and privacy.

Primary Source Materials

Warren, S., and Louis Brandeis. 1890. "The Right to Privacy."
Harvard Law Review **4: 193–200.**

> That the individual shall have full protection in person and in property is a principle as old as the common law; but it has been found necessary from time to time to define anew the exact nature and extent of such protection. Political, social, and economic changes entail the recognition of new rights, and the common law, in its eternal youth, grows to meet the new demands of society. Thus, in very early times, the law gave a remedy only for physical interference with life and property, for trespasses *vi et armis*. Then the "right to life" served only to protect the subject from battery in its various forms; liberty meant freedom from actual restraint; and the right to property secured to the individual his lands and his cattle. Later, there came a recognition of man's spiritual nature, of his feelings and his intellect. Gradually the scope of these legal rights broadened; and now the right to life

has come to mean the right to enjoy life—the right to be let alone; the right to liberty secures the exercise of extensive civil privileges; and the term "property" has grown to comprise every form of possession—intangible, as well as tangible. . . . Recent inventions and business methods call attention to the next step which must be taken for the protection of the person, and for securing to the individual what Judge Cooley calls the right "to be let alone." Instantaneous photographs and newspaper enterprise have invaded the sacred precincts of private and domestic life; and numerous mechanical devices threaten to make good the prediction that "what is whispered in the closet shall be proclaimed from the house-tops." For years there has been a feeling that the law must afford some remedy for the unauthorized circulation of portraits of private persons; and the evil of invasion of privacy by the newspapers, long keenly felt, has been but recently discussed by an able writer. The alleged facts of a somewhat notorious case brought before an inferior tribunal in New York a few months ago, directly involved the consideration of the right of circulating portraits; and the question whether our law will recognize and protect the right to privacy in this and in other respects must soon come before our courts for consideration.

REFERENCES

Clarke, Roger. 1988. "Information Technology and Dataveillance." *Communications of the ACM* 31 (5): 498–512.

———. 1997. "Introduction to Dataveillance and Information Privacy, and Definitions of Terms." www.anu.edu.au/people/Roger.Clarke/DV/Intro.html.

Federal Trade Commission. 2012. *Protecting Consumer Privacy in an Era of Rapid Change: Recommendations for Business and Policymakers.* https://www.ftc.gov/sites/default/files/documents/reports/federal -trade-commission-report-protecting-consumer-privacy-era-rapid-change-recommendations/120326 privacyreport.pdf.

Gavison, Ruth. 1980. "Privacy and the Limits of Law." *Yale Law Journal* 89 (3): 421–71.

Inness, Julie. 1992. *Privacy, Intimacy, and Isolation.* New York: Oxford University Press.

Nissenbaum, Helen. 2009. *Privacy in Context: Technology, Policy, and the Integrity of Social Life.* Stanford, CA: Stanford University Press.

Prosser, William. L. 1960. "Privacy." *California Law Review* 48: 383–423.

Regan, Priscilla. 1995. *Legislating Privacy: Technology, Social Values, and Public Policy.* Chapel Hill, NC: University of North Carolina Press.

Solove, Daniel. 2005. "A Taxonomy of Privacy." *University of Pennsylvania Law Review* 154: 477–564.

Solove, Daniel J. 2008. *Understanding Privacy.* Cambridge, MA: Harvard University Press.

Sprenger, Polly. 1999. "Sun on Privacy: Get over It." *Wired,* January 26. https://www.wired.com/1999/01/ sun-on-privacy-get-over-it/.

Tavani, Herman. 2009. "Informational Privacy: Concepts, Theories, and Controversies." In *The Handbook of Information and Computer Ethics,* edited by Kenneth Himma and Herman Tavani, 131–64. New York: John Wiley and Sons, Inc. http://onlinelibrary.wiley.com/doi/10.1002/9780470281819.ch6/ summary.

Warren, S., and Louis Brandeis. 1890. "The Right to Privacy." *Harvard Law Review* 4: 193–200.

Westin, Alan F. 1970. *Privacy and Freedom.* New York: Atheneum.

ADDITIONAL RESOURCES

Bennett, Colin J., and Charles D. Raab. 2006. *The Governance of Privacy: Policy Instruments in Global Perspective.* Cambridge, MA: MIT Press.

boyd, danah, and Alice Marwick. 2011. "Social Privacy in Networked Publics: Teens' Attitudes, Practices, and Strategies." *A Decade in Internet Time: Symposium on the Dynamics of the Internet and Society.* http://papers.ssrn.com/s013/papers.cfm?abstract_id=1925128.

Capurro, Rafael. 2005. "Privacy: An Intercultural Perspective." *Ethics and Information Technology* 7 (1): 37–47.

DeCew, Judith. 2015. "Privacy." In *The Stanford Encyclopedia of Philosophy,* edited by Edward N. Zalta, Metaphysics Research Lab, Stanford University. https://plato.stanford.edu/archives/spr2015/entries/privacy/.

Givens, Cherie L. 2014. *Information Privacy Fundamentals for Librarians and Information Professionals.* Lanham, MA: Rowman and Littlefield Publishers.

Gormley, K. 1992. "One Hundred Years of Privacy." *Wisconsin Law Review,* 1335.

Jones, Meg Leta. 2016. *Ctrl + Z: The Right to Be Forgotten.* New York: NYU Press.

Krotoszynski, Ronald J. 2016. *Privacy Revisited: A Global Perspective on the Right to Be Left Alone.* New York: Oxford University Press.

Richards, Neil. 2015. *Intellectual Privacy: Rethinking Civil Liberties in the Digital Age.* New York: Oxford University Press.

Solove, Daniel J., and Paul M. Schwartz. 2011. *Privacy, Information, and Technology.* Aspen Publishers.

Zimmer, Michael. 2008. "The Externalities of Search 2.0: The Emerging Privacy Threats When the Drive for the Perfect Search Engine Meets Web 2.0." *First Monday* 13 (3). http://firstmonday.org/htbin/cgiwrap/bin/ojs/index.php/fm/article/view/2136/1944.

CHAPTER 6

Ethics of Discourse

John M. Budd

It should be mentioned at the outset of this essay that "discourse analysis" will not be delved into deeply here. For some treatment of that aspect of discourse, refer to Budd (2006a). The attention here, naturally, will be on the ethics of discourse, which will necessarily entail the ethics of discourse analysis. It should be noted that the initial essays in this volume address the fundamentals of ethics and information and communication, an issue I have tackled elsewhere (Budd 2006b). As Alisdair MacIntyre (1984) emphasizes, the political and the moral do not have separate histories (or presents, for that matter). Theorizing and belief are both political and moral actions. "Every action is the bearer and expression of more or less theory-laden beliefs and concepts; every piece of theorizing and every expression of belief is a political and moral action" (61). Michel Foucault (1997) also speaks of the fundamentals of ethics:

> [One aspect is] what I call the mode of subjectivation . . . , that is, the way in which people are invited or incited to recognize their moral obligations. . . .
>
> [Another aspect is] what are the means by which we can change ourselves in order to change in order to become ethical subjects?
>
> [Yet another is] which is the kind of being to which we aspire when we behave in a moral way? (264–65)

The background to the ethics of discourse also relies on what Foucault expresses as the difference between an archaeological approach and traditional intellectual history:

> The analysis of the discursive field is oriented in a quite different way; we must grasp the statement in the exact specificity of its occurrence; determine its conditions of existence, fix at least its limits, establish its correlations with other statements that may be connected with it, and show what other forms of statements it excludes (1972, 28).

Foucault (1972) further states:

> It is both reinforced and accompanied by whole strata of practices such as pedagogy—naturally—the book-system, publishing, libraries, such as the learned societies in the past, and laboratories today. But it is probably even more profoundly accompanied by

the manner in which knowledge is employed in a society, the way in which it is exploited divided and, in some ways, attributed. (219)

For more on the application of discourse analysis in general, see Budd and Raber (1996).

ON DISCOURSE ETHICS

Conversational Analysis Ethics

There are severe limits on what can be addressed in this essay, so attention will focus on two elements of discourse—*conversational analysis* and *discourse ethics*. Brown and Yule (1983) refer to what I am calling conversational analysis as "transactional language." "In primarily transactional language we assume that what the speaker (or writer) has primarily in mind is the efficient transference of information" (Brown and Yule 1983, 2). Each of these elements of discourse has a history and an analytical background, but those backgrounds will not be delved into in detail here. For further background on conversational analysis see, for example, Deborah Schiffrin (1994). The primary purpose of the method is the analysis of the actual language employed in two-person or other conversations. I have previously (2006a) provided a brief example:

> Suppose two people are conversing and a portion of their exchange is as follows:
>
> A: Did you hear what he said?
> B: Yeah, but I don't buy it.
> A: I don't know; he seemed to know what he's talking about.
> B: Yeah, right.

It would be difficult for native English speakers in today's American society to assume that B is actually agreeing with A. At work is what Grice calls "conversational implicature" (1989, 26); the conversational context determines the meaning of some words, so "Yeah, right" in the above example is not taken as literal information (Budd 2006a, 67). This example is only intended to illustrate the nature of conversational analysis. I have written, "Applied discourse analysis of the type we are focusing on here is, perhaps first and foremost, *not* an ideation of human behavior. . . . As a method in our field, this kind of discourse analysis includes not merely *what* is said but also *how* it is said" (Budd 2006a, 69; italics in original).

Ethical considerations come into play in, for example, the reference interview in libraries. Many of the reference interviews that take place in libraries are generally straightforward and are not ethically problematic. However, there are times when the kinds of questions asked can raise ethical issues. The employment of language in this kind of discourse is, as Norman Fairclough (1989) notes, a social practice. Fairclough asserts, "Firstly, that language is a part of society, and not somehow external to it. Secondly, that language is a social process. And thirdly, that language is a socially conditioned process, conditioned that is by other (non-linguistic) parts of society" (22). As a social exchange—and embodying all that society means—discourse as conversation can definitely be ethically fraught. Case study one, below, will demonstrate both the ethical nature of this kind of discourse, as well as the kinds of difficulties that can arise in conversation.

An analyst, especially an analyst of the ethics of conversational situations, has a set of challenges that must be addressed. For example, Robin Wooffitt (2001) notes,

> whereas intuition fails the analyst, recordings of actual events, and detailed transactions of them, permits capture of the detail of participants' conduct. The analyst is relieved of the near impossible task of trying to imagine what goes on during the interaction: the analyst can actually find out by listening to the [recording], and investigation of the subsequent transcript (50–51).

Not all of the challenges can be dealt with here, but one that is important is consequentialism. This idea holds that ethics should take into account the consequences of all that we say and do. That is, all of this carries the weight of outcomes that we call consequences, and the consequences are of import especially to the "other" in any exchange. The other person may act upon what we say and do, which can make a material difference to that person and her or his life. There is an alternative to consequentialism, though. I have previously discussed the alternative—an agent-centered ethic:

> Samuel Scheffler (1994) argues for an agent-centered prerogative that must be infused into any ethical theory and that is absent from all consequentialist theories. Recognition of individual integrity, according to Scheffler, is vital to realization of human agency and authenticity. Based on that recognition, agents must be free to not always produce the best results or outcomes for society as a whole (Budd 2006b, 261).

The recognition of human agency, in keeping with Scheffler, is of utmost importance in acting ethically in situations such as those represented by case study one.

Another challenge to be faced is that of the semiotic or symbolic structure of the exchange. Not only are all of the linguistic utterances to be considered signs, but so too are the nonlinguistic ones (following Fairclough). There are many ways to examine the signs that appear in the exchange; one of the most fundamental is supplied by Ferdinand de Saussure. For one thing, Saussure (1959) makes a distinction between *langue* (or language)—what *could* be said, and *parole* (or speech)—what *is* said. Case study one illustrates the difference; each participant *could* have said any number of things, but they engaged in specific speech, which has ethical import. The examination of the signs, in this instance, must take ethics into account. As John Gumperz (1982, 11) explains, "While all information on language ultimately derives from speech, the assumption is that the raw information collected in situ must first be sifted and recoded in more general form before it can be utilized in the linguist's generalizations." In the present predicament, the examiner must take into account all speech and all signs (what is said and what is done) in order to reach answers to the questions asked at the conclusion of case study one. The speech itself must rely on, among other things, speech-act theory, as articulated by J. L. Austin (1975) and John Searle (1969). Space constraints prohibit exposition of the theory here, but Searle reminds us that sets of definitions and methods of study depend on the utterances that actually exist.

The semiotic analysis, with ethical examination in mind, can also draw from James Williams's idea of process semiotics. He takes a different view of the definition of signs:

> First, a sign is a selected set, where selection is an ongoing process rather than the settled outcome of a choice. The process of selection emphasizes a series of changing

relations between all things brought about by a selection of some of them. It is therefore to pick out things by altering their relations, yet without detaching them from all others (2015, 75).

The concentration, for Williams, is on "selection." The "process" semiotics depends upon the interpreter assessing the signifier and the signified and then selecting the most appropriate meaning for the sign (with respect to a given situation). There is a process of speculation on the part of the interpreter; signs are processes just as are other interpretable probabilities. In other words, there are choices to be made within a dialectical set of selections that are neither purely scientific nor purely antithetical to the sciences. As Williams writes, "The process account has no need for the distinction of signifier and signified, or expression and content, since these are replaced by a multiplicity of changing intensive relations between any selected things" (2015, 116). Though he does not address ethics directly, the selection process must include ethical considerations. The interpretation of a sign, as is indicated in the case study one, frequently requires ethical selection as part of the process. In fact, certain circumstances require that ethical consideration come to the fore. When discourse is less than entirely explicit (and sometimes when it *is*), there is a decided need for ethics to be integral to the selection process.

Discourse Ethics

The second aspect of the ethics of discourse that will be treated in this essay is quite specific and draws primarily from the thought and work of Jürgen Habermas. He asserts some norms that govern discourse ethics and the people who would acquiesce to such ethics:

> (D) Only those norms can claim to be valid that meet (or could meet) with the approval of all affected in their capacity *as participants in a practical discourse* (p. 66; emphasis in original).

For the moment, we can stress "practical discourse." There are numerous instances where, in organizations like libraries and other information organizations, discursive practice carries ethical import. The ethics includes both content and process. The content element may be most apparent to librarians and archivists because the concerns that involve the content of work, services, and communities are common topics of discussion. Awareness of the process element may arise only during meetings or discussions, when the process is faulty. In addition to Habermas (more about whom will be said later), Foucault speaks to the matter of discursive practice: "The analysis of the discursive field is oriented in a quite different way; we must grasp the statement in the exact specificity of its occurrence; determine its conditions of existence, fix at least its limits, establish its correlations with other statements that may be connected with it, and show what other forms of statements it excludes" (1972, 28).

To return to Habermas, he addresses discourse ethics in some detail: "Discourse ethics, then, stands or falls with two assumptions: (a) that normative claims to validity have cognitive meaning and can be treated *like* claims to truth and (b) that the justification of norms and commands requires that a real discourse be carried out and thus cannot occur in a strictly monological form, i.e., in the form of a hypothetical process of argumentation occurring in the individual mind" (1990, 68).

These assumptions are powerful and essential. The first carries the presumption of claims to truth, which places a burden upon speakers in organizational settings (as well as elsewhere). There is much that could be said about truth, but a summary of what truth is and can do will suffice for the purposes of discourse ethics (and ethics in discourse generally). Michael Lynch provides such a summary that is very effective for the present: "that truth is objective; that it is good to believe what is true; that truth is a worthy goal of inquiry; and that truth is worth caring about for its own sake" (2004, 4). Discourse ethics, in the ideal, relies on just these kinds of elements for organizational communication to be successful.

In order to follow Habermas when it comes to a full and complete conception of discourse ethics, one should adopt all the conditions that Habermas imposes. It should be stated that these conditions are extensive and are integral to the operations of practical discourse under ethical conditions. He states:

> My programmatic justification of discourse ethics requires all of the following:
>
> 1. A definition of a universalization principle that functions as a rule of argumentation
>
> 2. The identification of pragmatic presuppositions of argumentation that are inescapable and have a normative content
>
> 3. The explicit statement of that normative content (e.g., in the form of discourse rules)
>
> 4. Proof that a relation of material implication holds between steps (3) and (1) in connection with the idea of the justification of norms (Habermas 1990, 96–97).

These rules should apply to any practical discourse, especially by groups. When there are differences of opinion, argumentation (rather than *dispute or debate*) should hold sway. As Habermas indicates, a pragmatics needs to be a foundation of the argumentation; this is ineluctably related to the normative nature of the content of argumentation. In summary, there is a normative process plus normative content to the argumentation. Human practical discourse should follow these ideals. [(Note that they are indeed *ideals,* as is ethical action itself.)]

Habermas sets up another group of ideals that are intended to guide practical discourse in real situations:

> (3.1) Every subject with the competence to speak and act is allowed to take part in a discourse.
>
> (3.2) a. Everyone is allowed to question any assertion whatsoever.
>   b. Everyone is allowed to introduce any assertion whatever into the discourse.
>   c. Everyone is allowed to express his attitudes, desires, and needs.
>
> (3.3) d.? No speaker may be prevented, by internal or external coercion, from exercising his rights as laid down in (3.1) and (3.2) (1990, 89).

What Habermas is espousing is reminiscent of classical liberalism, in the tradition of Mill, Rawls, and others. One may disagree with the demands that are placed on subjects, but the demands also articulate ideal action for participants in practical discourse, including the discursive practices that take place in organizations like libraries.

The case study two, below, is intended to present, as closely as possible, the kind of predicament that can be faced in a library organization. The discursive practices described at the outset should seem familiar to those who work in complex human organizations such as libraries. An objective in these kinds of organizations is the efficient and effective resolution of matters that affect the functioning of the library (in as timely a manner as possible). When there are disputes in meetings, the processes of productive argumentation can fall by the wayside. The questions asked, then, are aimed at prompting analysis of both of the processes of argumentation and the content of the matter to be resolved. Both elements carry ethical aspects for action; in fact, practical discourse demands ethical action. The action required entails listening as well as speaking; there is a demand for each participant to weigh what is said and evaluate it according to the content element. The argument that follows speaking and listening can be said to be Aristotelean in nature. The various speech acts are to be assessed according to logic and ethics. That is, the assessment cannot stop with what may make sense; it must continue on to what is right for the organization, the people in it, and the communities served. The foregoing places a particular responsibility upon the participants. As each person listens, that person must keep an open mind to what is said and to weigh it according to the process and content requirements. This is not an easily met responsibility. As Habermas says, the actions of the participants are not hypothetical; they are genuine and are to be met within the social structure of the event (1990, 104). He further states that practical discourse involves the application of the norms that are established *a priori*. The processes described above are agreed upon before the event of something like a meeting. The results or outcome is to be judged according to the degree to which the processes are held intact and foster the success of ethical practical discourse (1990, 103).

Perhaps the most effective summary and evaluation of Habermas's program has been offered by Donald Moon:

> Habermas has presented one of the most powerful accounts of a discourse-based morality; it is grounded in an understanding of practical reason which explains how the validity of norms can be tested, thereby demonstrating their cognitive character. According to Habermas, valid norms can be freely accepted by all of the individuals who are affected by them. Thus, a society where institutions and practices were governed by valid norms would instantiate the ideal of a moral community (1995, 143).

Moon captures the entirety of Habermas's ideas and emphasizes that not only are the norms carriers of validity, they contribute to the establishment and maintenance of a moral community. An objective of practical discourse of this sort is creation, not only of institutional practices, but of an ethically based community.

Not everyone, it should be mentioned, accepts Habermas's discourse ethics as entirely valid (although even critics admit to the efficacy of the fundamental ideas of the idea). Todd Hedrick is one such sympathetic critic. He writes:

> Many of [Habermas's] long-standing concerns about the technocratization of politics and the depoliticization of citizens stems from what he sees as Western modernity's unfortunate tendency to treat social coordination problems that could be solved consensually as technical problems to be solved through the application of bureaucratic power; this is an aspect of the lifeworld (2010, 96).

The elements of discourse theory mentioned above are less technical and less bureaucratic than Hedrick critiques, but when Habermas turns his attention to politics he does add a technical aspect both to problems of communication and to their solutions. This criticism is noted here in the interest of full disclosure; the ethics of discourse does have a foundation in the aforementioned characteristics of formal discourse ethics.

DISCUSSION

Two quite different types of discourse ethics have been treated here. Although there are nominal differences between the two, there are some obvious similarities. The most pertinent and powerful is that both are instances of practical discourse. They are examples of the kinds of discursive practices in which people actually engage. Whether the focus is on conversational analysis or discourse ethics, the emphasis is on the practices that people engage in as they live their lives. Foucault adds to the similarity by articulating two essential questions: "What are the means by which we can change ourselves in order to become ethical subjects?" and "Which is the kind of being to which we aspire when we behave in a moral way?" (1997, 265). Although it is Habermas who speaks directly of *lifeworld,* the concept applies to conversational analysis as well. Lifeworld refers, in part, to the lived experiences of human agents, of subjects. There is not space here to delve deeply into the complexities of the idea of lifeworld, but a few tenets, propounded first by Edmund Husserl (1972), must be mentioned. Habermas states, "the phenomenological concept of lifeworld suggests a conception of world constitution borrowed from epistemology. . . .. 'Lifeworld' shall therefore be introduced as a complementary concept to communicative action" (1998, 239). Lifeworld likewise applies to conversational analysis, because it is also communicative action among subjects. As Habermas notes, lifeworld, for Husserl, is not an idealization; rather, it represents real interactions among human agents in the course of lived experiences in the world, and with one another.

Two elements of discourse (or discursive practice) are imbued with ethical import. In particular, the humans who engage in the practices have ethical responsibilities, and those responsibilities are necessities for action and work. In fact, the examination of discursive practice is possible if the analyst comprehends the situatedness of the practice, the arrangement of the practice in time, place, etc. As Gary Radford reminds us, "like any statement, whether it be a book on the library shelf or a single sentence within this article, historical documents do not speak for themselves. Their significance lies in their place within a greater discursive formation, that is, in the ways they are combined and arranged with other documents/statements" (2003, 14).

CASE STUDY 1

A young woman, appearing to be of high school age, enters a public library and approaches a reference librarian. She seems uncomfortable and, eyes downcast, asks the librarian if she could get some books on biology. The librarian responds, "Certainly, we have many books on a variety of topics related to biology. Is there a particular aspect you'd like information on?" The young woman, still not making eye contact, says, "I suppose something on human biology would be what I want." This answer does narrow the topic down, but it is still quite broad. The librarian, taking the cue, says, "That helps. Would you prefer some historical, something that speaks to the nature of human development?" The young woman simply shakes her head. The librarian, remaining patient, asks, "Is the book you need something that would be used in a class assignment?" The young woman raises her head slightly and answers, "Uh, [pause] no, this isn't for school work." The librarian is beginning to wonder what the purpose of the request really is and hopes she can close the apparent gap a bit; she states, "There are many, many approaches to human biology; it would help greatly if we could narrow the topic down somewhat." The young woman shuffles her feet and doesn't say anything for a moment. Finally, she makes some more eye contact and says, slowly, "I guess [pause] what I really what is something about human reproduction." The librarian's concern heightens, and she begins to search the library catalog. It takes little time to retrieve materials on human reproduction. She shows some of the items to the young woman, asking, "Do any of these items look like what you want?" The young woman looks carefully at the list of hits and, saying nothing, very slowly points to a title on pregnancy. The librarian is alerted by the user's selection; she asks, "Would you like to see other items on this topic; for example, we have materials such as pamphlets from health organizations?" The young woman nods her head.

Questions

What could be the next response by the librarian? What responsibilities would a librarian have in such an exchange? Are there limits to what can be said to someone such as the young woman? In short, what does the librarian do to assist the user?

CASE STUDY 2

A sizable committee in an academic library is meeting to discuss an important policy matter that will, in the end, affect all units and all personnel in the library. The meeting, as is typical of most meetings, has an established agenda. As is also typical of many meetings, agendas can be quite general. In this instance, the agenda indicates which items are informational and which are action items. Because this agenda is based on major policy matters, it is to be expected that members of the committee might have associations and allegiances that could emerge in the course of the meeting. In fact, the allegiances do emerge in the discussion of the action items, with individual committee members standing up for their departments, functions, and communities. Disagreement comes to the fore as the committee members adhere to their allegiances. At times the disagreement becomes heated, with voices being raised and people attempting to speak over others. The meeting is on the verge of becoming chaotic, and a couple of the committee members attempt to dominate discussion and silence others. Further, the verity of some of the statements are open to challenge. This, unfortunately, is not an uncommon scenario.

Questions

What can discourse ethics contribute to render the discussion more effective? Can there be a commitment to item (D) (quoted above) prior to the beginning of the meeting? Should there also be a commitment to truth claims? Are there ways to avert the problems of such a meeting and create a setting where discourse ethics can flourish?

REFERENCES

Austin, J. L. 1975. *How to Do Things with Words,* 2nd ed. Cambridge, MA: Harvard University Press.

Brown, Gillian, and George Yule. 1983. *Discourse Analysis.* Cambridge: Cambridge University Press.

Budd, J. M. 2006a. "Discourse Analysis and the Study of Communication in LIS." *Library Trends* 55 (1), 65–82.

_____. 2006b. "Toward a Practical and Normative Ethics for Librarianship." *Library Quarterly* 73 (3), 251–69.

Budd, J. M., and D. Raber. 1996. "Discourse Analysis: Method and Application in the Study of Information." *Information Processing and Management* 32, 217–26.

Fairclough, N. 1989. *Language and Power.* London: Longman.

Foucault, M. 1972. *Archaeology of Knowledge and the Discourse on Language.* Translated by A. M. S. Smith. New York: Pantheon.

_____. 1997. *Ethics: Subjectivity and Truth.* Edited by P. Rabinow. New York: New Press.

Grice, P. 1989. *Studies in the Way of Words.* Cambridge, MA: Harvard University Press.

Gumperz, J. J. 1982. *Discourse Strategies.* Cambridge: Cambridge, UK University Press.

Habermas, J. 1990. *Moral Consciousness and Communicative Action.* Translated by C. Lenhardt and S. W. Nicholsen. Cambridge, MA: MIT Press.

_____. 1998. *On the Pragmatics of Communication.* Edited by M. Cooke. Cambridge, MA: MIT Press.

Hedrick, T. 2010. *Rawls and Habermas: Reason, Pluralism, and the Claims of Political Philosophy.* Stanford, CA: Stanford University Press.

Husserl, E. 1972. *The Crisis of the European Sciences.* Edited by D. Carr. Evanston, IL: Northwestern University Press.

Lynch, M. P. 2004. *True to Life: Why Truth Matters.* Cambridge, MA: MIT Press.

MacIntyre, A. 1984. *After Virtue.* 2nd ed. Notre Dame, IN: University of Notre Dame Press.

Moon, J. D. 1995. "Practical Discourse and Community Ethics." In *The Cambridge Companion to Habermas,* edited. by S. K. White. Cambridge, UK: Cambridge University Press, 143–64.

Radford, G. P. 2003. "Trapped in Our Own Discursive Formations: Toward an Archaeology of Library and Information Science." *Library Quarterly* 73 (1): 1–18.

Saussure, F. de. 1959. *Course in General Linguistics.* New York: Philosophical Library.

Scheffler, S. 1994. *The Rejection of Consequentialism.* Oxford, UK: Oxford University Press.

Schiffrin, D. 1994. *Approaches to Discourse.* Oxford, UK: Blackwell.

Searle, J. R. 1969. *Speech Acts.* Cambridge, UK: Cambridge University Press.

Williams, J. 2015. *A Process Philosophy of Signs.* Edinburgh: Edinburgh University Press.

Wooffitt, R. 2001. "Researching Psychic Practitioners: Conversation Analysis." In *Discourse as Data: A Guide for Analysis,* edited by M. Wetherell, S. Taylor, and S. J. Yates, 49–92. London: SAGE.

CHAPTER 7

Intellectual Property Ethics

Kathrine Andrews Henderson

This chapter examines intellectual property rights as a matter of law and from the perspective of how an owner can assert his or her rights under these various forms of protection. Although it is critical not to conflate law and ethics, without some background about the relevant law, we cannot begin to determine if the law is ethical, fair, and justified in and of itself, and further, if the application of the law is also fair and just. This is a task that truly cannot be contained in these few pages!*

ETHICAL CONSIDERATIONS FOR INTELLECTUAL PROPERTY

It is important to note that professionals are expected to be law-abiding citizens even when we recognize that merely abiding by the law is not sufficient to ensure one is behaving ethically. Professional codes of conduct call for us to respect the rule of law, even as one advocates for change. For example, the American Library Association's (ALA) Code of Ethics states that "We respect intellectual property rights and advocate balance between the interests of information users and rights holders." Copyright, as noted by ALA, "is the aspect of intellectual property most pertinent for libraries. Further, copyright, as established by the U.S. Constitution and the Copyright Act, is a system of rights granted by the law combined with limitations on those rights."(ALA 2008).

All forms of intellectual property can be described as a system of rights that are constrained in various ways. These laws and systems are designed to protect creators and, at least indirectly, the public and businesses from certain harms in the marketplace, financial loss, damage to reputation, fraudulent goods, and so forth. Patents, trademarks, and trade secrets differ in that these systems focus on protecting the rights of the creator or owner and do not include countervailing rights for information users such as the right of first sale and exceptions like the Fair Use Doctrine or the TEACH Act, as found in copyright law. On the face of it, it seems reasonable to say that patent protections encourage invention, design, and scientific discovery; trademarks ensure that the public is purchasing goods and services from a specific supplier in which they have placed its trust with regard to quality; and that trade secret protection helps to ensure companies remain viable, thus protecting the livelihoods of their owners and employees.

Justifications for such systems of intellectual property echo the natural rights case for individual property ownership over what would otherwise be held in common. John Locke, for example, argued that man could be justified in accumulation of land and other goods provided he took no more than he could use before it spoiled, and what remained was both "good" and "enough for others," and if such property was accumulated through his own labor (*Stanford Encyclopedia of Philosophy* 2016). This justification for owning physical objects, especially land, is carried over to objects of the mind. Inventions and designs, expressions of ideas through works of literature, and works of art naturally belong to their creator. The difficulty in this application of the "sweat of the brow" justification arises because unlike physical property, when ideas, inventions, and creative works are revealed by the creator, they leave the creator, as Abraham Lincoln noted relative to patent, "with no special advantage over his own invention" (Lincoln 1859). "From the beginning, the United States recognized the critical need to protect authors and inventors from free riders—[who] have . . . taken the liberty of printing, reprinting, and publishing, or causing to be printed, reprinted, and published, books and other writings, without the consent of the authors or proprietors of such books and writings (8 Anne, c. 19, 1710) or those who have . . . without the consent of the patentee or patentees . . . devised, made, constructed, used, employed or vended such contraptions or conceived these breakthroughs through their own ingenuity" (Copyright Act, 1 Statutes At Large, 124, 1790).

The natural right of private property is one way of examining the ethics of the laws protecting the various types of intellectual property. However, another approach might also be applied—"justice as fairness." Justice as fairness is a political theory of society, promulgated by John Rawls, in which each citizen has the same basic rights and works cooperatively within an egalitarian economic system. Rawls argues that reasonable citizens, so long as they have the same basic rights, will be willing to go along with fair terms of cooperation even if it is not in their own best interest if others are also willing to do so. That is, the citizen has a sense of justice. Moreover, Rawls also argues that reasonable citizens have the capacity to understand what is valuable to others in society—a sense of the "good." These two complementary moral principles taken together allow for the development of public goods and these public goods are desired by all (*Stanford Encyclopedia of Philosophy* 2017).

Intellectual property protection schemes, copyright and patent in particular, have been enacted because they serve a significant social purpose—to promulgate and advance knowledge to enlighten and inform the public. By and large, reasonable citizens go along with the terms of cooperation—seeking permission, entering into licensing agreements, and so forth. In the case of copyright, this involves making fair use of works and taking advantage of exceptions to the exclusive rights delineated in the Copyright Act. However, as with all human enterprises, there are points of contention.

Justice as fairness is particularly useful in ethical considerations surrounding copyright especially when we analyze for example, the Digital Millennium Copyright Act of 1998. Many argued that the extension of the copyright term was so long that is was essentially perpetual rather than limited as called for within the Constitution. Moreover, technologies that have given rise to the sharing culture and social media make enforcement of protections more complex.

INTELLECTUAL PROPERTY

In the simplest terms, governments protect intellectual property—that is, the expressions of ideas, innovations, and designs dreamt up by authors, artists, writers, musicians, inventors, scientists, and scholars—from others who would sell or otherwise use these works without the permission of or compensation for the creator for his or her labor.

In actuality, intellectual property is an amazingly large and complex topic that impacts people globally. For many, these encounters take place every day, sometimes several times a day—including right now as you read this sentence in a copyrighted work. However, intellectual property is not something most people think about in their daily lives even though they encounter all sorts of things, every single day, that are governed by intellectual property laws. Consider for a moment a tall building with which one is familiar. Think back to before it was built, when the architect was designing the facade and other architectural elements. Think about the advanced tools and machinery, with their logos or brands prominently displayed, used by the workers as they constructed the building according to the blueprints. Then later, the "coming soon" posters, designed by graphic artists that advertised retail shops and restaurants, followed by tenants moving into the offices and apartments on the higher floors, the art and photography hanging on the walls, the sculpture in the lobby, the books on shelves, the music wafting out of speakers, the computers and smart devices with programs and applications—even the medicines in the bathroom cabinets are all in one way or another protected by different types of intellectual property schemes.

There are several ways intellectual property is protected—copyright, patent, trademarks and trade secrets, and related rights such as the right of publicity and the right of privacy. Each of these has its own characteristics, which help to ensure rights holders can monetize their creative works and inventions by protecting these works and inventions from infringement and/or other market harms.

The next few pages detail the history and the laws and legal characteristics of several forms of intellectual property. Although this chapter focuses primarily on intellectual property in the United States, one would be remiss to not recognize that intellectual property ethics and law is a global issue.

INTELLECTUAL PROPERTY HISTORY AND LAW

Accordingly, it is a fact, as far as I am informed, that England was, until we copied her, the only country on earth which ever, by a general law, gave a legal right to the exclusive use of an idea. In some other countries it is sometimes done, in a great case, and by a special and personal act, but, generally speaking, other nations have thought that these monopolies produce more embarrassment than advantage to society; and it may be observed that the nations which refuse monopolies of invention, are as fruitful as England in new and useful devices.

—*Thomas Jefferson (1813)*

With the notable exception of trade secrets, intellectual property rights have been established in law for hundreds of years, not only in the United States but in other parts of the world as well. Early examples of intellectual property laws include Britain's Statute of Anne, enacted in 1710, which is the basis of United States copyright law. Another important example is The Berne Convention of 1886, an international agreement under which contracting countries must provide a minimum standard of protection for each work and grant certain rights to authors relative to his or her own works. In addition, Berne also provides for "moral rights," that is, "the right to claim authorship of the work and the right to object to any mutilation, deformation or other modification of, or other derogatory action in relation to, the work that would be prejudicial to the author's honor or reputation" (World Intellectual Property Organization 2017).

Both the United States Copyright Act and Patent Act were established through the Patent and Copyright Clause of the United States Constitution, which empowers Congress to create laws, "to promote the Progress of Science and useful Arts, by securing for limited Times to Authors and Inventors the exclusive Right to their respective Writings and Discoveries." (U.S. Const. Art. 1. sec. 8. cl. 8).

The US Copyright Act of 1790

The US Copyright Act traces back to what is believed to be the first copyright law, Britain's Statute of Anne, "An act for the encouragement of learning, by vesting the copies of printed books in the authors or purchasers of such copies, during the times therein mentioned" (8 Anne, c. 19, 1710). So too goes the Copyright Act of 1790, "An Act for the encouragement of learning, by securing the copies of maps, Charts, And books, to the authors and proprietors of such copies, during the times therein mentioned." (Copyright Act, 1 Statutes At Large, 124, 1790).

Section I of the Statute of Anne specifically describes the situation that the act would remedy, "Whereas printers, booksellers, and other persons have of late frequently taken the liberty of printing, reprinting, and publishing, or causing to be printed, reprinted, and published, books and other writings, without the consent of the authors or proprietors of such books and writings, to their very great detriment, and too often to the ruin of them and their families: for preventing therefore such practices for the future, and for the encouragement of learned men to compose and write useful books . . ." (8 Anne, c. 19) The Copyright Act also notes the detrimental effects of other persons copying said works and provides exclusive copyrights and sets forth the idea of infringement, "That any person or persons who shall print or publish and manuscript, without the consent and approbation of the author or proprietor thereof, first had and obtained as aforesaid, (if such author or proprietor be a citizen of or resident in these United States) shall be liable to suffer and pay to the said author or proprietor all damages occasioned by such injury . . ." (Copyright Act, 1 Statutes At Large, 124, 1790).

Although it has been amended many times, significantly by the Copyright Act of 1976 (below) and significantly and controversially by the Digital Millennium Copyright Act, which extended "limited times" to what many considered perpetual; copyright's original purpose endures.

The Copyright Act of 1976

Copyright law was amended, "in its entirety" via Public Law 94-553, which is more commonly cited as the Copyright Act of 1976 (17 USC §§ 101 et seq.). This act is the modern legal framework for copyright protection in the United States. It is often the focal point of ethical concerns especially when one considers copyright's essential purpose is to promulgate science and the useful arts and its protections were meant to be limited. Some specific sections that are of substance and concern to information professionals include the following sections.

17 USC § 102. This section identifies seven categories of authorship. These categories are (1) literary works; (2) musical works, including any accompanying words; (3) dramatic works, including any accompanying music; (4) pantomimes and choreographic works; (5) pictorial, graphic, and sculptural works; (6) motion pictures and other audiovisual works; and (7) sound recordings (17 USC § 102). An eighth category was added December 1, 1990, for architectural works (United States Copyright Office Circular 41).

17 USC § 106. This section describes the five exclusive rights found in copyrighted works. Unless one's use falls under an exception such as fair use (found in 17 USC § 107), copyright owners are solely able "(1) to reproduce the copyrighted work in copies or phono-records; (2) to prepare derivative works based upon the copyrighted work; (3) to distribute copies or phonorecords of the copyrighted work to the public by sale or other transfer of ownership, or by rental, lease, or lending; (4) in the case of literary, musical, dramatic, and choreographic works, pantomimes, and motion pictures and other audiovisual works, to perform the copyrighted work publicly; and (5) in the case of literary, musical, dramatic, and choreographic works, pantomimes, and pictorial, graphic, or sculptural works including the individual images of a motion picture or other audiovisual work, to display the copyrighted work publicly." (17 USC § 106, 1976).

17 USC § 107. This section provides for a key exception to the exclusive rights of the copyright holder, fair use. The fair use exceptions allow others to make non-infringing uses of copyrighted works "including such use by reproduction in copies or phonorecords or by any other means specified by that section, for purposes such as criticism, comment, news reporting, teaching (including multiple copies for classroom use), scholarship, or research." In addition, the section includes the four factors that are considered in determining if a use is, indeed, fair: "(1) the purpose and character of the use, including whether such use is of a commercial nature or is for nonprofit educational purposes; (2) the nature of the copyrighted work; (3) the amount and substantiality of the portion used in relation to the copyrighted work as a whole; and (4) the effect of the use upon the potential market for or value of the copyrighted work." (17 USC § 107, 1976).

Under current law, the term of copyright for works created after 1978 are as follows: For a single author, the author's life plus an additional seventy years. For a "joint work prepared by two or more authors who did not work for hire," the term lasts for seventy years after the last surviving author's death. For works made for hire and anonymous and pseudonymous works, the duration of copyright is 95 years from first publication or 120 years from creation, whichever is shorter (United States Copyright Office Circular 15A).

Other important changes contained in the 1976 revision include the removal of registration requirements and the transfer of copyright ownership.

The Patent Acts of 1790 and 1793

The patent system added the fuel of interest to the fire of genius.

—*Abraham Lincoln*

Patent is another form of legal protection for intellectual property emerging from the same constitutional clause that empowered Congress to establish copyright. The Patent Act of 1790 is, "An act to promote the progress of useful Arts." (1 Stat. 109–112, 1790). This early public law authorized the US Attorney General and the Secretary of State to grant patents, if such requests met the requirements described therein; established exclusive rights to the patent holder and legal process to remedy infringement of these exclusive rights. The Patent Act of 1790, while not expressly recognizing that more than one inventor might apply for a patent, did consider the possibility that an applicant might falsely claim to be an inventor, "If it shall appear that the patentee was not the first and true inventor or discoverer, judgment shall be rendered by such court for the repeal of such patent or patents." (1 Stat. 109–112, 1790). However, The Patent Act of 1793 clarified and settled the issue that there is no legal requirement for patents to be granted to the first to invent. Section 9 of the act states, "That in case of interfering applications, the same shall be submitted to the arbitration of three persons, one of whom shall be chosen by each of the applicants, and the third person shall be appointed by the Secretary of State; and the decision or award of such arbitrators, delivered to the Secretary of State, in writing and subscribed by them, or any two of them, shall be final, as far as respects the granting of the patent . . ." (1 Stat. 318, 1793).

In the United States, "The right conferred by the patent grant is, in the language of the statute and of the grant itself, 'the right to exclude others from making, using, offering for sale, or selling' the invention in the United States or 'importing' the invention into the United States." (United States Patent and Trademark Office 2015).

Many other countries grant patent protection for inventors, but may use different terminology to express the same type of protection. There are a number of international agreements relating to patents and inventors can patent their inventions in more than one country. However, there is not a specific international patent for which one can apply.

Patent is quite different from copyright in that not all inventions and designs are patentable and the process by which one is awarded a patent is rigorous and time-consuming. For an invention to receive a patent, it must be new, novel, and/or nonobvious and it may not exist in prior art—that is there must not be any evidence that the invention already exists or has been conceived. Evidence need not be a physical version of the invention nor must the invention exist physically or be commercially available. Most countries including the United States have a grace period from six months to a year, depending on the jurisdiction that allows for the invention to have been presented at conference or discussed in other specific kinds of communications. It can take months if not years to obtain a patent.

There are three types of patents under United States Law (United States Patent and Trademark Office 2015):

1) Utility patents may be granted to anyone who invents or discovers any new and useful process, machine, article of manufacture, or composition of matter, or any new and useful improvement thereof;

2) Design patents may be granted to anyone who invents a new, original, and ornamental design for an article of manufacture; and

3) Plant patents may be granted to anyone who invents or discovers and asexually reproduces any distinct and new variety of plant.

In the United States, the current patent term for inventions (called utility patents) and for plant patents is twenty years, while the term for design patents is fifteen years (United States Patent and Trademark Office 2015).

Although most library and information professionals will not be confronted with ethical dilemmas related to patent, it is important to have a basic understanding of this form of intellectual property protection. Patents are valuable assets to companies and universities and increasingly investors, such as venture capitalists, who are concerning themselves with the market value of patents and how patents are or could be monetized through licensing. Although patents are frequently subject to litigation for infringement, patent holders may prefer to bring infringers into the fold through licensure agreements.

In addition to laws protecting creative works and inventions, two other forms of intellectual property are trademark and trades secrets, which also play an important role specific to commerce.

The Lanham Act of 1946

There were laws governing trademark prior to the Lanham Act of 1946; however, most trademarks that are currently in use in commerce fall under this act. The authority is found in the Commerce Clause, which empowers Congress "to regulate commerce with foreign nations, and among the several states, and with the Indian tribes" (U.S. Const. art. 1. sec. 8. cl. 3). The Lanham Act is also called the Trademark Act and "it provides for a national system of trademark registration and protects the owner of a federally registered mark against the use of similar marks if such use is likely to result in consumer confusion, or if the dilution of a famous mark is likely to occur." (Legal Information Institute 2017). Although the Lanham Act provides the most extensive trademark protection, there is also state common law governing trademark protection (Legal Information Institute 2017).

Trade and service marks (herein trademarks or marks) include words, phrases, symbols, and designs that are used to differentiate among companies and their goods and services (United States Patent and Trademark Office 2017). Marks, in one form or another, have been around for a very long time; essentially, once we had commerce we had marks ostensibly to protect the buyer from shoddy workmanship or to help the buyer to identify the goods and services of one particular seller over another.

In the United States, trademark rights arise from the use of a particular mark in commerce; as long as a mark continues to be used in commerce, the trademark will not "expire." In other words, unlike patent and copyright, there is no "limited time" associated with trademarks.

There is no requirement to register a mark; however, it is advantageous to register one's mark with the United States Trademark and Patent Office. Registering the mark notifies the public of the claim to ownership of the mark, a presumption of legal ownership throughout the United States, and the exclusive right to use the mark in commerce. Trademark registrations do not expire (United States Patent and Trademark Office 2017).

The standard for trademark infringement is the "likelihood of confusion" on the part of the consumer about the source of goods and services sold under a particular mark. Using identical marks to sell the same product is clearly infringement under this standard. Generally, though, the situation is more muddled, and so to determine infringement the court considers several factors: (1) the strength of the mark; (2) the proximity of the goods; (3) the similarity of the marks; (4) evidence of actual confusion; (5) the similarity of marketing channels used; (6) the degree of caution exercised by the typical purchaser; and (7) the defendant's intent (Berkman Klein Center 2017).

In addition to trademark infringement, the Lanham Act also protects trademark owners from dilution (Berkman Klein Center 2017). Under federal law, a finding of dilution is only available to marks that are "famous." Courts determine whether or not a mark is famous by considering several factors including, but not limited to, the distinctiveness of the mark, its duration of use, and whether or not the mark is registered. Under state laws a mark is not required to be famous for a finding of dilution. Dilution is characterized in two ways. The first is "blurring," which occurs when a famous mark is weakened because it is associated with dissimilar goods or services. The second is "tarnishment," which happens when a famous mark is associated with something objectionable—for example, a trademark associated with a family-friendly entertainment center is associated with a business that provides adult entertainment (Berkman Klein Center 2017; United States Patent and Trademark Office 2017).

Defend Trade Secrets Act of 2016

Trade secrets are just that, secrets that are held by a particular firm that are valuable to the firm so long as they remain a secret. There are a wide variety of trade secrets from "secret recipes" for fried chicken and soda to business methods and marketing plans to research and development activities. Because these secrets are valuable, firms will take a variety of steps to ensure that these secrets are not disclosed.

Prior to the enactment of the Defend Trade Secrets Act of 2016, companies whose trade secrets were misappropriated had limited options. Companies could only seek redress in the state courts or if applicable, take action under the Economic Espionage Act of 1996, which was limited to international situations. Definitions and remedies and application of these laws varied from state to state, which was problematic for firms dealing with misappropriation. Fortunately, the Defend Trade Secrets Act provides a legal definition of a trade secret which allows for a broad range of proprietary information to be protected under the statute as long as

> (A) the owner thereof has taken reasonable measures to keep such information secret; and (B) the information derives independent economic value, actual or potential, from not being generally known to, and not being readily ascertainable through proper means by, another person who can obtain economic value from the disclosure or use of the information (Cohen, Renaud, and Armington 2016). The statute further provides guidance as to acts that constitute a misappropriation and provides penalties and increases the maximum penalty for trade secret theft (currently $5 million) to the greater of $5 million or three times the value of the stolen trade secret (Defend Trade Secrets Act S.1890 2015).

CASE STUDY

Case studies provide an opportunity to apply one's ethical and legal understanding to a particular situation. The following case study includes issues of fair use, in particular, transformative use and the impact of a particular use on the "market."

Hope was an overarching message of President Barack Obama's national campaign. An artist called Shepard Fairey was inspired by Obama and created a now infamous poster, the design of which featured an image of Obama and in bold type, the word *HOPE*. Fairey used a stock photograph of Obama that he had found online for his design. The photograph was one of hundreds a photographer, Mannie Garcia, had taken of Obama; it was reported in the media that the photographer did not recognize his own photograph until someone pointed it out to him. The HOPE design was ubiquitous and appeared everywhere from street corners to T-shirts. Fairey believed he had made a fair use of the photograph because his design was a transformative use of the photograph. In addition, Fairey has stated that he did not profit from the work and that the money from the work was donated to the Obama campaign. The Associated Press, determined to be the owner of the photograph as it was a "work made for hire," accused Fairey of copyright infringement because he had used the image without its express permission. Ultimately, Fairey and the Associated Press settled its dispute without disclosing the financial terms. The settlement leaves unanswered the question of whether or not the Obama HOPE poster constitutes a transformative use and whether or not a use is commercial if the creator does not profit.

GLOSSARY OF TERMS

Fair Use—A legal doctrine that allows for the use of copyrighted works without the permission of the owner for certain purposes is not an infringement. Such purposes include criticism, comment, news reporting, teaching (including multiple copies for classroom use), scholarship, or research. Four factors are used to determine if a use is fair: the purpose and character of the use; the nature of the copyrighted work; the amount and substantiality of the portion used in relation to the copyrighted work as a whole; and the effect of the use upon the potential market for or value of the copyrighted work (17 U.S. Code § 107).

Natural right—a right considered to be conferred by natural law. A natural law is a body of law or a specific principle of law that is held to be derived from nature and binding upon human society in the absence of or in addition to positive law (Merriam Webster 2017).

Free rider—an individual or group takes advantage of a common resource or public good while contributing little or nothing (*Stanford Encyclopedia of Philosophy* 2003).

REFERENCES

American Library Association. "Code of Ethics." Last modified January 22, 2008. www.ala.org/tools/ethics.

Berkman Klein Center for Internet and Society at Harvard University. "Overview of Trademark Law." https://cyber.harvard.edu/metaschool/fisher/domain/tm.htm.

Cohen, Bret A., Michael T. Renaud, and Nicholas W. Armington. "Explaining the Defend Trade Secrets Act." Last modified September 9, 2016. www.americanbar.org/publications/blt/2016/09/03_cohen.html.

Commerce Clause, U.S. Const. art. 1. sec. 8. cl. 3. Legal Information Institute, Cornell Law School. www.law.cornell.edu/wex/commerce_clause.

Copyright Act, 1 Statutes At Large, 124, (1790). United States Copyright Office. www.copyright.gov/history/1790act.pdf.

_____. 17 USC. §§ 101 et seq. (1976). United States Copyright Office. www.copyright.gov/history/p194-553.pdf.

Defend Trade Secrets Act, S.1890—114th Congress (2015-2016). Congress.gov. Last modified May 11, 2016. www.congress.gov/bill/114th-congress/senate-bill/1890.

Intellectual Property Clause, U.S. Const. art. 1. sec. 8. cl. 8. Legal Information Institute, Cornell Law School. www.law.cornell.edu/wex/intellectual_property_clause.

Lanham Act, 15 U.S.C. §§ 1051 et seq. Legal Information Institute, Cornell Law School.
www.law.cornell.edu/wex/lanham_act.

Lincoln, A. 1859. "Second Lecture on Discoveries and Inventions." In *Collected Works of Abraham Lincoln 1809–1865* 3. University of Michigan Library. . https://quod.lib.umich.edu/cgi/t/text/text-idx?c =lincoln;idno=lincoln3.

Merriam Webster Law Dictionary. s.v. "natural right." www.merriam-webster.com/legal.

Patent Act. 1 Stat. 109-112, (1790). University of New Hampshire School of Law. www.ipmall.info/sites/ default/files/hosted_resources/lipa/patents/Patent_Act_of_1790.pdf.

———. 1 Stat. 318, (1793). University of New Hampshire School of Law. www.ipmall.info/sites/default/files/ hosted_resources/lipa/patents/Patent_Act_of_1793.pdf.

Stanford Encyclopedia of Philosophy. s.v. "The Free Rider Problem." Last modified May 21, 2003. https://plato.stanford.edu/entries/free-rider/.

———. s.v. "John Rawls." Last modified January 9, 2017. https://plato.stanford.edu/entries/rawls/.

———. s.v. "Locke's Political Philosophy." Last modified January 11, 2016. https://plato.stanford.edu/entries/ locke-political/.

The Statute of Anne. The Avalon Project, New Haven, CT: Lillian Goldman Law Library, Yale University. Last modified 2008. http://avalon.law.yale.edu/18th_century/anne_1710.asp.

United States Copyright Office. "Circular 15A: Duration of Copyright." Last modified August 2011. www.copyright.gov/circs/circ15a.pdf.

——— . "Circular 41: Copyright Claims in Architectural Works." Last modified September 2012. www.copyright.gov/circs/circ15a.pdf.

United States Patent and Trademark Office. "About Trademarks" Last modified September 15, 2017. www.uspto.gov/about-trademarks.

———. "About Trademark Infringement" Last modified September 29, 2014. www.uspto.gov/page/ about-trademark-infringement.

———. "General Information Concerning Patents" Last modified October 20, 2016. www.uspto.gov/patents -getting-started/general-information-concerning-patents.

World Intellectual Property Organization. "Berne Convention for the Protection of Literary and Artistic Works." www.wipo.int/treaties/en/ip/berne/.

FURTHER RESOURCES

Basic Facts about Trademarks and *About Trademarks,* prepared by the United States Patent and Trademark Office. www.uspto.gov/sites/default/files/documents/BasicFacts.pdf and www.uspto.gov/ about-trademarks. In addition to providing general information on trademarks, these pages provide links to searchable databases and other tools required for research.

Copyright Law of the United States, prepared by the United States Copyright Office. See in particular *Law and Guidance.* This part of the website includes historic versions of copyright laws which were used in this chapter as well as *Circulars* (www.copyright.gov/circs/), which provide current and authoritative information on United States Copyright law. www.copyright.gov/title17/.

General Information Concerning Patents, prepared by the United States Patent and Trademark Office. www .uspto.gov/patents-getting-started/general-information-concerning-patents. This website provides an extensive list of topical links related to patents including information on the patent office and patent process.

John Rawls' *Justice as Fairness: A Restatement.* Harvard University Press, 2003.

---

* *Disclaimer:* The information contained in this chapter does not constitute legal advice. The author is a librarian and not an attorney. If legal advice is required, one should seek the assistance of a licensed attorney.

CHAPTER 8

Data Ethics

Peter Darch

DEFINING DATA

Although widely used, the definition of *data* is difficult to pin down. Often, data are conceptualized as a collection of numbers, or strings of zeroes and ones, or symbols. However, this conceptualization is too restrictive because it excludes many ways in which people and organizations learn about the world. Instead, the definition here is adapted from Borgman's definition of data, "Entities used as evidence of a phenomenon for a particular purpose," which was formulated for data used in scholarly research (Borgman 2015).

This definition has two implications of particular interest. One is that it includes a wide range of entities that could become data, including text and images. A second implication is that an entity only becomes data in relation to its use, which ensures we focus on the actions and intentions of those using the data, and the effects of use of the data when considering data ethics.

THE AGE OF BIG DATA

The term *big data* is widely used and much hyped. Recent years have seen rapid technological developments that allow for production, collection, aggregation, processing, and analysis of datasets on an increasingly large scale. The news media, governments, and businesses all hail the potential benefits that arise from big data analytics.

Definitions

As with the term *data,* no single definition of *big data* exists. One common definition uses the "3Vs"—volume, variety, and velocity—as dimensions along which big data can be characterized (McAfee et al. 2012). Over time, other dimensions have been added, such as variability, veracity, value, and complexity (Bedi, Jindal, and Gautam 2014):

- **Volume:** The sheer size of datasets being created and used is much larger than ever before. Whereas traditional methods of data collection often involve sampling the group of people being studied, data about entire populations can often now be collected and analyzed.
- **Variety:** Technologies now allow the collection and integration of multiple types of data in a single analysis.

- **Velocity:** New data are often being generated rapidly, and those using big data analytics frequently need to integrate these new data quickly to respond to changing situations.
- **Veracity:** Sometimes a trade-off exists between the size and quality of datasets: whereas traditional approaches to data collection usually involve careful planning and rigorous methods, the imperative to collect as much data as possible can compromise data quality.
- **Value:** Large scale datasets can have great value for their users, but these datasets' value is only realized through the way in which they are used.
- **Variability:** What data actually mean can change according to context. For instance, two separate tweets may contain the same words, but their meaning can still be very different, for instance, if one tweet is intended seriously and the other is satirical.
- **Complexity:** Performing analyses using big data is challenging. Particular difficulties involve how to integrate different types of data; how to manage large-scale datasets; and how to assess, and deal with, data quality issues.

Uses of Big Data

Big data is becoming increasingly prevalent across a wide range of societal endeavors, including (but certainly not limited to):

- **Business:** including targeting online advertising, and monitoring employees;
- **Politics:** political parties make use of demographic data to identify likely supporters, their propensity to vote in elections (and how to increase voter turnout), and potential donors;
- **Health care:** including self-monitoring devices (e.g., activity trackers), electronic health records, and decisions made by health insurance companies;
- **Surveillance by government:** including, for instance, the collection and analysis of telecommunications data to identify potential terrorist activity;
- **Crime prevention and policing:** including, for example, where potential crime hotspots are predicted in advance, with the aim of preventing crime;
- **Academic research:** including astronomy, where telescopes generate gigabytes or even terabytes of data per day; climate science, where many different types of data are integrated; and social science, when making use of data from social media sites such as Twitter;
- **Social media:** where algorithms determine what activities of other people you can see, and *search engines,* which use algorithms to determine which websites are displayed most prominently in response to search queries.

ACTIVITIES INVOLVING DATA

The term *data curation* refers to the range of activities performed on a dataset through its entire lifecycle, from original generation through to what happens to it after it is used (Ball 2012). These activities include:

- **Generation.** In some cases, the production of data is deliberately planned and executed for specific purposes (e.g., a scientific experiment or a survey of people's opinions). In other cases, the data were not originally intended as data (e.g., a dataset comprising social media posts), but are collected together.
- **Recording and storage.** Choices are made about how data are recorded and stored (e.g., what formats and units are used to record data, what storage media are used, who can access the stored data) have profound implications for how the data are subsequently used.
- **Processing and analysis.** Many steps must be applied to data for them to become information that can be meaningfully used. These include retrieval, searching or querying, integration with other data, statistical analysis, and visualization. *Data mining* is particularly applied to processing of large datasets.
- **Use.** Data can be used for many purposes (see above). *Primary data* refers to data that are used for the original purpose for which they were generated. *Secondary data* is where data are used for a different purpose.
- **Dissemination.** Data may be distributed to other people or organizations. Some dissemination is intentional, with the data owner choosing whether, how, and to whom to transfer data; in other cases dissemination may be inadvertent if data are accidentally released through human or technical error or obtained by hackers. Data can be disseminated via many different methods, including physical media, electronic communication, and deposition in a repository or database.
- **Archiving or destruction.** After it has been used, a dataset may be subject to one of many fates. In some cases, steps are actively taken to preserve and archive the dataset so that it continues to exist in its current form and may be used in the future. In other cases, the dataset may be intentionally destroyed, for instance, in accordance with data protection laws. In other cases, the data may simply be neglected: over time, these data may get lost, or resurface unexpectedly.

CHANGES RESULTING FROM BIG DATA

The challenges of producing, handling, and analyzing big data require new computational tools, methods, information systems, and infrastructure. However, the changes accompanying big data are not just about the underlying technologies.

Big data can produce changes in terms of how we understand the world around us. Advocates of big data suggest that if datasets are large enough, we may be able to identify relationships among different phenomena simply by detecting patterns or correlations in datasets; we may not need to understand the underlying mechanisms that produce these relationships (Anderson 2008). Our understandings of the phenomena themselves may also change, with new and different types of data enabling us to see phenomena in new ways (boyd and Crawford 2012).

Big data can also contribute to changes to the ways in which society is organized, with implications for issues such as career structure and the nature of work (Levy 2015). For instance, businesses often now devote significant resources to building and operating information systems to exploit big data analytics. In turn, new career paths are opening up for individuals to build these systems. Some of these systems are used by organizations to monitor employee activities and productivity, which significantly changes employees' experiences in the workplace. Other systems may be used to target advertising or new products at potential customers, providing significant commercial advantages to those businesses that are able to exploit big data analytics at the expense of businesses that cannot.

It is these—and other—changes that have profound ethical implications.

HISTORY OF DATA ETHICS

Data ethics is very much a concern within information ethics that has emerged concurrently with the explosion in collection, storage, and use of data (Floridi and Taddeo 2016). The history of data ethics is thus to a large extent the history of other concerns within information ethics like as privacy, information access, and intellectual property. However, current thought in data ethics is also shaped by concerns about the ethics of research that involve collecting and using data about humans, such as in medical and social science research.

Concerns about medical experimentation on humans strengthened after World War II when details emerged of human experimentation conducted by the Nazi regime. In 1947 at the Nuremberg trials of Nazi party leaders, judges formulated the Nuremberg Code, a list of ten points intended to guide medical researchers. This code addressed the principle of informed consent of the research subjects, including the ability for subjects to leave the trial of their own volition; the avoidance of unnecessary physical and mental suffering; and the pursuit of positive results for society. Although not widely enforced, the Nuremberg Code informed the Declaration of Helsinki, a set of principles for medical research first established in 1964 (and revised multiple times subsequently). The Declaration also emphasized that research subjects' welfare should always take precedence over any perceived benefits of the study to society as a whole and must supersede local laws.

Although influential, the Helsinki Declaration has never been legally binding. In the United States, a series of controversial experiments and studies caused great concern in the late 1960s and early 1970s. One major example is the Tuskegee Syphilis Study, which ran from 1932 to 1972. This study aimed to track the progress of syphilis through the human body. It recruited participants in Tuskegee, Alabama, a poor, largely African American community, who were promised health care in exchange for participation. However, participants who contracted syphilis were not informed they had done so and, left untreated, many died or suffered serious health problems. This study raised major ethical concerns about exploitation of vulnerable or marginalized groups of people, issues of justice around the distribution of harms and potential benefits of the study, and honest conduct of researchers (Katz, Capron, and Glass 1972).

Following this and other scandals, the US Department of Health, Education and Welfare commissioned the *Belmont Report,* published in 1978. This report established three ethical principles for human subjects research:

1. **Respect for persons:** Autonomy—the idea that individuals should have freedom of action and freedom of choice—should be respected by a commitment to informed consent (the assumption that research subjects

are competent to make their own decisions), to the dignified treatment of subjects, and that lying, deception, and the withholding of information related to subjects' welfare should be avoided by researchers.

2. **Beneficence:** The benefits of research to society and to the research subjects should be maximized, while the harms to research subjects are minimized.

3. **Justice:** The benefits and costs of research should be distributed fairly and equally, and research should be nonexploitative.

These principles are reflected in legislation and individual organizations' (e.g., universities') codes of conduct about research involving human subjects.

MAJOR THINKERS

Jacob Katz (1922-2008). Originally trained as a physician, Jacob Katz (United States) was a professor of psychiatry and law at Yale University. Following his service on a federal inquiry into the Tuskegee Syphilis Study, Katz highlighted the exploitation of marginalized people as research subjects and their vulnerability to deception and concealment of potential research harms (Katz, Capron, and Glass 1972).

Luciano Floridi (1964-). A professor in Oxford University's Internet Institute, Luciano Floridi (Italy) has made numerous major contributions to information philosophy. He developed the argument that entities such as software and computer systems should be considered as moral agents (Floridi and Sanders 2004). This argument, and subsequent work on distributed morality, has influenced how accountability and responsibility are understood when people suffer harm in situations involving complex technological systems (Floridi 2016).

Kate Crawford. A professor at New York University and researcher at Microsoft, Kate Crawford (Australia) has made major contributions to a range of issues in data ethics. One example is her research using large datasets drawn from social media. She draws attention to tensions between using publicly accessible data for beneficial research and to issues of consent, privacy, and potential harm to data subjects. She also argues that these large-scale datasets must be interpreted with care so decision-makers are not mislead into pursuing harmful courses of action (boyd and Crawford 2012; Crawford and Finn 2015).

Lucas Introna (1961-). A professor at Lancaster University's Management School, Introna (Great Britain and South Africa) has published widely on the ethical and social consequences of algorithms. His work demonstrates that supposedly neutral algorithms are instead often biased, systematically favoring some people and organizations over others (Introna and Nissenbaum 2000; Introna and Wood 2002).

Christine L. Borgman (1951–). A professor in Information Studies at the University of California at Los Angeles, Borgman (United States), drew on social scientific case studies across multiple scientific disciplines to articulate the key rationales for promoting the sharing of research data (Borgman 2012; 2015). Borgman's work has proven highly influential in shaping thinking about how to devise policies, practices, and infrastructures for research data curation.

Solon Barocas. An assistant professor in the Department of Information Sciences at Cornell University, Barocas (United States) explores issues of justice and fairness in data- and algorithmic-based decision-making. His work addresses how this decision-making can widen existing patterns of socioeconomic, racial, gender, and other forms of inequality (Barocas and Selbst 2016; Barocas et al. 2017).

ONGOING CONCERNS

Privacy

People and organizations must make decisions related to privacy at every stage of data curation: what categories and level of detail of data get collected?

- How should the data be stored (e.g., should it be anonymized or pseudonymized)?
- Who should have access to stored data and under what circumstances?
- Who is responsible for the security of data and for ensuring that procedures and policies relating to data privacy are followed and enforced?
- Can data be disseminated or shared with others, and if so, should the data be modified in any way (e.g., should personally identifiable information be used?)
- How long should different categories of data be retained by a person or organization, and what steps need to be taken to delete or destroy data?
- What control or rights do data subjects have over the data that are collected or stored about them?

These decisions are ethically significant because they influence the risk that data subjects will experience breaches of privacy. These breaches can result in substantial harm for people, groups, and organizations. In some cases, the organization that collected the data will release it publicly, so that others may use the data. An example is where data collected by physicians are released to biomedical researchers. To protect individuals' privacy in these cases, the data may be de-identified, with personally identifying information removed. However, no de-identification technique is foolproof: a highly skilled individual could aggregate the de-identified data with data from other sources to re-identify individuals in the dataset (Narayanan and Felten 2014). In other cases, data release can be unintended, even when that organization has sophisticated procedures and technologies in place to prevent data "spills" (Schafer 2016). For instance, databases may be hacked, or people may accidentally leave laptops or thumb drives containing data in public places.

Addressing ethical issues relating to data privacy is often difficult. Principles of informed consent suggest that subjects of data should be informed about how these data will be curated and used, and be given control over their data (e.g., being able to specify when it is deleted). However, this approach is extremely challenging to realize in practice. The majority of people do not read existing terms and conditions (which typically cover data collection and processing) when using online services (Luger, Moran, and Rodden 2013). It is very hard for people to conceptualize how data about them will be used, particularly in relation to secondary uses of data. Furthermore, users of the internet generate so much data when they interact with websites that they simply cannot keep track of all the data that exist about them.

Narayanan, Huey, and Felten (2016) argue for a precautionary approach, whereby the burden for ensuring privacy protection falls squarely on the people and organizations who handle data. This approach shifts the burden away from the data subjects. One example of a deontological argument in favor of this approach is that a person has an absolute right to privacy, and the organization should therefore never release data in a way that could compromise this right, especially given that once data are released, it can never be taken back.

A consequentialist argument against this precautionary principle approach is that it could lead to inadvertent and harmful consequences. For instance, the fear of being held responsible for any privacy breach could deter organizations from releasing data for use in important biomedical research. Instead, decisions about whether and how to release data need to balance potential risks of harms resulting from privacy breaches with potential benefits of data release (Mann, Savulescu, and Sahakian 2016).

Data Sharing in Academic Research

Data is central to scientific research. However, collecting or producing scientific data often requires a great deal of time, money, and effort. Once the scientist has used a dataset, it very often remains inaccessible to others and may even get lost over time. Recent years have seen growing interest in increasing the sharing of datasets by scientists, both with other scientists and with the public (Heidorn 2008).

A number of rationales exist for data sharing (Borgman 2015). These rationales implicate multiple ethical perspectives (Darch and Knox 2017). A consequentialist argument for data sharing is that it will resort to more and better science. Other scientists may be able to make good use of a dataset, thereby increasing the return on the initial investment incurred when producing the dataset. Data sharing can also allow for different datasets to be aggregated, enabling scientists to pursue research questions that were previously not answerable. Another benefit is making science more trustworthy: scientists making their data available enables other scientists to check that data for errors or fraud. Meanwhile, a deontological argument for data sharing is that members of the public have a right to access the products of research that they have paid for via taxation.

There are also ethical arguments against data sharing. Collecting or producing scientific data often requires a great deal of resources (time, effort, money). Scientists' careers depend on using data to make new scientific discoveries. A deontologist may argue it is only fair that the person or organization that invested the resources in data production should be allowed to use that data first. A consequentialist may argue that requiring data sharing reduces scientists' incentives to produce new data because they can access data produced by others rather than going to the effort of producing their own, thereby ultimately harming the progress of science.

Some approaches to addressing the above dilemmas include giving the data producer a period of time to exploit the data for their own purposes before they are required to share the data; and ensuring the original data producer is given credit for scientific discoveries made by other scientists who use the data (Wallis, Rolando, and Borgman 2013).

The Data Divide

People and organizations use data to pursue their own interests. Consequently, the distributional consequences of data are ethically significant. Who benefits or is harmed by the use of data is determined both by who is (and is not) able to access and use data, and by who is (and is not) represented in datasets that form the basis of subsequent decision-making.

Divides emerge or deepen between those who are able to access and use data and those who cannot (Manovich 2011). Building and using tools and infrastructure to collect, process, and analyze data require resources such as money and skills. Those who possess these resources can benefit from using data whereas those who lack these resources cannot. An online bookseller like Amazon is able to profitably leverage big data analytics, for instance to identify books to recommend to customers or to formulate promotional and pricing strategies. Small independent booksellers, meanwhile, cannot.

Divides can also emerge or deepen between those who are collecting and using data, and those people who are the subject of data (Andrejevic 2014). Indeed, the former may be able to use their access to these data to increase their power or accumulate more resources at the expense of those who are the subjects of the data. One example is the case of employers who collect and use data to monitor employee behavior and performance. The more detailed the data collected, the more an employer can regulate employee behavior, thus impacting how employees experience their work environment (Levy 2015).

Finally, divides can also emerge or deepen between those who are represented in datasets and those who are not (Lerman 2013). When datasets are used as the basis of decision-making, the difference between a person or group being represented or not being represented can affect whether their interests and needs are taken into account by decision-makers. One example is that of StreetBump, a smartphone app used in Boston that recorded when a user drives over a pothole. The app notified the Mayor's Office of potholes so that they could be fixed. Economically disadvantaged areas of the city were underrepresented in the data generated by the app, because poorer residents were more likely to use public transport rather than drive and were less likely to have access to smartphones. A consequence is that pothole repair crews were more likely to be directed to wealthier areas (United States and Podesta 2014).

Such data divides can reproduce and reinforce existing divisions in society, such as those relating to race, gender, sexuality, and socioeconomic status (Ajunwa 2016). These divisions can be built into the data cycle from the start of data production and then persist as data are analyzed, processed, and used. For instance, data collected for medical research has often classified people either as male or female. This classification can render transgender people who do not fit into this binary invisible to people or organizations, such as physicians or insurance companies, who make decisions on the basis of this research. In turn, this can lead to comparatively poorer treatment outcomes for transgender people, causing further harm to an already marginalized group of people.

Accountability and Redress

Systems that involve big data decision-making can very often cause substantial harm to individuals, organizations, or social groups. The ability to identify who or what is responsible when things go wrong is important for a number of reasons, including deterring negligence or wrongdoing, ensuring victims can seek appropriate redress, and identifying actions that can be taken to reduce the risk of things going wrong again in the future.

Systems involving big data are usually very complicated, involving many components. Some components are technical, such as hardware and code. Other components are human, including people who work on the system (designing, building, maintenance, operation); people responsible for system security; and users of the system. Sometimes things go wrong due to internal flaws or errors in the system. Other times, things go wrong due to external actors, such as hackers.

Identifying what caused the system to go wrong (i.e., who or what is accountable or responsible) can be a very difficult task, given the system's complexity (Leonelli 2016). Often, the system's failure cannot be reduced to a single cause, but instead results from a complex series of interactions between human and technical components. A small, seemingly insignificant mistake or action by a single person can rapidly develop into a catastrophic failure with significant negative consequences for many people and organizations; in such cases, it can be very unfair to hold this person solely or largely to blame for the failure.

The concept of *distributed moral responsibility* is useful for thinking about such a scenario (Floridi 2016). Rather than assigning blame to a single person or a small group, we should think about how responsibility is distributed throughout the entire collection of components involved in the system and the scenario.

Algorithmic Power and Bias

In computer science, an algorithm is a program that uses a specific set of procedures or rules to transform input data into an output. Algorithms are being used by an increasing range of people and organizations for automated decision-making. Examples of use include loan application decisions by banks; sentencing decisions in the justice system, where algorithms are used to estimate an offender's chance of reoffending; determining the order in which internet search engines display results in response to a search query; and choices about what advertisements to display to internet users.

Algorithms are a special instance of the generation, analysis, and use of data to make decisions. The ethical issues discussed already in this chapter apply in the case of algorithmic decision-making, but often more acutely and urgently.

Decisions that may have enormous consequences for individuals are being made with no humans involved in the decision-making process. A single algorithmic system may make decisions far more quickly than humans can feasibly monitor. Algorithms can reflect and reinforce existing biases in society because these biases can be deeply embedded in the data the algorithms use (Barocas and Selbst 2016). People may be scarcely—if at all—aware of what algorithmic decisions are being made and the effect of these algorithms on their lives. People or groups who are harmed by algorithmic decisions may not be aware of the ways in which they are being harmed. Even when they are aware of this harm, they may have no way to rectify the harm, hold anyone accountable for causing them harm, or prevent more harm from being done to them in the future.

The issue of algorithmic accountability is a growing concern among many researchers. However, how to audit an algorithm is still an open question. One approach is for people to inspect the algorithm's code to understand how it works. However, this approach is extremely difficult (Burrell 2016). Code can stretch to thousands of lines and be difficult to interpret. Additionally, many companies are concerned about maintaining competitive advantages over their rivals and are thus reluctant to make their algorithms' code publicly available.

Sandvig et al. (2016) argue that consequentialist approaches offer the most promising avenue for algorithmic accountability. Focusing on the outcomes of algorithmic decision-making can help us to identify what algorithms are causing harm to particular groups of people. However, this approach cannot prevent people from being harmed in the first place; instead, Sandvig et al. challenge the reader to think deontologically and devise norms that can be followed by those people and organizations devising or implementing algorithms.

CASE STUDY 1: ACCESS TO SCIENTIFIC DATA

The Large Synoptic Survey Telescope (LSST) is currently under construction and is due to come online in 2022. It will produce twenty terabytes of data every night for ten years. This scale of data will be unprecedented and will lead to novel, and likely groundbreaking, scientific discoveries.

LSST data will be used by astronomers, who will access and analyze these data for their own research. LSST will cost approximately $1.1 billion to build and operate. Most of the money for LSST comes from US federal government agencies and is thus supplied by US taxpayers. One of the conditions for funding this telescope is that access to LSST data will be restricted to researchers at universities in Chile (where the telescope will be physically located) and the United States. Researchers in other countries will have very restricted, or no, access to the data.

Questions

1. Should access to the data be restricted to US- and Chilean-based astronomers? Why or why not?
2. What are consequentialist, deontological, and justice-based arguments for and against limiting access?

CASE STUDY 2: ETHICS OF USING HACKED DATA

Two social science researchers were studying crowdfunding websites where individuals ask members of the public to make donations to help fund a project. These researchers intended for their research findings to contribute to future improvements in crowdfunding efforts.

In October 2015, Patreon, a major crowdfunding site, was illegally hacked. The hackers made the entire site—including all data about all projects on the site for which funds were being raised and users' private messages and email addresses—publicly available on the internet.

Initially, the two researchers were divided about whether they should use the hacked data in their own research. Case study adapted from Poor and Davidson (2016).

Questions

1. Should the researchers be able to use the hacked data in their research?
2. Should hacked data ever be used for any purpose? What criteria should determine in which circumstances it is appropriate to use hacked data?

CASE STUDY 3: WHO IS RESPONSIBLE FOR REPUTATIONAL HARM?

(This is a fictional case, based on the real-world hacking of online dating service Ashley Madison) Jane, a journalist, created a profile on a dating website aimed at married people. She created her profile solely for research purposes, because she was considering writing an article about online dating (which she did not, in the end, write). Jane never used the website to contact other users.

When registering for the website, users were presented with a lengthy list of terms and condition, including a statement that the website would store personal information given by users in the sign-up process. Jane did not read this list.

Jane was able to fully delete her profile from the website. However, she did not realize that personal details about her (e.g., the email address she used to sign up) were retained on the site's internal database.

A few years later, this website's database was hacked. The hackers publicly released information about people who had registered for the website, including their names and emails. Although no one has yet been prosecuted for this hack, there are suspicions that the hacker is an IT contractor who worked for a short period in the dating website's offices and thereby became familiar with the website's technical and security features.

Included in the release were Jane's name and email address. This email address is one that she continued to use with friends, family, work colleagues, and members of a local religious nonprofit organization of which Jane is a board member. A computer programmer set up a simple online search tool that allows anyone to check whether a particular email address was part of the hacked data. Someone with a grudge against Jane entered Jane's email address into this search tool and anonymously tipped off other members of the nonprofit's board. Jane is devastated by this exposure and her potential loss of reputation.

Questions

1. Who or what is responsible for what happened to Jane?
2. Who or what should be held accountable for what happened to Jane?
3. What measures can be taken to lessen the risk of similar instances in the future? Are any of these measures likely to prove fail-safe?

REFERENCES

Ajunwa, Ifeoma. 2016. "Genetic Data and Civil Rights." *Harvard Civil Rights-Civil Liberties Law Review* 51 (1): 75–114.

Anderson, Chris. 2008. "The End of Theory: The Data Deluge Makes the Scientific Method Obsolete." *Wired*, June 23. www.wired.com/2008/06/pb-theory/.

Andrejevic, Mark. 2014. "Big Data, Big Questions| the Big Data Divide." *International Journal of Communication* 8: 17.

Ball, Alexander. 2012. "Review of Data Management Lifecycle Models." http://opus.bath.ac.uk/28587/.

Barocas, Solon, Elizabeth Bradley, Vasant Honavar, and Foster Provost. 2017. "Big Data, Data Science, and Civil Rights." *arXiv Preprint arXiv: 1706.03102.* https://arxiv.org/abs/1706.03102.

Barocas, Solon, and Andrew Selbst. 2016. "Big Data's Disparate Impact." *California Law Review* 104 (3): 671-732. https://doi.org/https://doi.org/10.15779/Z38BG31.

Bedi, Punam, Vinita Jindal, and Anjali Gautam. 2014. "Beginning with Big Data Simplified." In *Data Mining and Intelligent Computing (ICDMIC), 2014 International Conference on,* 1-7. IEEE. http://ieeexplore .ieee.org/abstract/document/6954229/.

Belmont Report: Ethical Principles and Guidelines for the Protection of Human Subjects of Research. 1978. Bethesda, MD: National Commission for the Protection of Human Subjects of Biomedical and Behavioral Research.

Borgman, Christine L. 2012. "The Conundrum of Sharing Research Data." *Journal of the American Society for Information Science and Technology* 63 (6): 1059-78. https://doi.org/10.1002/asi.22634.

_____. 2015. *Big Data, Little Data, No Data: Scholarship in the Networked World.* Cambridge, MA: MIT Press. http://mitpress.mit.edu/big-data.

boyd, danah, and Kate Crawford. 2012. "Critical Questions for Big Data: Provocations for a Cultural, Technological, and Scholarly Phenomenon." *Information, Communication and Society* 15 (5): 662-79. https://doi.org/10.1080/1369118X.2012.678878.

Burrell, Jenna. 2016. "How the Machine 'Thinks': Understanding Opacity in Machine Learning Algorithms." *Big Data and Society* 3 (1).

Crawford, Kate, and Megan Finn. 2015. "The Limits of Crisis Data: Analytical and Ethical Challenges of Using Social and Mobile Data to Understand Disasters." *GeoJournal* 80 (4): 491-502.

Darch, Peter T., and Emily J. M. Knox. 2017. "Ethical Perspectives on Data and Software Sharing in the Sciences: A Research Agenda." *Library and Information Science Research* 39 (4): 295-302.

Floridi, Luciano. 2016. "Faultless Responsibility: On the Nature and Allocation of Moral Responsibility for Distributed Moral Actions." *Philosophical Transactions of the Royal Society A* 374 (2083).

Floridi, Luciano, and Jeff W. Sanders. 2004. "On the Morality of Artificial Agents." *Minds and Machines* 14 (3): 349-79.

Floridi, Luciano, and Mariarosaria Taddeo. 2016. *What Is Data Ethics?* The Royal Society. http://rsta.royal societypublishing.org/content/374/2083/20160360.abstract.

Heidorn, P. Bryan. 2008. "Shedding Light on the Dark Data in the Long Tail of Science." *Library Trends* 57 (2): 280-99.

Introna, Lucas, and Helen Nissenbaum. 2000. "Shaping the Web: Why the Politics of Search Engines Matters." *The Information Society* 16 (3): 169-85. https://doi.org/10.1080/01972240050133634.

Introna, Lucas, and David Wood. 2004. "Picturing Algorithmic Surveillance: The Politics of Facial Recognition Systems." *Surveillance and Society* 2 (2/3). https://queens.scholarsportal.info/ojs-archive/ index.php/surveillance-and-society/article/view/3373.

Katz, Jay, Alexander Morgan Capron, and Eleanor Swift Glass. 1972. *Experimentation with Human Beings: The Authority of the Investigator, Subject, Professions, and State in the Human Experimentation Process.* Russell Sage Foundation. https://books.google.com/s?hl=en&lr=&id=9Zy6AwAAQBAJ&oi=fnd&pg=PR1 3&dq=jay+katz&ots=EC91RzjWBQ&sig=FX0Q4YrKXQgzB8h9DqG13LFpmck.

Leonelli, Sabina. 2016. "Locating Ethics in Data Science: Responsibility and Accountability in Global and Distributed Knowledge Production Systems." *Philosophical Transactions of the Royal Society A* 374 (2083): 20160122.

Lerman, Jonas. 2013. "Big Data and Its Exclusions." SSRN Scholarly Paper ID 2293765. Rochester, NY: Social Science Research Network. https://papers.ssrn.com/abstract=2293765.

Levy, Karen E. C. 2015. "The Contexts of Control: Information, Power, and Truck-Driving Work." *The Information Society* 31 (2): 160–74. https://doi.org/10.1080/01972243.2015.998105.

Luger, Ewa, Stuart Moran, and Tom Rodden. 2013. "Consent for All: Revealing the Hidden Complexity of Terms and Conditions." In *Proceedings of the SIGCHI Conference on Human Factors in Computing Systems,* 2687–96. CHI '13. New York, USA: ACM. https://doi.org/10.1145/2470654.2481371.

Mann, Sebastian Porsdam, Julian Savulescu, and Barbara J. Sahakian. 2016. "Facilitating the Ethical Use of Health Data for the Benefit of Society: Electronic Health Records, Consent and the Duty of Easy Rescue." *Philosophical Transactions of the Royal Society A* 374 (2083): 20160130.

Manovich, Lev. 2011. "Trending: The Promises and the Challenges of Big Social Data." *Debates in the Digital Humanities* 2: 460–75.

McAfee, Andrew, Erik Brynjolfsson, Thomas H. Davenport, and others. 2012. "Big Data: The Management Revolution." *Harvard Business Review* 90 (10): 60–68.

Narayanan, Arvind, and Edward W. Felten. 2014. "No Silver Bullet: De-Identification Still Doesn't Work." http://randomwalker.info/publications/no-silver-bullet-de-identification.pdf.

Narayanan, Arvind, Joanna Huey, and Edward W. Felten. 2016. "A Precautionary Approach to Big Data Privacy." In *Data Protection on the Move,* 357–85. Dordrecht, NL: Springer. http://link.springer.com/chapter/10.1007/978-94-017-7376-8_13.

Poor, Nathaniel, and Roei Davidson. 2016. "The Ethics of Using Hacked Data: Patreon's Data Hack and Academic Data Standards." New York: Data & Society. http://bdes.datasociety.net/wp-content/uploads/2016/10/Patreon-Case-Study.pdf.

Sandvig, Christian, Kevin Hamilton, Karrie Karahalios, and Cedric Langbort. 2016. "Automation, Algorithms, and Politics: When the Algorithm Itself Is a Racist: Diagnosing Ethical Harm in the Basic Components of Software." *International Journal of Communication* 10, 19.

Schafer, Burkhard. 2016. "Compelling Truth: Legal Protection of the Infosphere against Big Data Spills." *Philosophical Transactions of the Royal Society A* 374 (2083): 20160114.

United States and John Podesta. 2014. *Big Data: Seizing Opportunities, Preserving Values.* Washington, DC: Executive Office of the President. www.whitehouse.gov/sites/default/files/docs/big_data_privacy_report_may_1_2014.pdf.

Wallis, Jillian C., Elizabeth Rolando, and Christine L. Borgman. 2013. "If we Share Data, Will Anyone Use Them? Data Sharing and Reuse in the Long Tail of Science and Technology." *PLoS ONE* 8 (7): e67332. https://doi.org/10.1371/journal.pone.0067332.

ADDITIONAL RESOURCES

Ethical Reasoning in Big Data: An Exploratory Analysis

Collmann, Jeff, and Sorin Adam Matei. 2016. *Ethical Reasoning in Big Data: An Exploratory Analysis.* Switzerland: Springer.

Handbooks for Ethical Data Practices in Business and Medicine

Business

Davis, Kord. 2012. *Ethics of Big Data: Balancing Risk and Innovation.* Sebastopol, CA: O'Reilly Media, Inc.

Medicine

Béranger, Jérôme. 2016. *Big Data and Ethics: The Medical Datasphere.* Oxford, UK: Elsevier.

Collmann, Jeff, and Sorin Adam Matei. 2016. *Ethical Reasoning in Big Data: An Exploratory Analysis.* Switzerland: Springer.

"Ten Simple Rules" for Good Data Practices

Goodman, Alyssa A., Alberto Pepe, Alexander W. Blocker, Christine L. Borgman, Kyle Cranmer, Merce Crosas, Rosanne Di Stefano, et al. 2014. "Ten Simple Rules for the Care and Feeding of Scientific Data." *PLoS Computational Biology* 10 (4): e1003542. doi: 10.1371/journal.pcbi.1003542.

Zook, Matthew, Solon Barocas, danah boyd, Kate Crawford, Emily Keller, Seeta Peña Gangadharan, Alyssa Goodman, et al. 2017. "Ten Simple Rules for Responsible Big Data Research." *PLOS Computational Biology* 13 (3): e1005399. doi: 10.1371/journal.pcbi.1005399.

White House Reports on Big Data

United States. 2016. *Big Data: A Report on Algorithmic Systems, Opportunity, and Civil Rights.* Washington, DC: Executive Office of the President. www.whitehouse.gov/sites/default/ files/microsites/ ostp/2016_0504_data_discrimination.pdf.

United States and John Podesta. 2014. *Big Data: Seizing Opportunities, Preserving Values.* Washington, DC: Executive Office of the President. www.whitehouse.gov/sites/default/files/docs/big_data_privacy _report_may_1_2014.pdf.

Data and Society

Founded by danah boyd in 2015, Data & Society is a research institute that addresses the ethical and societal implications of data. Data & Society researchers publish journal articles, press articles, white papers, reports, and short primers about the role of data in many aspects of society, including labor, privacy, and civil and human rights. https://datasociety.net/.

CHAPTER 9

Cybersecurity Ethics

Jane Blanken-Webb, Imani Palmer, Roy H. Campbell, Nicholas C. Burbules, and Masooda Bashir

The critical need to secure cyberspace is one of the most significant challenges of our time (National Academy of Engineering n.d.). As we grow ever more dependent on digital and web-based interfaces to conduct the business of our daily lives, we are increasingly vulnerable to the threat of cyberattack. Beyond our personal activities, critical infrastructures on which society depends have also been shown to be vulnerable. At the same time, we face a global shortfall of skilled cybersecurity professionals that has been predicted will number 1.5 million by 2019 (Furnell, Fischer, and Finch 2017). There is an urgent need to prepare a generation of cybersecurity professionals who are technologically equipped to defend and secure digital infrastructures. However, addressing this need involves cultivating powerful capabilities in students who are often young and inexperienced—students who will be on the forefront of ethical and technological challenges that stand to shape the future of society. It is vital that we prepare this workforce to be able to manage the ethical challenges and the burden of responsibility that comes along with its increased technological skills and its access to highly sensitive networks. In this chapter, we will address the emerging realm of cybersecurity ethics in order to help to guide instructors in developing course content that will speak to this vital area of concern.

Cybersecurity, by its nature, is ethically challenging. To protect a system, cybersecurity professionals must determine where it is vulnerable. They need to understand—and often times figure out how—to break in. In this sense, they need to be hackers. When successful in uncovering a vulnerability, the ethical waters become muddier still. They hold a powerful secret, and resolving the concern is often not straightforward. Implementing a fix takes time and often involves drawing further attention to the problem. This can put users at risk. The release of a security patch, for example, can tell intruders exactly where a system is vulnerable. And because users are often slow to update their systems, this creates a perfect window of opportunity for exploitation. But sitting on it, keeping it secret, means that the vulnerability is lying in wait for someone else to discover. Meanwhile, there is a global market for these kinds of secrets and some will pay top dollar for the information cybersecurity professionals possess.

We would like to acknowledge the contributions of the following people who have provided valuable insight and guidance in developing this work: Michael Bailey, John Bambenek, Martha Crosby, Stephen Downie, Suyup Kim, Katie Kramer, Young Li, Michael Loui, Eugene Spafford, Richard L. Wilson, and Tim Yardley.

Cybersecurity professionals are uniquely situated to face ethically complex scenarios that can have profound implications for the rest of society. Unlike more established professions like medicine or law, cybersecurity does not have codified standards of ethics—nor is cybersecurity anywhere near establishing such standards. The few laws we do have in this area, chief among them being the 1986 Computer Fraud and Abuse Act (CFAA), struggle to "regulate a space where, fundamentally, some of the activities we want to encourage among the good guys—finding new vulnerabilities in computer systems, testing the security of software and devices—are largely indistinguishable from the activities that we want to discourage when undertaken by the bad guys" (Wolff 2016).

Investigations into cyberattacks rarely lead to prosecutions and therefore have little deterrence value: "In comparison to other federal crimes, CFAA offenses are not charged frequently—and prosecuting someone engaged [in] computer security research is *extremely rare*" (Bailey 2015, original emphasis). At the same time, researchers in cybersecurity do not agree on common ethical principles and some remain unconvinced of the possibility of establishing a universal framework that can address the realm of cybersecurity at all (Kenneally and Bailey 2014). In the ever-evolving realm of cybersecurity, where universal rules do not neatly apply and where the intricate web of consequences are not easily foreseen, new possibilities of what *can* be done open up new questions about what *should* be done. Cybersecurity ethics thus poses many more questions than it offers definitive answers.

DEFINING CYBERSECURITY ETHICS

In order to grasp the concept of cybersecurity ethics it can be helpful to look first at its constituent parts: cybersecurity and ethics.

Cybersecurity has been defined in various ways for differing purposes (Kissel 2011; Joint Task Force 2016; International Telecommunications Union 2008). However, one of the most comprehensive definitions has been proposed by Rossouw von Solms and Johan van Niekerk: "Cyber security can be defined as the protection of cyberspace itself, the electronic information, the [Information and Communication Technologies (ICTs)] that support cyberspace and the users of cyberspace in their personal, societal, and national capacity, including any of their interests, either tangible or intangible, that are vulnerable to attacks originating in cyberspace" (2013, 101).

What is significant about this definition is its holistic emphasis on protecting cyberspace, which includes not only information and technology, but also those who function within cyberspace. This expands the scope beyond the classic CIA triad consisting of confidentiality, integrity, and availability of information (Olivier 2002). This expansion opens up the concept further to include humans and society at large who make use of ICTs. And by expanding the concept of cybersecurity in this way, the need for ethical consideration enters into the picture of cybersecurity with even more immediate force. It is not just the confidentiality, integrity, and availability of *information* that is at stake in cyberspace—*people*, can be directly harmed. Rossouw von Solms and Johan van Niekerk demonstrate this in pointing to the case of cyberbullying, as "the target of such activities is the user him/herself" (2013, 99). Dramatic harm can also occur in the case of cyberattacks that target cyber-physical systems such as health care devices (Leavitt 2010), hospitals (Harris et al. 2017) and national power grids (Greenberg 2017). As we become more and more dependent upon these cyber-systems, it is not just our information and ICTs that are at risk, but also individual people, nation states, and potentially humanity at large. Recognizing this broad terrain of cybersecurity is important because it brings the need for ethical consideration to the fore.

In contrast to considerations of morality, where *morality* refers to local, sometimes cultural, standards of good behavior, *ethics* concern broader ambitions such as the search for objective, generalizable principles of conduct, or fundamental questions about what it means to live a good life. The Western philosophical tradition offers three overarching ethical frameworks including deontological ethics, utilitarian ethics, and virtue ethics (for a full description of these three approaches, see Baron, Pettit, and Slote 1997). Although all of these frameworks offer valuable (and competing) perspectives for thinking about ethical concerns, they are all limited—and the bleeding-edge nature of cybersecurity pushes up against their limitations from many different angles. Additional frameworks can help when thinking about the realm of cybersecurity. Among many additional frameworks from around the globe, these might include Confucian ethics (Ames 2011), rights and social contract theory (Rawls 2009), feminist ethics of care (Noddings 2013, Gilligan 1982), and pragmatist ethics (Dewey 1920, Dewey 2003/1932).

Cybersecurity ethics is a practice-based realm of philosophical inquiry engaging ethical issues related to cybersecurity. As a subcategory of computer and information ethics, cybersecurity ethics is a branch of applied and professional ethics that concerns standards of good practice in cybersecurity. By extension, cybersecurity ethics also concerns the education of future cybersecurity professionals. An interesting backdrop to cybersecurity ethics is the hacker culture, which in some sense both gave rise to the need for and the professional practice of, cybersecurity. Cybersecurity ethics calls for nuanced approaches that can account for the subtleties of cyber space. Despite being an area of study with a distinct lineage that dates back to the ancient Greeks, ethics, in this realm, is "forever new" (Harter 2011, 18.)

INTELLECTUAL HISTORY AND MAJOR THINKERS

Tracing the intellectual history and major thinkers of cybersecurity ethics involves exploring three lineages: the hacker ethic, cybersecurity professional practice, and philosophical inquiry related to computer and information ethics.

The Hacker Ethic

Although the term *hacker* is widely used to describe a person who uses computer and information technologies to conduct illegal activities, among computer enthusiasts the term has long carried a positive association (Hollinger 1991; for a full discussion of a classification system of hackers, see Zhang et al. 2015). Broadly speaking, the term hacker refers to a person who uses his or her technical knowledge to circumvent or overcome an obstacle. In terms of cybersecurity, hackers use their knowledge of systems, networks, and sometimes people to accomplish objectives like gaining access to networks and data. Sometimes this involves participating in illegal activities, but the term hacker can be used to describe activities that are legal as well, as in the case of "white hat hackers" (Caldwell 2011). Overall, it can be said that the hacker culture is rooted in curiosity and the belief that knowledge should be free (The Cyberpunk Project). Indeed, the hacker ethic is grounded in the free software movement (FSM) formally founded by Richard Stallman in 1983 with the launch of the GNU Project. The FSM aims to ensure that software users can freely study, change, and redistribute software with or without changes. The hacker ethic is further defined by Eric S. Raymond (n.d.), who says that the hacker ethic entails:

1. The belief that information-sharing is a powerful positive good, and that it is an ethical duty of hackers to share their expertise by writing open-source code and facilitating access to information and to computing resources wherever possible.
2. The belief that system-cracking for fun and exploration is ethically OK as long as the cracker commits no theft, vandalism, or breach of confidentiality.

This view is widely but not universally accepted among hackers. Although most hackers agree with statement 1, many argue that statement 2 is unethical. However, it should be noted that statement 1 stands in conflict with professional practice where classified or proprietary information—by definition—is deemed secret and is expected to remain so.

The hacker ethic continued to grow and was better formulated by Steven Levy (1984) in his book *Hackers: Heroes of the Computer Revolution*. While still rooted in the belief that sharing and access to computer and information should be free and unlimited, Levy's account indicates the growing distrust for authority as well as belief in meritocracy. A related sentiment was later passionately expressed in a post in *Phrack* (Blankenship 1986) magazine called "The Conscience of a Hacker." This short essay later became known as "The Hacker Manifesto." Written in response to the then teen-aged author's arrest, the essay argues that hacking is not about causing harm to others, but is rather an expression of curiosity and intelligence that is not adequately encouraged by schools: "we've been spoon-fed baby food at school when we hungered for steak . . . the bits of meat that you did let slip through were pre-chewed and tasteless . . . . The few that had something to teach found us willing pupils, but those few are like drops of water in the desert" (Blankenship 1986).

The hacker ethic has been summarized to place great value on individualism, autonomy, libertarian freedom, and subjectivity. Considered in light of the experience of programming—an experience that lends itself toward feeling all powerful and omnipotent within the bounds of a computer program—the hacker ethic's emphasis on individualism has raised concerns about experiences of self-other relationships and the ethical implications entailed therein (Warnick 2004). This concern seems to suggest the value of care ethics (Noddings 2013), in particular, for analyzing ethical concerns in cybersecurity. It may be precisely a lack of care that is encouraged by this radically individualistic orientation.

Cybersecurity Professional Practice

The notion of the ethical hacker grew out of hacker culture as it engaged with the professional realm. As awareness of the dangers posed by cyberattacks began to grow, the concept of ethical hacking took root. Ethical hacking refers to professionals who use the same tools and techniques as intruders in order to evaluate a target system's degree of security and then report back vulnerabilities so that they may be remedied (Palmer 2001, 770). The importance of thinking like an intruder to protect systems was first posed in an influential paper by Dan Farmer and Wietse Venema (1993, 2): "By showing what intruders can do to gain access to a remote site, we are trying to help system administrators to make informed decisions on how to secure their site—or not."

Throughout hacker history, ethics has been a core issue. Ethical thinking in this arena grew from discussions among individual hackers and hacker groups in online publications and the eventual creation of guidelines and certifications used in industry. The task of setting guidelines for the ethical hacking of various systems came from organizations and companies instead of individuals. The Open Web Application Security Project released the Testing Guide in order to aid in the development of secure web applications (Meucci, Keary, and Cuthbert 2008). The Penetration Testing Execution Standard (PTES n.d.) offers businesses and security services a scope for performing penetration testing, sparked by the determined value of penetration testing industry. The International Council of Electronic Commerce Consultants (EC-Council) is a professional certification body with the well-known certification Certified Ethical Hacker (CEH). The CEH provides students with the tools and techniques used by hackers to break into organizations. It also requires that its students sign an agreement stating they will not use the skills acquired from this certification in illegal or malicious manners.

Two main overarching professional organizations are the Institute of Electrical and Electronics Engineers (IEEE) and the Association for Computing Machinery (ACM), both of which have established codes of ethics for the engineers who belong to their organizations. However, there is a lack of consensus among shared values, as evidenced by the growing frustration among researchers, program committees, and professional organizations (Allman 2008). At the same time, there is a growing frustration among researchers, professional organizations, industry, and the government about the limits of ethical research and about who is responsible for the enforcement of these frameworks and guidelines (Dittrich, Bailey, and Dietrich 2009).

Philosophical Inquiry Related to Computer and Information Ethics

Alongside these developments, philosophical consideration of computer and information ethics can be traced back to Norbert Wiener's (1948) publication of *Cybernetics*. Although Wiener envisioned his work as a new branch of applied science dealing with interactions between living things and machines, the implications for ethics in Wiener's work abound: "Apparently, no one—not even Wiener himself—recognized the profound importance of his ethical achievements; and nearly two decades would pass before some of the social and ethical impacts of information technology, which Wiener had predicted in the late 1940s, would become obvious to other scholars and to the general public" (Bynum 2016). Wiener understood early on that the newly invented computer and information technologies would revolutionize society and would place human beings "in the presence of another social potentiality of unheard-of importance for good and for evil" (1948, 27). Notably, the significance of Wiener's work has also been appreciated within the field of cybersecurity, with the identification of prominent links between the two fields (Adams et al. 2013; Anjaria and Mishra 2017).

It would take nearly three decades before other scholars began to recognize the ethical significance of computers. In 1976, Walter Maner proposed a new field he termed "computer ethics" to study the new ethical problems that are aggravated, transformed, or created by computer technology (Bynum 2016). This set the stage for a core debate within the field of computer ethics about whether computers generate ethically unique problems or whether the problems that emerged from the use of computers are just new spins on old ethical dilemmas. James H. Moor (1985) posed what has come to be known as the Standard

Account in his influential paper called "What Is Computer Ethics?" In it, Moor argued that computers are creating new possibilities for ethical action that exposes policy vacuums. He envisioned the role of computer ethics to examine these new possibilities in order to fill the policy vacuums, which involves addressing what he termed "conceptual muddles." In contrast, Deborah G. Johnson, who wrote the first, and one of the most influential, textbooks in computer ethics, is a key figure in these debates, arguing that computers are not posing wholly new problems, but rather "new species of old moral issues" (Johnson 1985).

Ethical consideration related to cybersecurity has emerged as a core theme within this philosophical lineage of ethical inquiry. Given the significant implications of cybersecurity for society at large and the urgent demand to prepare a new generation of cybersecurity professionals, cybersecurity ethics has emerged as an area of study that now calls for its own distinct focus.

CONTINUING ISSUES AND CONCERNS

In a field founded on the reality that we are never fully secure, continuing issues and concerns abound. Three prominent themes have emerged in recent years.

Hiring Formerly Convicted Hackers

Cybersecurity is unique in that it is not uncommon for convicted cybercriminals to be tasked by the government to help catch other cybercriminals in exchange for a shorter prison sentence or even employment (Wiener-Bronner 2014; Leyden 2013). Security is, above all, a mindset. While technical knowledge is obviously needed in cybersecurity, being able to think like an intruder is fundamental in order to put technical knowledge and skills to good use. Convicted hackers have proven their ability to leverage their technical abilities in thinking like an intruder—but can they be trusted?

Hacking Back

It has been estimated that cybercrime will cost an average of $6.1 trillion *every year* through 2021 (Eubanks 2017). Although there are laws that aim to protect against cyberattacks, the reality is that cybercriminals are rarely prosecuted for their crimes and therefore offer little deterrence value. Furthermore, cyberattacks are not only concerning from a business perspective, but are a matter of national security. According to Stewart Baker (2013), former general counsel of the US National Security Agency, "We will never defend our way out of the cybersecurity crisis. I know of no other crime where the risk of apprehension is so low, and where we simply try to build more and thicker defenses to protect ourselves. . . .. Sometimes the best defense is really a good offense." Given the current state of affairs, in which cyberattackers often "win," questions arise about whether hacking back could be justified? (For a full analysis of this issue, see Lin 2016).

Ransomware

A type of malware that locks users' machines, ransomware renders users' files inaccessible until they pay a ransom in order to recover their files. Although it is clearly unethical to hold someone's files hostage in demand for a ransom to be paid, there is a very real lingering question as to whether or not paying the ransom is the right thing do. In paying the ransom, victims are no doubt supporting this unethical practice. However, if they don't pay, they are likely to lose their files if sufficient backups do not exist. Shockingly, the FBI recommends that users pay the ransom (Roberts 2015), though there is no guarantee that doing so will recover users' files. Ransomware has been known to take advantage of disclosed vulnerabilities, as in the case of the recent WannaCry virus (Fruhlinger 2017). What would you do if your computer was infected by ransomware? How does the existence of ransomware inform issues of responsible disclosure of vulnerabilities?

However, underlying these themes are larger, more profound ethical issues that strike at the very root of the responsibilities of an individual to society. When and under what conditions is whistle blowing the right thing to do in cybersecurity? The suppression of cybersecurity knowledge and concerns better supports cyber technology translation, transfer, and adoption. However, ignoring whistleblower claims can lead to retaliation, increasing regulatory policies, and risk. Also, recent events and public awareness raise, in a broader scope, the question of how we are to ethically evaluate cybersecurity when social engineering can impact people's decisions, including the use of targeted and pervasive memes on social media. In the coming years, the confluence of artificial intelligence and active cybersecurity defense creates a dynamic with an underlying problem of how to build autonomous systems that incorporate an ethical view of their actions. But perhaps the ultimate edge case in cybersecurity involves *cyberwar*. Carl von Clausewitz claims that "War is simply the continuation of political intercourse with the addition of other means" (1989, 89). Cyberwar could range from fabrication, distortion, or removal of information to death and destruction. Microsoft president Brad Smith suggested global rules in the form of "a Digital Geneva Convention" for cyberattacks at the RSA 2017 Conference. The NATO Tallinn Manual (Schmitt 2013) studied how international law might apply to cyberconflicts and cyberwarfare. But as of today, there are no widely accepted legal or ethical frameworks to guide humanity when political intercourse is continued by means of cyberattack.

SUMMARY

This chapter introduces some of the major issues concerning cybersecurity ethics that we currently face. However, the open-ended nature of cybersecurity raises more questions than it answers. In our review and analysis, a key observation is that automation is accelerating and diversifying the occurrence of cybersecurity ethical issues and are central to the question of how to deploy cyber technology for the benefit of mankind. Our best institutional mechanisms that respond to these issues, both legal and academic, are ponderous at best. At worst, they ignore major issues or end up stymied by the element of surprise or lack of practical enforcement. The subject is offered to the readers as a serious problem worthy of practice and study.

CASE STUDY 1: THE MORRIS WORM

In 1988, Cornell graduate student Robert Morris created and unleashed one of the first widespread computer worms (Orman 2003). This worm infected and effectively shut down about 10 percent of the computers connected to the internet at that time (Graham 2005).

Although the creator's intended purpose is unknown it is assumed the main goal was to establish access to as many machines as possible (Orman 2003). The US Government Accountability Office estimated the cost of the damage at $100,000 to $10,000,000. Robert Morris was the first person tried and convicted of violating the Computer Fraud and Abuse Act (*United States v. Morris* 1991). Although illegal and highly disruptive, this worm caused no lasting damage to infected machines and served as a wakeup call to the need for security on the internet. As a result, many companies and organizations began thinking about cybersecurity and formed their own cybersecurity teams. The research community responded with the invention of new computer languages, automated tools, and mechanisms to improve computer security. The Morris worm case is seminal in the field of cybersecurity and raised many lasting ethical questions.

Questions

To what extent is gaining unauthorized access to computer systems analogous to breaking and entering in the physical world? Does the fact that Morris was an inexperienced student at the time of the worm's launch impact judgments about the ethical quality of his action? Could Morris's action be considered ethical if we believe that, over time, the Morris worm led to greater security on the internet?

CASE STUDY 2: THE SAN BERNARDINO SHOOTER'S IPHONE CASE

On December 2, 2015, fourteen people were killed in a mass shooting and an attempted bombing at the Inland Regional Center in San Bernardino, California. After the attack, the Federal Bureau of Investigation identified the attackers and began an extensive investigation (Volz and Hosenball 2016). When the FBI discovered it was unable to unlock one of the mobile phones recovered, the FBI requested the help of the National Security Agency (NSA). The NSA reportedly was unable to fulfill the request because it "has to prioritize its resources in a utilitarian way—in that it will focus its resources on cracking the popular devices among suspected criminals, rather than the more popular devices, like iPhones" (Whittaker 2016). The FBI then requested Apple Inc. to create a new operating system in order to disable certain security features and gain access to the data on the phone. Apple declined, and the FBI issued a court order mandating Apple to create the requested operating system (Blankenstein 2016). The use of legislation to compel Apple to write up new software was unprecedented and a milestone moment in the Crypto Wars and the privacy debate. While the debate continues, many questions loom.

Questions

Should law enforcement require legislation to access a personal device? Who is responsible for privacy enforcement? Do you own your own personal data? What is the cost of violations of privacy?

REFERENCES

Adams, Michael D., Seth D. Hitefield, Bruce Hoy, Michael C. Fowler, and T. Charles Clancy. 2013. "Application of Cybernetics and Control Theory for a New Paradigm in Cybersecurity." *arXiv preprint arXiv: 1311.0257.*

Allman, Mark. 2008. "What Ought a Program Committee to Do?" *Workshop on Organizing Workshops, Conferences, and Symposia for Computer Systems* 8 (2008): 1–5.

Ames, Roger T. 2011. *Confucian Role Ethics: A Vocabulary.* Chinese University Press.

Anjaria, Kushal and Arun Mishra. 2017. "Relation between Cybernetics and Information Security: from Norbert Wieners' Perspectives." *Kybernete.* 46 (10), 1654–73, https://doi.org/10.1108/K-04-2017-0129.

Association for Computing Machinery Council. "Code of Ethics and Professional Conduct," October 1992. www.acm.org/about/code-of-ethics.

Bailey, Leonard. 2015. "Bring a Hacker to Work Day: How the Justice Department Uses the Computer Fraud and Abuse Act." Presentation given at black hat, August 15. www.blackhat.com/docs/us-15/materials/us-15-Bailey-Take-A-Hacker-To-Work%20Day-How-Federal-Prosecutors-Use-The-CFAA.pdf.

Baker, Stewart. 2013. "The Department of Homeland Security at 10 Years: Examining Challenges and Achievements and Addressing Emerging Threats." Testimony before the US Senate Committee on Homeland Security and Governmental Affairs. September 11. www.hsgac.senate.gov/download/?id=AD53570C-3682-45DF-91B1-E1D60F003CF7.

Baron, M. W., Pettit, P., and Slote, M. 1997. *Three Methods of Ethics: A Debate.* Malden, MA: Blackwell Publishers Inc.

Blankenship, Loyd. 1986. "The Conscience of a Hacker." *Phrack Magazine* 18 (1986).

Blankenstein, Andrew. 2016. "Judge Forces Apple to Help Unlock San Bernardino Shooter iPhone." *NBC News.* Feb. 16. www.nbcnews.com/storyline/san-bernardino-shooting/judge-forces-apple-help-unlock-san-bernardino-shooter-iphone-n519701.

Bynum, Terrell 2016. "Computer and Information Ethics." In *Stanford Encyclopedia of Philosophy.* Stanford, CA: The Metaphysics Research Lab. https://plato.stanford.edu/entries/ethics-computer/.

Caldwell, Tracey. 2011. "Ethical Hackers: Putting on the White Hat." *Network Security* 7, 10–13.

Clausewitz, Carl von. 1989. *On War.* Edited and translated by Michael Howard and Peter Paret. Princeton, NJ: Princeton University Press.

Cyberpunk Project. "The Hacker's Ethics." http://project.cyberpunk.ru/idb/hacker_ethics.html.

Dewey, J. 2003a. *Reconstruction in Philosophy* (1920), in *The Middle Works of John Dewey (1899–1924),* edited by Jo Anne Boydston Vol. 12 (Carbondale and Edwardsville: Southern Illinois University Press).

———. 2003b. *Ethics* (1932). In *The Later Works of John Dewey (1925–1953),* edited by Jo Anne Boydston Vol. 7 (Carbondale and Edwardsville: Southern Illinois University Press).

Dittrich, David, Michael Bailey, and Sven Dietrich. 2009. "Towards Community Standards for Ethical Behavior in Computer Security Research." *Stevens CS Technical Report* (April 20). http://mdbailey.ece.illinois.edu/publications/dbd2009tr1.pdf.

Eubanks, Nick. 2017. "The True Cost of Cybercrime for Businesses." *Forbes,* July 13. www.forbes.com/sites/theyec/2017/07/13/the-true-cost-of-cybercrime-for-businesses/#52867b4b4947.

Farmer, Dan, and Wietse Venema. 1993. "Improving the Security of Your Site by Breaking into It." www.dcs.ed.ac.uk/home/rah/Resources/Security/admin_guide_to_cracking.pdf.

Fruhlinger, Josh. 2017. "What Is WannaCry Ransomware, How Does It Infect, and Who Was Responsible?" *CSO,* September 27. www.csoonline.com/article/3227906/ransomware/what-is-wannacry-ransomware-how-does-it-infect-and-who-was-responsible.html.

Furnell, S., P. Fischer, and A. Finch. 2017. "Can't Get the Staff? The Growing Need for Cyber-Security Skills." *Computer Fraud and Security,* 2, 5–10.

Gilligan, Carol. 1982. *In a Different Voice.* Cambridge, MA: Harvard University Press.

Graham, Paul. 2005. The Submarine. www.paulgraham.com/submarine.html#f4n.

Greenberg, Andy. 2017. "Hackers Gain Direct Access to US Power Grid Controls." *Wired,* September 16. www.wired.com/story/hackers-gain-switch-flipping-access-to-us-power-systems/.

Harris, Dan, et al. 2017. "Fears of Hackers Targeting US Hospitals, Medical Devices for Cyber Attacks." *ABC News,* June 29. http://abcnews.go.com/Health/fears-hackers-targeting-us-hospitals-medical-devices -cyber/story?id=48348384.

Harter, Nathan. 2011. "Toward What End? Three Classical Theories." In *Information Assurance and Security Ethics in Complex Systems: Interdisciplinary Perspectives,* edited by Melissa Jane Dark, 17-29. Hershey, PA: ITI Global.

Hollinger, Richard C. 1991. "Hackers: Computer Heroes or Electronic Highwaymen?" *ACM SIGCAS Computers and Society* 21 (1): 6-17.

Institute of Electrical and Electronic Engineering Board of Directors. "Code of Ethics." Feb. 2006. www.ieee.org/portal/pages/iportals/aboutus/ethics/code.html.

International Telecommunications Union (ITU). 2008. Overview of Cybersecurity. ITU-TX.1205: series X: data networks, open system communications and security: telecommunication security. www.itu.int/ rec/T-REC-X.1205-200804-I.

Johnson, Deborah G. 1985. *Computer Ethics.* Englewood Cliffs, New Jersey: Prentice-Hall.

Joint Task Force on Cybersecurity Education. "Defining Cybersecurity." Aug. 2016. www.csec2017.org.

Kenneally, E., and Bailey, M. D. 2014. "Cyber-Security Research Ethics Dialogue and Strategy Workshop." *Computer Communication Review* 44 (2): 76-79. https://doi.org/10.1145/2602204.2602217.

Kissel, Richard, ed. 2011. *Glossary of Key Information Security Terms.* Collington, PA: Diane Publishing.

Leavitt, Neal. 2010. "Researchers Fight to Keep Implanted Medical Devices Safe from Hackers." *Computer* 43 (8): 11-14.

Levy, Steven. 1984. *Hackers: Heroes of the Computer Revolution.* Vol. 14. Garden City, NY: Anchor Press/ Doubleday.

Leyden, John. 2013. "U.K. Government Open to Hiring EX-CON Hackers for Cyber Reserves." *The Register,* October 23. www.theregister.co.uk/2013/10/23/hacker_wanted_uk_cyber_reserve_squad/.

Lin, Patrick. 2016. *Ethics of Hacking Back: Six Arguments from Armed Conflict to Zombies.* Washington, DC, US National Science Foundation. http://ethics.calpoly.edu/hackingback.pdf.

Meucci, Matteo, Eoin Keary, and Daniel Cuthbert. 2008. "The OWASP Testing Guide v2." *OWASP Foundation* 16.

Moor, James H. 1985. "What Is Computer Ethics?" *Metaphilosophy* 16 (4): 266-75.

National Academy of Engineering. n.d. 14 Grand Challenges for Engineering in the 21st Century: Secure Cyberspace. www.engineeringchallenges.org/challenges/cyberspace.aspx.

Noddings, Nel. 2013. *Caring: A Relational Approach to Ethics and Moral Education.* University of California Press.

Olivier, Martin S. 2002. "Database Privacy: Balancing Confidentiality, Integrity and Availability." *ACM SIGKDD Explorations Newsletter* 4, (2): 20-27.

Orman, Hilarie. 2003. "The Morris Worm: A Fifteen-Year Perspective." *IEEE Security and Privacy* 99 (5): 35-43.

Palmer, Charles C. 2001. "Ethical Hacking." *IBM Systems Journal* 40 (3): 769-80.

Penetration Testing Execution Standard (PTES). n.d. www.pentest-standard.org/index.php/Main_Page.

Raymond, Eric S. "Hacker Ethic." n.d. www.catb.org/jargon/html/H/hacker-ethic.html.

Rawls, John. *A Theory of Justice,* rev. ed. Cambridge, MA: Harvard University Press, 2009.

Roberts, Paul. 2015. "F.B.I.'s Advice on Ransomware? Just Pay the Ransom." *The Security Ledger.* October 22. https://securityledger.com/2015/10/fbis-advice-on-cryptolocker-just-pay-the-ransom/.

Schmitt, Michael N., ed. 2013. *Tallinn Manual on the International Law Applicable to Cyber Warfare.* Cambridge, UK: Cambridge University Press, 2013.

Smith, Brad. 2017. "Protecting and Defending against Cyberthreats in Uncertain Times." *RSA 2017 Conference.* www.rsaconference.com/events/us17/agenda/sessions/7577-protecting-and -defending-against-cyberthreats-in.

Stallman, R (1983). "New UNIX Implementation," https://groups.google.com/forum/#!msg/net.unix -wizards/8twfRPM79u0/1xlglzrWrU0J.

Volz, Dustin, and Mark Hosenball. 2016. "FBI Director Says Investigators Unable to Unlock San Bernardino Shooter's Phone Content." *Reuters,* February 9. www.reuters.com/article/us-california -shooting-encryption/fbi-director-says-investigators-unable-to-unlock-san-bernardino-shooters -phone-content-idUSKCN0VI22A.

Von Solms, Rossouw, and Johan Van Niekerk. 2013. "From Information Security to Cyber Security." *Computers and Security* 38, 97–102.

Warnick, Bryan R. 2004. "Technological Metaphors and Moral Education: The Hacker Ethic and the Computational Experience." *Studies in Philosophy and Education* 23 (4): 265–81.

Whittaker, Zack. 2016. "NSA Finally Admits Why It Couldn't Hack San Bernardino Shooter's iPhone." *ZDNet,* June 10. www.zdnet.com/article/nsa-comes-clean-on-why-it-couldnt-hack-san-bernardino -shooters-iphone/.

Wiener, Norbert. 1948. *Cybernetics: or Control and Communication in the Animal and the Machine.* New York: Technology Press/John Wiley and Sons.

Wiener-Bronner, Danielle. 2014. "Hacker Freed from Prison after Helping the FBI Catch Other Hackers." *The Atlantic,* May 27. www.theatlantic.com/technology/archive/2014/05/hacker-sabu-freed-from -prison/371649/.

Wolff, Josephine. 2016. "The Hacking Law that Can't Hack It." *Slate,* September 27. www.slate.com/ technology/2018/03/with-apples-face-id-its-time-to-look-at-facial-recognition-techs-problematic -past.html.

Zhang, Xiong, Alex Tsang, Wei T. Yue, and Michael Chau. 2015. "The Classification of Hackers by Knowledge Exchange Behaviors." *Information Systems Frontiers* 17 (6): 1239–51.

ADDITIONAL RESOURCES

Ess, Charles. 2013. *Digital Media Ethics.* Cambridge ; Malden, MA: Polity.

Johnson, Deborah G., with Keith W. Miller. 2009. *Computer Ethics: Analyzing Information Technology.* Upper Saddle River, New Jersey: Prentice Hall.

Library Freedom Project. https://libraryfreedomproject.org/.

Quinn, Michael J. 2014. *Ethics for the Information Age.* Boston, MA: Pearson.

Spinello, Richard. 2010. *Cyberethics: Morality and Law in Cyberspace.* Burlington, MA: Jones and Bartlett Learning.

Tavani, Herman T. 2013. *Ethics and Technology: Controversies, Questions, and Strategies for Ethical Computing.* Hoboken, NJ: John Wiley and Sons.

Vallor, Shannon. 2016. *Technology and the Virtues: A Philosophical Guide to a Future Worth Wanting.* Oxford, UK: Oxford University Press.

CHAPTER 10

Cognitive Justice and Intercultural Information Ethics

Rachel Fischer and Erin Klazar

Cognitive justice recognizes the right of different forms of knowledge to co-exist, but adds that this plurality needs to go beyond tolerance or liberalism to an active recognition of the need for diversity. It demands recognition of knowledges, not only as methods but as ways of life. This presupposes that knowledge is embedded in ecology of knowledges where each knowledge has its place, its claim to a cosmology, its sense as a form of life. In this sense knowledge is not something to be abstracted from a culture as a life form; it is connected to livelihood, a life cycle, a lifestyle; it determines life chances.

—*Shiv Visvanathan*, The Search for Cognitive Justice, *2009*

Shiv Visvanathan (2009) asserts that cognitive justice emphasizes the importance of different forms of knowledges and their right to coexist. To develop this, an international dialogue to establish a fraternity among these different forms must take place to allow for the expansion of an individual's horizons. This means that previously subjugated expressions from the "Global South" and previously colonized countries are given the platform to express their unique points of view on matters of development, politics, and ethics, without these expressions becoming representative of "primitive" examples of thinking and living.

The objective of this chapter is not to enter the debate on whether cognitive justice is representative and supportive of relativism nor whether it argues that all forms of knowledge have valid and instrumental value. Instead, it is a scholarly analysis of cognitive justice and what it entails within the broader information ethics theoretical framework. As such, the aim of this chapter is to provide an overview of key terms relating to cognitive justice and major thinkers that have contributed to this concept. As a key component of information ethics, intercultural information ethics (IIE) is proposed as the means by which these dialogues can take place. Situating the importance of social justice, indigenous knowledge, and IIE central to the theme and the use of appropriate case studies will assist in demonstrating how practitioners, academics, and students can use this chapter to improve their understanding of the topic and apply it in practice.

KEY TERMS AND CONCEPTS

Abyssal Thinking and Border Thinking

Conceptualized by Boaventura de Sousa Santos, *abyssal thinking* refers to the "epistemological dominance of the West," which segregates different social realities and knowledge systems (Santos 2014). It is connected to inclusion and exclusion, where knowledges and ways of thinking that are alternative or not dominant are excluded and hence cease to exist. In relation to cognitive justice, Santos indicates the two different sides, namely the (Global) North (truth, universality, rational, scientific knowledge) and the (Global) South (traditional and indigenous knowledge, beliefs, opinions, intuition) (Zembylas 2017). By addressing this, post-abyssal thinking allows for the co-presence of all forms of knowledge.

Border thinking, or border gnosis, is the process of bringing previously repressed knowledges to the foreground, allowing them to become areas of research in their own right. Border thinking also encourages participation among academics and civil society, allowing for cross-industry dialogue. This is emancipatory multiculturalism, where the recognition of difference, and of the right to difference and the coexistence or construction of a common way of life that extends beyond the various types of difference occurs whilst still retaining the autonomy of the various agents involved in these dialogues (Zembylas 2017).

Cognitive Justice

This is the recognition of different forms of knowledge as equal to other forms of knowledge, together with the right to exist alongside these. Cognitive justice proposes not only mere tolerance but also requires active endeavors towards inter- and intracultural dialogues and the recognition of diversity (Visvanathan 2009), as well as the reorganization of various research and development strategies between communities and experts (Hoppers 2009). The global and ubiquitous nature of information and communication technologies (ICTs) also means that cognitive justice is realized through "open and flexible designs that do justice to different ways of knowing and being in the world" (Van der Velden 2009).

Ecology of Knowledges, Diatopical Hermeneutics, and Alternative Discourses

The ecology of knowledges is central to the discourse on cognitive justice. It implies the concept of "epistemological diversity of the world, [which is] the recognition of the existence of a plurality of knowledges beyond scientific knowledge" (Santos 2007). This complements post-abyssal thinking, where the abyss is crossed by stimulating intercultural dialogues. It enables one to transcend one's own prejudices about understanding other ways of knowing, thinking, and doing. In this sense, it links with *diatopical hermeneutics,* which encompasses the notion of identifying similar concerns between two or more cultures together with the various responses to these concerns, without delegitimizing one culture's knowledge. It is a recognition of radical "Otherness," which also involves alternative discourses within and between different cultures (Griffioen 2002). By engaging in such dialogical approaches, the space is created for the development and representation of definitions, content, solutions, and so on, which are relevant for local conditions (Coleman and Dionisio 2009).

Epistemicide

Epistimicide is also known as "the murder of knowledge," which implies the subjugation and even death of other forms of knowledge by more dominant forces (e.g., Western, Eurocentric and colonial). This not only impacts the knowledge itself, but also the demise of those cultures that held it—their beliefs, traditions, and local knowledge (Zembylas 2017).

Grassroots Globalization

The concept of grassroots globalization is linked with hegemonic globalization (and counter-hegemonic globalization). Hegemony is the dominance of one system or group over another; it is usually characterized by a power struggle and subsequently becomes legitimized ideologically, politically, socially, and culturally. Grassroots globalization extends the notion that representation of knowledge should also happen bottom-up, towards giving a voice to previously suppressed forms of knowledge (and hence be counter-hegemonic). Since it is a form of cognitive injustice to perceive globalized areas of the world as being more advanced, one must be aware of the hegemonic implications of the use of the word *globalization,* even for purposes of legitimizing local ways of knowing (Coleman and Dionisio 2009), which undermines the aim of cognitive justice.

Indigenous Knowledge

Indigenous knowledge is the awareness and celebration of knowledge systems found in traditional and local practices. It is found in practices of medicine and healing, knowledge about the natural environment and even eating, lifestyle, and cooking habits. Indigenous knowledge is usually dominated by the preference for "Western" or scientific forms of knowledge hence practitioners of cognitive justice's endeavor to reintroduce it in global, inclusive dialogues.

According to Catherine A. Odora Hoppers, the use of the term "indigenous knowledge systems" differs in various parts of the world. She situates her understanding of the term in the South African landscape, where it encompasses "systems of knowledge in philosophy, science, technology, astronomy, education, mathematics, engineering, etc. [which] are grounded in the total cultural heritage of a nation or society and maintained by communities over centuries" (Hoppers 2009). She further underscores that not only do these indigenous knowledge systems need to be recognized, but they must be actively engaged with.

This meaning links with cognitive justice in the sense that the engagement is achieved by the fraternity of dialogue among different forms of knowledge systems. Therefore, these different knowledge systems contain both the process of self-reflection as well as the active engagement towards considering new horizons of human and societal possibilities that are found in the "multiplicity of worlds and forms of life" (Hoppers 2009). Indigenous knowledge is not about museumizing local, tribal, and traditional knowledge that seek to be preserved, digitized, and archived. It is rather an active endeavor towards knowledge sharing (Van der Velden 2009).

Intercultural Information Ethics

Intercultural information ethics (IIE) encourages cross-cultural dialogues on matters arising from the life cycle of information and ICTs. In doing so it addresses not only local, but also global issues brought about by ICTs. By supporting this dialogue without giving preference to a dominant or any specific knowledge system, it sustains indigenous knowledge, local traditions, and customs and makes it available to the global community. The premise of IIE is to take (information) ethical issues and seek universal responses to them without detracting from local experiences.

According to Rafael Capurro (2008), IIE can be defined in both a narrow and a broad sense. The narrow sense considers how ICTs impact on different cultures; not only how these cultures utilize ICTs but also how ICTs change the behavioral and communication patterns among individuals with different cultural backgrounds. It also analyzes how different cultures respond to information ethical issues. In a broad sense, Capurro (2008) looks at how IIE addresses ethical questions raised by digital and other information and communication media. Furthermore, IIE explores methods to develop ethical guidelines for society, while remaining sensitive to how culture affects these guidelines and of the potential conflicts between information and culture.

Therefore, this global dialogue considers cultural differences as well as similarities in how ICTs are implemented and experienced. IIE becomes aligned with cognitive justice by the call for inter- and intracultural dialogues. However, it is also a diversion from the primacy of Western and scientific reasoning towards the recognition of other knowledge systems.

INTELLECTUAL HISTORY

Social Justice

Social justice is inextricably linked to cognitive justice and that is why an approach to cognitive justice must include the struggle for social justice (Zembylas 2017). Social justice is "a concept based upon the belief that each individual and group within a given society has a right to civil liberties, equal opportunity, fairness, and participation in the educational, economic, institutional, social, and moral freedoms and responsibilities valued by the community" (Disman and Degan n.d.).

Social justice finds its foundations in John Rawls's book *A Theory of Justice* (1973). In the development of information ethics, it has been applied by Johannes J. Britz (2004; 2008) in his analyses of information poverty as an issue of justice, where justice is used as a moral tool to assess it. According to Rawls, justice is a virtue for social institutions and ought to be utilized in the process of evaluating any institutions or societies. In so doing, social justice creates awareness within and among communities about practices that are both just and unjust and seeks to set out guidelines for the fair and equal treatment of all people within communities (Britz 2004). In his reflection on information poverty, Britz applies these principles of social justice to reveal why information poverty is an issue of justice. Knowledge is power, and by not having access to crucial information and by not being able to represent one's local knowledge, the knower becomes excluded by dominant discourses, whether Western, state, or even capitalist. To address this, Britz identifies the following categories of justice in his application to information poverty (Britz 2004; 2008):

- justice as recognition
- justice as reciprocity
- justice as participation
- justice as enablement
- justice as distribution
- justice as contribution
- justice as retribution

If social justice is the "ideal condition in which all members of a society have the same basic rights, security, opportunities, obligations and social benefits" (Hoppers 2009), then investigating the mechanisms that hinder inclusion, a global dialogue (considering the preceding seven categories) will contribute towards understanding and addressing cognitive and social in/justices.

MAJOR THINKERS

Shiv Visvanathan. An Indian intellectual, anthropologist, and human rights researcher, Visvanathan (OP Jindal Global University, Sonepat, India) was one of the first scholars to write about the issues that cognitive justice seeks to address. His collection of essays, *A Carnival for Science: Essays on Science, Technology and Development,* published in 1997, is frequently referenced. Visvanathan calls for a "democracy of knowledges" that allows for a plurality of voices, civic participation, resistance, and dialogue and for him cognitive justice achieves this (Visvanathan 2009). According to Visvanathan, the following are the principles for cognitive justice (Van der Velden 2004):

- All forms of knowledge are valid and should coexist in a dialogic relationship to each other;
- Cognitive justice implies the strengthening of the "voice" of the defeated and marginalized;
- Traditional knowledges and technologies should not be museumized;
- Every citizen is a scientist. Each layperson is an expert;
- Science should help the common man/woman; and
- All competing sciences should be brought together into a positive heuristic for dialogue.

Therefore, this plurality of voices and diversity of knowledges is exemplified in cognitive justice made manifest in constructive intercultural dialogue.

Boaventura de Sousa Santos. A Portuguese academic and sociologist at the Centre for Social Studies, University of Coimbra, Portugal, Santos critiques marginalization and delegitimation specifically in regard to human rights and hence also social in/justices. He challenges the dominant discourses emanating from Western, Eurocentric, and colonial epistemological foundations. He argues these discourses tend to suppress and delegitimize other approaches from the Global South, Third World, and indigenous knowledges (Zembylas 2017). To address this he calls for counter-epistemologies and counter-hegemonic globalization. Scientific knowledge is a product of abyssal thinking and hence also a product of colonial, imperial, and Western thinking. The continuous manifestation of abyssal thinking is not conducive for cognitive justice if it is argued that scientific knowledge must be distributed equally and fairly, because there will always be those who have more, and those that have less access to this knowledge due to the digital divide. Santos, however, argues that emphasizing nonscientific knowledge as an instance of an ecology of knowledges does not presuppose the discrediting of scientific knowledge; rather, it calls for its counter-hegemonic use (Santos 2007). The counter-hegemonic uses consist of two dimensions: (1) the exploration of the "internal plurality of science" or alternative scientific practices, and (2) the promotion of "interaction between scientific and nonscientific knowledges" (Santos 2007), which in this instance can also be construed as intercultural and inter-disciplinary dialogues.

Catherine A. Odora Hoppers. DST/NRF Chair in Development Education, University of South Africa, South Africa, Hoppers examines the implications of culture and society in a globalizing world on education. Important themes in her research are indigenous knowledge, cognitive justice, and the coexistence of different knowledge systems. Looking at the roles of cultural diversity and citizenship, she emphasizes equal access, equality, and social justice that is achieved by universal respect (Hoppers 2009). Referring to both African and global contexts, she recognizes the importance "that knowledge primarily rests in people rather than in ICTs, databases or services"; hence, for Africa, and other communities, it is imperative that local knowledge, with full participation by rural and urban communities, be built simultaneously with global knowledge (Hoppers 2017). She agrees with Visvanathan that universities have a central role to play as institutes of lifelong learning and representatives of rural, local, and global knowledge. This can be achieved through:

- Universities as the environment where the "Other" is enabled by dialogue;
- Universities as a forum where different knowledge systems are examined to understand its origins, current and future practices;
- Critical examination of research and interdisciplinary studies such as indigenous knowledge, education policies, citizenship education, science, politics, and philosophy;
- Engagement with issues such as democracy and human rights from various local and global points of view; and
- Collaboration among academics, practitioners, and civil society to broaden understanding towards alternative and multiple perspectives.

Themes of inclusive dialogue, intercultural debates, and social justice are critical to achieve transformation within education and communities.

Jennifer Chan-Tiberghien of the Department of Educational Studies, University of British Columbia, Canada, considers the cultural diversity and global citizenship education in light of cognitive justice. She reiterates that social justice is not possible without cognitive justice, and that different systems of knowledge should be given the equal opportunity to achieve representation and interpretation. Themes of counter-neoliberal globalization, culture-capitalism, cosmopolitan culturalism, decolonizing methodologies, democratic deliberations and cultural narratives feature in her research (Chan-Tiberghien 2006). She seeks to interlink the concepts of critical pedagogy (which will not be discussed here), cognitive justice, and decolonizing methodologies. Although she agrees with Santos that "there will be no global social justice without global cognitive justice," she argues that the affirmation of cognitive justice is not enough to restore oppressed knowledge systems. To address restoration, she refers to Linda Tuhiwai Smith's concept of "decolonizing methodologies" (Smith 2012) as a means to address "Western imperial scientific research on indigenous and local populations" (Chan-Tiberghien 2010). Twenty-five decolonizing methodologies are recommended through which local communities can engage. Chan-Tiberghien lists the following: "claiming, testimonies, storytelling, celebrating survival, remembering, indigenizing, intervening, revitalizing, connecting, reading, writing, representing, gendering, envisioning, reframing, restoring, returning, democratizing, networking, naming, protecting, creating, negotiating, discovering, and finally sharing." It becomes imperative for non-governmental and civil society organizations to engage, as a social responsibility, in local and global citizenship education (Chan-Tiberghien 2010).

Maja van der Velden. Affiliated with the Department of Informatics, University of Oslo, Norway, Van der Velden engages with cognitive justice to the extent of examining the neutrality and impact of ICTs in knowledge sharing and the equal treatment of different knowledge systems. Her investigation into the neutrality of ICTs is aligned with the notions of social justice and information poverty because the ethical agency of "creators" and "users" are questioned. For her, "ethical agency is the capability to act responsibly towards the 'other,'" and as such cognitive justice is achieved by open and flexible designs (Van der Velden 2009) by taking into consideration not only the needs of the users, but also how the values of the developers are translated into their designs. Her viewpoint that technology is never neutral encourages design for a common world. By acknowledging different knowledge systems and ways of understanding the world by encouraging responsible dialogues, cognitive justice can be achieved. A call for decolonization and democratization of knowledge *vis-a-vis* Visvanathan is made where diversity in the sciences must take place due to the dominance of Western forms of scientific knowledge. In this regard, civil society also has a role to encourage inclusive dialogues on diversity and diverse forms of local and global knowledge. Civil society can champion a bottom-up approach to social justice by enabling an environment of dialogue. In this space, local knowledge is celebrated, accompanied by the utilization of ICTs as a supporting tool for the exchange of information and facilitation of communication across communities.

CONTINUING ISSUES AND CONCERNS

Universalism versus Relativism

Hoppers states that the call for global interaction among diverse cultures and knowledge systems, and the practicalities thereof, do have inherent challenges. Her solution is based on what Seyla Benhabib calls a "content-based and an interactive form of universalism" (Benhabib 1996), which views individuals as "concrete others and as fully competent moral beings" (Hoppers 2009). To ensure that integrity is maintained along with cultural diversity, the notion of universal respect is emphasized to ensure multicultural societies.

However, when considering the philosophical dichotomy between universalism and relativism, Soraj Hongladarom proposes an alternative approach. This approach, situated within the discussions around intercultural information ethics, is a pragmatic consideration to ask, "which set of values serve the existing goals and fit with the desires of the people for a particular period of time and place more than other values?" (Hongladarom 2016). Cognitive justice is the acknowledgment of different knowledge systems and thus also different value sets. Values, especially when addressed in light of the information society and the impact of ICTs on individuals and communities, will invariably be different across cultures—not all values can be universalized. So instead of asking which values should be universalized, or delegating values to a relativistic standpoint where they are merely relative to what is cherished by communities, he recommends investigating solutions to intercultural information ethics based on what works for the given society. Hence, he does not argue for an overarching truth value, but instead focuses on how our goals can be reached. In this sense, the aim of cognitive justice is interlinked with intercultural information ethics because it motivates multi-, inter-, and intracultural dialogues—discussions of differences and similarities—without subjugating any approach to a dominant theory. Therefore, neither cognitive justice nor intercultural information ethics seek to find universally valid arguments, but rather emphasize the importance of including all cultures and communities in the debate.

CASE STUDY: STATE CAPTURE

The hegemonic characteristics of *state capture,* a condition that damages dialogue and democracy within a state and undermines cognitive and social justice, can be seen in the definition originally used by the World Bank to describe "the appropriation of decision making by small corrupt groups determined to strengthen their own economic position through the influence they wielded over governments and decision makers" (Hellman et al. 2000). Similar situations of state capture have been experienced in Asia, Latin America, and the Soviet Union. Further studies of state capture emphasized the similarities among the behavior of these individuals and those of oligarchies. The term *oligarchy* has its roots in the Greek term *oligarchia,* originally used by Aristotle to describe leadership exercised unjustly by bad men, rather than the best men for the position. It is "a hereditary social grouping that is set apart from the rest of society by religion, kinship, economic status, prestige, or even language" (Britannica 2017).

The most recent example of a country battling these dominant negative forces is South Africa. As a very young democracy, in 1994 South Africa freed itself from the oligarchy and hegemonic system of apartheid. Pre-1994, the ability to share knowledge, to form individual opinions, and to contribute towards a true democracy was stifled by the ruling elite, thus preventing grassroots globalization and inclusive dialogue. Post-apartheid, there was hope for emancipatory multiculturalism. The promotion of cognitive and social justice stood on the foundation of a robust constitution, as can be seen in this excerpt from the preamble of the Constitution of the Republic of South Africa (1996):

> Believe that South Africa belongs to all who live in it, united in our diversity. We therefore, through our freely elected representatives, adopt this constitution as the supreme law of the Republic so as to—Heal the divisions of the past and establish a society based on democratic values, social justice and fundamental human rights; Lay the foundations for a democratic and open society in which government is based on the will of the people and every citizen is equally protected by law; Improve the quality of life of all citizens and free the potential of each person; and Build a united and democratic South Africa able to take its rightful place as a sovereign state in the family of nations.

However, twenty-three years later, South Africa appears to be suffering once again from a new oligarchy or hegemonic structure, that of state capture. It appears that once again, a small, self-serving group of people in power have strengthened their own economic position through the abuse of state resources, primarily infrastructure based state-owned entities (SOEs). The estimated cost of these actions ranges between 100 billion and 250 billion rand (roughly equal to between 7.5 billion and 19 billion 2017 US dollars); however, the true losses are difficult to measure. What is perhaps unique in the South African context is the way in which the activities of state capture have been exposed. Driven mainly by revelations in the press and the more recent #Guptaleaks,[1] the role of ICTs and social media have been placed in the spotlight. One of the core dialogues around in South Africa is the role of the British public relations organization Bell Pottinger, and its campaigns to generate racial tension in South Africa. By manipulating the dialogue on social media through use of fake bloggers, Twitter accounts, and "fake news," Bell Pottinger ran multiple campaigns promoting racism and causing dissension in intercultural dialogue. This, to some extent, can be viewed as an internal epistemicide, whereby the validity of the cultural knowledge of the various communities within South Africa were being questioned and subsequently undermined.

As stated previously, knowledge is power. When a community is denied access to the dominant discourse it is more susceptible to being misled by "fake news" or censorship, and therefore members of that community ultimately do not enjoy the same "basic rights, security, opportunities, obligations and social benefits" as those with access to the dominant discourse (Hoppers 2009).

Questions

Part 1. The Effects of State Capture (Hegemonic System) on Cognitive and Social Justice

What is the impact of state capture on access to information?
What is the impact of state capture on access to reliable and accurate information?
What risk does state capture pose to the concept of community?
Looking at the definition of social justice, how does a systemic threat such as state capture prevent each of the rights and freedoms outlined?

How would the systemic threat of state capture hinder the seven categories of justice identified by Britz?

Part 2. How ICTs Have Changed the Landscape of IIE and Fighting against Social (In) Justice

The #Guptaleaks were like a localized form of Wikileaks, focusing purely on corrupt practices by a particular group of individuals in both private and public sectors. These leaks have formed the basis for a number of investigations into acts of state capture. This trove of emails, containing both company and personal emails related to the Gupta family and their businesses, raise a number of ethical questions. This is of particular concern because of the general perception that anyone mentioned in the leaks or connected to any business related to the Gupta family is considered guilty by association. Some questions that should be asked include:

Had the entire email trove been publicly released, what could the impact have been on the local business, government community, and established relationships?

What is the responsibility of those in possession of the information in releasing and managing the information?

How have ICTs changed the manner in which the injustices within a particular community are exposed?

Part 3. Information Ethical Responsibility of Media in the Influence of Culture

The media play a vital role in revealing the actions of those who cause injustices. However, there are concerns around the authenticity of stories published in the media and online space. In light of that:

How has the use of ICTs and social media changed the behavioral and communication patterns between individuals and communities of different backgrounds?

How have ICTs altered the way in which communities respond to particular issues such as access to these email leaks and the fake news spread by organizations such as Bell Pottinger?

What do you think are the major concerns faced by the media and civil society in ensuring responsible release of information?

How do we ensure that communities are taught to identify fake versus authentic information?

NOTE

1. "Earlier in 2017, investigative journalists obtained an enormous trove of emails and documents from the heart of the Gupta business empire. The subsequent exposés, dubbed the #GuptaLeaks, appear to confirm the state capture hypothesis that journalists have been chipping away at for years." http://amabhungane.co.za/article/2017-08-09-why-you-should-care-about-the-guptaleaks-an-international-view.

REFERENCES

Benhabib, Seyla. 1996. *Democracy and Difference: Contesting the Boundaries of the Political.* New York: Princeton University Press.

Britannica.com. 2017. s.v. "Oligarchy Government." www.britannica.com/topic/oligarchy.

Britz, Johannes J. 2004. "To Know or Not to Know: A Moral Reflection on Information Poverty." *Journal of Information Science* 192–204.

———. 2008. "Making the Global Information Society Good: A Social Justice Perspective on the Ethical Dimensions of the Global Information Society." *Journal of the American Society for Information Science and Technology* 1171–83.

Capurro, Rafael. 2008. "Intercultural Information Ethics." In *The Handbook of Information and Computer Ethics,* by Kenneth E. Himma and Herman T. Tavani, 639–65. Hoboken, NJ: Wiley.

Chan-Tiberghien, Jennifer. 2006. "Cultural Diversity as Resistance to Neoliberal Globalization: The Emergence of a Global Movement and Convention." *Review of Education* 52, 89–105.

———. 2010. "Towards a 'Global Educational Justice' Research Paradigm: Cognitive Justice, Decolonizing Methodologies and Critical Pedagogy." *Globalisation, Societies and Education* 191–213.

Coleman, W. D., and Dionisio, J. 2009. "Globalization, Collaborative Research and Cognitive Justice." *Globalizations* 6 (3): 389–403.

Disman, R., and M. Degan, M. n.d. *Social Justice: Useful Definitions.* www.google.co.nz/url?sa=t&rct =j&q=&esrc=s&source=web&cd=9&cad=rja&uact=8&ved=0ahUKEwjhiP _akf7VAhVD2LwKHT4qAoYQFghHMAg&url=http%3A%2F%2Fvibrantcanada.ca%2Ffiles%2Fsj _defs.pdf&usg=AFQjCNEOtelLFqiYODN5MtLV06JgMp68-A.

Griffioen, H. 2002. *Is the Notion of Intercultural Dialogue a Western Concept?* www.dhdi.free.fr/recherches/ theoriedroit/articles/griffioen.htm.

Hellman, Joel S., Geraint Jones, Daniel Kaufmann, and Mark Schankerman. 2000. "Measuring Governance, Corruption, and State Capture: How Firms and Bureaucrats Shape the Business Environment in Transition Economies." Policy Research Working Paper 2312. The World Bank and European Bank for Reconstruction and Development. http://siteresources.worldbank.org/INTWBIGOVANTCOR/ Resources/measure.pdf.

Hongladarom, Soraj. 2016. "Intercultural Information Ethics: A Pragmatic Consideration." In *Information Cultures in the Digital Age: A Festschrift in Honor of Rafael Capurro,* edited by Matthew Kelly and Jared Bielby, 191–206. Springer VS.

Hoppers, Catherine A. Odora. 2009. "Education, Culture and Society in a Globalizing World: Implications for Comparative and International Education." *Compare: A Journal of Comparative and International Education* 39 (5): 601–14.

———. 2017. "Transformation and Change in Knowledge Generation Paradigms in the African and Global Contexts: Implications for Education Research in the 21st Century." *Educational Research for Global Change* 6 (1): 1–11.

Rawls, John. 1973. *A Theory of Justice.* Oxford, UK: Oxford University Press.

Santos, Boaventura de Sousa. 2007. "Beyond Abyssal Thinking: From Global Lines to Ecologies of Knowledges." *Review, Fernand Braudel Center* 30 (1): 45–89.

———. 2014. *Epistemologies of the South: Justice against Epistemicide.* Boulder, CO: Paradigm.

Smith, Linda Tuhiwai. 2012. *Decolonizing Methodologies: Research and Indigenous Peoples.* Dunedin, NZ: Otago University Press.

Van der Velden, Maja. 2004. "From Communities of Practice to Communities of Resistance: Civil Society and Cognitive Justice." *Development* 47 (1): 73–80.

———. 2009. "Design for a Common World: On Ethical Agency And Cognitive Justice." *Ethics Information Technology* 11 (1): 37–47.

Visvanathan, Shiv. 2009. *The Search for Cognitive Justice.* India Seminar. www.india-seminar.com/2009/
    597/597_shiv_visvanathan.htm.

Zembylas, Michalinos. 2017. "The Quest for Cognitive Justice: Towards a Pluriversal Human Rights
    Education." *Globalisation, Societies and Education* 15 (4): 1-13.

ADDITIONAL RESOURCES

Santos, Boaventura de Sousa. *The World Social Forum: Toward A Counter-Hegemonic Globalisation* (Part I).
    www.boaventuradesousasantos.pt/media/wsf_JaiSenPart1.pdf.

_____ . *The World Social Forum: Toward A Counter-Hegemonic Globalisation* (Part II).
    https://pdfs.semanticscholar.org/0931/749f4fb530d9e82f2ed58d8ef652c387d9a3.pdf.

_____ . 2006. *The Rise of the Global Left: The World Social Forum and Beyond.* London: Zed Books, 2006.

_____ . 2007. *Cognitive Justice in a Global World: Prudent Knowledge for a Decent Life.* Lanham, MD:
    Lexington Books.

_____ . 2014. *Epistemologies of the South: Justice against Epistemicide.* Boulder, CO: Paradigm.

Visvanathan, Shiv. 1997. *A Carnival for Science: Essays on Science, Technology and Development.* Delhi: Oxford
    University Press.

CHAPTER 11

Global Digital Citizenship

Margaret Zimmerman

Global digital citizenship is an emerging concept in academic thought. In an effort to describe contemporary issues related to the freedom to partake in acts of global citizenship over digital means, a special volume of the *Journal of Information Ethics* comprised of literature pertinent to these concerns was published in the spring of 2016. Currently, very little scholarly literature utilizes the specific terminology "global digital citizenship." Instead, global digital citizenship must be examined not as a singular, concrete phrase already used within the vernacular of scholarship, but as an expression of concepts related to citizenship in a global world that occurs via digital mediums. Just as the initial precise terminology was too restrictive, this widening can encompass an incredible latitude of actions pertinent to political participation and civic engagement in a digital world. Therefore, this chapter will explore issues that Samek and Shultz (2016, 13) refer to as the "intersections and patterns between acts and scales of citizenship, and the way information is created, exchanged, surveilled, and controlled."

A conclusion drawn by Buschman (2016) in his examination of the term *citizenship*, is that today it is an act that requires a democratic government and implies individual or collective agency. To engage in citizenship presupposes a supportive political structure and the requisite informational resources required. This is in agreement with Seymour Martin Lipset's (1960) conception of citizenship, which broadly states that citizenship is comprised of those who are included in a government's circle of full political participation. Another definition explains citizenship as "a form of political identity that consists in the identification with the political principles of . . . democracy, namely, the assertion of liberty and equality for all" (Mouffe 1995, 378). From these three perceptions of the term it appears that citizenship implies individual or collective political agency, which ideally occurs within a supportive democratic structure.

Although there is a lack of literature specifying global digital citizenship as coined terminology, there is an abundance of scholarly writing that discusses the repercussions of nations exerting control over the flow of information and the subsequent impact on citizens of these states. This work comprises the background of the term and, therefore, creates the intellectual history Samek and more recent scholars have built upon to establish current writing in this area. Therefore, this chapter will focus on a conception of global digital citizenship that examines the relationship of the state to information access and the implications of this relationship on individuals. First, current scholarship on concepts relevant to global digital citizenship will be examined in an attempt to define the term. Following this will be an examination of the intellectual history of literature germane to the development of global digital citizenship and inclusive of some of the most important concepts in this area. This will include scholarship concerned with the human right to information. The remainder of this chapter will be concerned with ongoing issues related to this concept, interspersed with real-life case studies to serve as examples of global digital citizenship.

DEFINITION OF CONCEPT

To define global digital citizenship as a concept, the older and more prevalent term "global citizenship" should first be examined. In order to appropriately draw a line around what global citizenship is, the Information Ethics Roundtable 2014 conference call for papers defined it as the development of citizens "who have a set of knowledge, skills and attitudes that make it possible for them to be actively involved in local, national and global institutions and systems that directly or indirectly affect their lives." (University of Alberta 2014). Schattle (2008, 9) offered another viewpoint, which states global citizenship is "a voluntary association with a concept that signifies ways of thinking and living within multiple cross-cutting communities—cities, regions, states, nations, and international collectives." Another definition of the term is expressed as "the dynamics of the economic, cultural, and ecological integration that are carrying human experience beyond its modernist phase of state/society relations" (Falk 1993, 40). Falk goes on to state the global citizen is concerned with what needs to happen in order to create a better world.

Digital citizenship, which is also relevant to this discussion, is a term that is explored in the realm of scholarly literature. Searson et al. (2015) describe it as characterized by the individual's collaborative behavior utilizing digital tools including computers and mobile devices. Choi, Glassman, and Cristol (2017) expand upon Searson's simplified concept of collaboration to recognize that digital citizenship allows for a perspective that is less confined geographically and allows for fewer restrictions on ideas based on place. Instead, Choi considers the digital citizen to be more globally aware and potentially more easily incited. This idea, that the digital citizen is able to explore citizenship across barriers of place, is prevalent in the literature. In fact, Searson et al. (2015) states that digital technology allows for interactive communities to be created based not on geographic location, but instead upon specific, highly specialized interests. Couldry et al. (2014) writes about digital citizenship and also discusses unique isolated communities. However, the authors' take on this concept is that digital citizenship has the ability to create connections through isolated communities within wider political cultures. Interestingly, this is an agreement with Falk's idea (1993) of global citizenship, which includes citizenship integrated across borders. Wellman et al. (2003) also stated that due to online communication, citizenship will be distributed based more on individual interests and agency, and less on local or cultural solidarity.

Looking at the two prior terms in connection with each other and combining them to a definition, a conclusion can be drawn that global digital citizenship must be comprised of actions that take place via digital means, such as computers and mobile devices, and that also encompass acts of citizenship that are not confined by geographic place and may occur both within and across physical, political, and cultural boundaries.

Having established a working definition of global digital citizenship, this chapter will now turn to examining literature relevant to this concept.

INTELLECTUAL HISTORY

The following, which is considered the basis for the concept of information as a human right, is an excerpt from Article 19 of the *Universal Declaration of Human Rights:* "Everyone has the right to freedom of opinion and expression; this right includes freedom to hold opinions without interference and to seek, receive and impart information and ideas through any media and regardless of frontiers" (UN General Assembly 1948).

In addition to being fundamental to the freedom of expression, the relationship between rights and information affects a myriad of other human rights, including issues of privacy, education, mobility, work, development, and peace (Jaeger, Taylor, and Gorham 2015). Walters (2002) describes three generations of human rights. First are civil and political rights against the encroachment of the state such as the right to life, personal integrity, and participation in government. Second, Walters lists economic, social, and cultural rights such as the right to work in favorable conditions and the right to education. Third are collective rights for society inclusive of the right to development, peace, and a healthy environment. When considering these three different generations of human rights, it is possible to see how the right to information interacts with each one. Accurate and available information is requisite to due process of law and participation in government, and certainly is a requirement of quality education. It is hard to imagine a collective society working for peace and development without the essential information to do so. When considered in this way, the human right to information is the right to the information that a person needs to live a fully actualized life (Kelmor 2016). Phrased another way, the ability to freely obtain, communicate, and disseminate information is vital for the attainment of many other human rights (Jaeger, Taylor, and Gorham 2015).

The idea of a human right to information is relevant to global digital citizenship in multiple ways. First, Choi (2016) describes four central categories of digital citizenship, two of which are relevant here. The ability to use the internet to participate in political activities, and also the ability of the citizen to challenge the status quo and promote social justice via the internet, are reliant upon the free flow of information. Peled and Rabin (2011) consider this to be a political-democratic justification to the right to information, which they state is required for citizen participation in the government, a fundamental requirement of democracy. Another justification listed by the authors is that the right to information, and particularly government-held information, is required for the accountability and transparency of the state. As Kelmor writes, "the most frequent method of finding a constitutional basis for such a right is finding that the right of access to information is a necessary corollary to constitutional grants of freedom of speech or other freedoms explicitly stated in the constitution" (Kelmor 2016, 102).

For individuals to fully participate as a citizen, they must have the information necessary to do so. If a government lacks transparency or constricts the flow of information to its people, it is not possible for citizenship activities to occur at any level—including global or digital domains. The ability of individuals to participate in discourse in which issues are decided on the public agenda is married to their ability to obtain relevant information (Peled and Rabin 2011). Parekh (2003) writes that globally oriented citizenship requires examination of one's own country and its policies, and an active interest in the affairs of other countries. It is clear that these actions cannot occur within an informational vacuum. Jaeger and Burnett state that "the most important information value in a democracy is the broadly agreed-upon belief that open access to information is not only a virtue but a necessity if a democratic information world is to succeed" (2010, 141). Having stated that a right to information is a requirement for individual participation in political practices, a logical line can be drawn to the fact that in order to fully participate as a global digital citizen, the freedom to pursue information without constriction from the state is of fundamental importance.

CONTINUING ISSUES AND CONCERNS

As predicted by Couldry in 2003, the internet has become a fundamental part of society's overall public communication space. Because of this, technology disparities have the potential to deepen existing geographically based inequalities, including the access to information and the ability to participate in the political spectrum. It is of critical importance that the global digital citizen has the ability to access technology that is capable of connecting the individual to both information and the greater world. One study reported that broadband in the home was critically important for digital citizenship (Mossberger, Tolbert, and Hamilton 2012). The authors went on to state that mobile and smart phones do not bridge the gaps or erase inequities present in disadvantaged communities. Norris (2001) writes about the democratic divide, in which individuals who do not have the internet are at great disadvantage in terms of lacking political capital and the ability to use political resources.

However, consistent in the literature is the aspiration of the internet to provide a soapbox for a previously silenced majority. Bennett, Wells and Rank (2009) state that many opportunities for meaningful civic learning and engagement exist online, including opportunities to use internet platforms for self-expression. Wellman et al. (2003) mention that a benefit of online communication is that it easily allows the inclusion of others. Palfrey and Gasser (2016) write that "the ability of networked activists to transform politics in some countries could prove to be the single most important trend in the global internet culture." The internet provides a medium for ordinary citizens to participate in creating the political dialogue. Howard refers to this as "cyber activism," which is defined as, "the act of using the internet to advance a political cause that is difficult to advance offline" (2010, 145).

Although technology itself is not a cause of social transformation (Toyama 2011), it does provide one means by which communication about political activism is possible given requisite access to both technology and informational resources. Therefore, the actions of a global digital citizen rely, in part, on the state's accordance with treating information and access to the internet as a human right. In the remainder of this chapter, some specific examples and issues concerning state control of information and acts of global digital citizenship will be discussed.

CASE STUDY 1

In May of 2013, following the use of tear gas on fifty unarmed, peaceful Turkish environmentalists protesting the destruction of Gezi Park (Dogan 2013), a new generation of activists took to the internet organizing protests with an efficiency unmatched by those that preceded. In addition to calling for support from their fellow countrymen, these cyber activists are able to leverage social media into an international platform, calling attention to the injustices taking place within their borders that the Turkish government was loath to publicize. As an example, during twenty-five days of revolt, Turkish protesters and international supporters produced 2.3 million tweets. An analysis of these tweets found that individuals responded to external political provocations by exhibiting collective action (Varol et al. 2014). This example of collective action spurred by global digital citizenship is also noteworthy in that it led to an increase in internet restrictions by the Turkish government—a depressingly common consequence of cyber activism. A law passed after the protests requires internet service providers to collect and retain individual data and grants the government the right to block websites at will (Krajeski 2014).

Reflection Questions

What movements can you think of that have utilized global digital citizenship? Has it made them more effective?

What increased restrictions has your own government implemented in response to citizen action?

Governments responding to citizen protests by cracking down on internet availability is a common tactic. The following countries are a few that have experienced government-created internet shutdowns during the past decade: China, Cameroon, India, Libya, Syria, and Egypt (Aouragh and Alexander 2011; Fisher 2012; "India: 20 Internet Shutdowns in 2017" 2017; Shaban 2017; So 2009; Sutter 2011). These are in addition to scores more that have experienced partial shutdowns or the blocking (temporarily or permanently) of social media sites including Facebook, YouTube, WhatsApp, and Twitter. Palfrey and Gasser (2016) report that more than two dozen countries are actively engaging in improving technology to censor and surveil citizens online. This includes using the internet not only to spy on citizens, but also to block their ability to send messages on specific topics and curtail their access to information. This is in part due to individual attempts at participation in what is referred to as "semiotic democracy." This is the idea that individual citizens, thanks to the power of participatory media such as blogs, wikis, podcasts, virtual communities, and social networks, now have the ability to create and alter political activity on a global scale (Bennett 2008; Palfrey and Gasser 2016).

However, it should not be taken lightly that such technology use and the data that results from it help to create a trail that the government can scrutinize. "While big data has the potential to be used in both productive and oppressive ways, the contract must be reevaluated to respect and limit the potential power embedded in such discovery" (Unsworth 2016, 95). In April of 2015, a company called Geofeedia assisted law enforcement in Baltimore, Maryland, to monitor and respond to protests that broke out after Freddie Gray died in police custody. This was done using a tool the company created that pulls data from Facebook, Twitter, Instagram, and nine other social media networks (Bromwich, Victor, and Isaac 2016). Following the trend of surveillance through social media, in the final days of writing this chapter the United States government released a modification to the Privacy Act of 1974 that allows the government to monitor and retain information from the social media accounts of immigrants and anyone linked to immigrants through these networks (Department of Homeland Security 2017). An excerpt from the Notice of Modified Privacy Act System of Records is included below:

The Department of Homeland Security, therefore, is updating the Department of Homeland Security/US Citizenship and Immigration Services, US Immigration and Customs Enforcement, US Customs and Border Protection-001 Alien File, Index, and National

File Tracking System of Records notice to "*Redefine which records constitute the official record of an individual's immigration history* to include the following materials and formats: expand the categories of records to include the following: country of nationality; country of residence; the USCIS Online Account Number; *social media handles, aliases, associated identifiable information, and search results;* and the Department of Justice (DOJ), Executive Office for Immigration Review and Board of Immigration Appeals proceedings information; expand the data elements used to retrieve records; *update the parameters for retention and disposal* of A-Files." (Department of Homeland Security 2017).

Unfortunately, these measures to collect and monitor the information of citizens should come as no surprise given that the government over recent years has had a steady increase in cases of denying freedom of information requests on the grounds of national security—from 3,805 cases in 2009 to 5,223 in 2013 (Kelmor 2016). Using only these examples, it is apparent that even if they occur behind a screen, acts of global digital citizenship can put the individual at risk.

Government suppression of the press is also a considerable concern in regard to the ability to participate in global digital citizenship. "Trust, in the government and commercial entities, relies upon open debate and transparency of actions" (Unsworth 2016, 91). Just as restrictions and rules regarding information created by governments are the most significant drivers of information availability in a society (Jaeger and Burnett 2010), media suppression is an invaluable tool for an authoritarian government to control both the information disseminated to its people and that which leaves its borders.

CASE STUDY 2

A peaceful protest turned violent in Lhasa, Tibet, on March 14, 2008. Reports vary, but the most common account seems to be that protestors began to riot after the police reportedly beat monks engaged in a peaceful protest. Once engaged in the riot, Tibetans set fire to a police car and a store owned by a Chinese shopkeeper (Yardley 2008). A regional protest erupted that lasted for nearly two weeks and resulted in the deaths and detainments of scores of people. Human rights groups claim that 140 people were killed during the uprising, while Chinese authorities put the number at 22. Likewise, international estimates of the number of people detained range well over a thousand, whereas Chinese authorities state that only 660 protesters were held (Barboza 2008). What is not in dispute is that shortly after the protests began, Western tourists and media were forced to leave the area. Journalists were not allowed to return until invited two weeks later and then accompanied by Chinese government officials. During this time, state-owned media broadcasted only images of Tibetan looting and violence against Han Chinese residents (Barboza 2008). Also published in China were angry reports of Western media demonstrating bias towards the Tibetan people (Jun 2008). These reports ignited a great deal of anti-Western and extreme nationalistic sentiment, both online and off (Xin 2010).

Reflection Questions

Should the press have full access to events currently under way at all times, or are there instances when they should be shut out?

Do you trust the reports of the media in your own country?

Do you believe that the government has undue influence over the press?

"Policies that limit information access serve multiple purposes, accomplishing both policy goals and partisan political goals" (Jaeger and Burnett 2010, 121). Limiting the freedom of the press can certainly aid governments in both suppressing the flow of information to and from those engaging in global digital citizenship and controlling the international discourse about internal events. Although the internet provides a means for citizens to help shape the story of current affairs and the way that they are told to an international audience (Palfrey and Gasser 2016), the curtailing of the freedom of the press is an aid to control the narration. This is a form of systemic oppression by governments with authoritarian policies.

In order to provide evidence of this point, ranking scores of the relative press freedom of each country were downloaded from the annual World Press Freedom Index (Reporters Without Borders 2017), and compared with datasets from the World Bank, the United Nations Development Program, and an organization called Freedom House, which works to promote human rights and civil liberties throughout the world. Correlation, using Taylor's scale (1990), was determined between the rankings of each country on the World Press Freedom Index and rankings of political rights and civil liberties (Freedom House 2017). Very strong correlation was found between the amount of press freedom in a given country and the amount of civil liberties and political rights afforded its citizens. If a country was ranked very low in the freedoms allotted the press, it also had low rankings for the other categories.

Interestingly, moderate correlations were also found for several other categories. When correlation was run between press freedom rankings and military expenditures as percentage of gross domestic product (World Bank 2017), a moderate relationship was found. There was also moderate correlation between the press index and the Human Development Index (United Nations Development Programme 2017).

From these findings, it can be determined that in countries where press freedom is more limited, military expenditures are higher, the human development index is lower, and political rights and civil liberties are more limited. These characteristics are accordant with some of those of totalitarian leadership (Linz 2000).

CASE STUDY 3

Here are four excerpts from Twitter:

My name is Bana, I'm 7 years old. I am talking to the world now live from East #Aleppo. This is my last moment to either live or die. —Bana (al-Abed, December 13, 2016)

One bomb hit very near to our house. I was very scared. I would like to thank everyone praying for us tonight as we sleep in fear. —Bana (al-Abed November 16, 2016)

Allow in food. Just allow, just. . . . Please allow it for the thousands starving here. Why is it a problem? —Fatemah #Aleppo (al-Abed November 25, 2016)

Dear world, this very beautiful babies died in the chemical attack. Dear @turkishairlines please give me your planes to evacuate the kids (al-Abed April 6, 2017)

Despite doubts about the authenticity of her tweets, Bana al-Abed has since been verified not only as a real child, but a seven-year-old who was, in fact, reporting live with the help of her mother from besieged East Aleppo beginning in November 2016 (Waters 2016). Bana and her family now live as refugees in Turkey.

Reflection Questions

Do you find the reports of citizen journalists on social media compelling? Do
  you think they motivate actual responses for helpful sources?
Are you skeptical of citizen journalists? Why or why not?

Reporting human rights atrocities is an act of global digital citizenship. Social media provides a tool for peer-to-peer communication among users, creating a medium by which large numbers of people can be reached (Khamis and Vaughn 2012). Social media has been used as an effective means by which to report human rights atrocities in many conflicts, including the disappearance of 276 schoolgirls in Nigeria in 2014, the current genocide and forced displacement of the Rohingya people of Burma, and the Arab Spring of 2011. "We argue that Facebook pages . . . can act as effective tools for supporting the capabilities of the democratic activists by . . . enabling ordinary citizens to document the protests and governmental brutality and to disseminate their own words and images" (Khamis and Vaughn 2012, 159). Although there is criticism that internet access does not level the playing field of power (Toyama 2011), the example of Bana al-Abed proves that the internet does provide ordinary citizens the ability to raise awareness of human rights violations (Jaeger, Taylor, and Gorham 2015). May they be heard.

REFERENCES

al-Abed, Bana. (@AlabedBana) Twitter, November 16, 2016, 11:54 a.m. https://twitter.com/AlabedBana/status/798977512504229903.
_____. Twitter, November 25, 2016, 9:01 a.m. https://twitter.com/AlabedBana/status/802195517518118912.
_____. Twitter, December 13, 2016, 1:06 a.m. https://twitter.com/AlabedBana/status/808599057794998272.
_____. Twitter, April 6, 2017, 9:22 a.m. https://twitter.com/AlabedBana/status/850020820294533120.
Aouragh, Miriyam, and Anne Alexander. 2011. "The Arab Spring| The Egyptian Experience: Sense and Nonsense of the Internet Revolution." *International Journal of Communication* 5, 15.
Barboza, David. 2008. "660 Held in Tibetan Uprising, China Says." *The New York Times.* March 26. www.nytimes.com/2008/03/27/world/asia/27tibet.html?mcubz=0.
Bennett, W. Lance, ed. 2008. *Civic Life Online: Learning How Digital Media Can Engage Youth.* Cambridge, MA: MIT Press.
Bennett, W. Lance, Chris Wells, and Allison Rank. 2009. "Young Citizens and Civic Learning: Two Paradigms of Citizenship in the Digital Age." *Citizenship Studies* 13 (2): 105–20.
Bromwich, Jonah Engel, Daniel Victor, and Mike Isaac. 2016. "Police Use Surveillance Tool to Scan Social Media, A.C.L.U. Says." *New York Times*, October 11. www.nytimes.com/2016/10/12/technology/aclu-facebook-twitter-instagram-geofeedia.html?mcubz=0&_r=0.

Buschman, John. 2016. "Citizenship and Agency Under Neoliberal Global Consumerism: A Search for Informed Democratic Practices/Response to Buschman." *Journal of Information Ethics* 25 (1): 38.

Choi, Moonsun. 2016. "A Concept Analysis of Digital Citizenship for Democratic Citizenship Education in the Internet Age." *Theory and Research in Social Education* 44 (4): 565-607.

Choi, Moonsun, Michael Glassman, and Dean Cristol. 2017. "What It Means to Be a Citizen in the Internet Age: Development of a Reliable and Valid Digital Citizenship Scale." *Computers and Education* 107, 100-12.

Couldry, Nick. 2003. "Digital Divide or Discursive Design? On the Emerging Ethics of Information Space." *Ethics and Information Technology* 5 (2): 89-97.

Couldry, Nick, Hilde Stephansen, Aristea Fotopoulou, Richard MacDonald, Wilma Clark, and Luke Dickens. 2014. "Digital Citizenship? Narrative Exchange and the Changing Terms of Civic Culture." *Citizenship Studies* 18 (6-7): 615-29.

Dogan, Duygu. 2013. "Raid on 'Occupy Taksim Park' Demonstrators Triggers Outcry." *Hurriyet Daily News,* May 30.

Falk, Richard. 1993. "The Making of Global Citizenship." *Global Visions: Beyond the New World Order* 39.

Fisher, M. 2012. "Web Monitor: 100 Percent of Syria's Internet Just Shut Down." *Washington Post Online,* November 29.

Freedom House. 2017. *Country and Territory Ratings and Statuses,* Washington, DC. https://freedomhouse .org/report-types/freedom-world.

Gorham, Ursula, Natalie Greene Taylor, and Paul T. Jaeger. 2016. "Perspectives on Libraries as Institutions of Human Rights and Social Justice." In *Perspectives on Libraries as Institutions of Human Rights and Social Justice,* edited by Ursula Gorham , Natalie Greene Taylor, and Paul T. Jaeger, iii (*Advances in Librarianship,* Volume 41), iii. Emerald Group Publishing Limited.

Howard, Philip N. 2010. *The Digital Origins of Dictatorship and Democracy: Information Technology and Political Islam.* Oxford, UK: Oxford University Press.

"India: 20 Internet Shutdowns in 2017." Human Rights Watch, June 15, 2017. www.hrw.org/news/2017/ 06/15/india-20-internet-shutdowns-2017.

Jaeger, Paul T., and Gary Burnett. 2010. *Information Worlds: Social Context, Technology, and Information Behavior in the Age of the Internet.* London: Routledge.

Jaeger, Paul T., Natalie Greene Taylor, and Ursula Gorham. 2015. *Libraries, Human Rights, and Social Justice: Enabling Access and Promoting Inclusion.* Lanham, MD: Rowman and Littlefield.

Jun, Ye. 2008. Lhasa Riot Reports Show Media Bias in West Comments. *China Daily,* March 22. www.chinadaily.com.cn/china/2008-03/22/content_6557738.htm.

Kelmor, Kimberli M. 2016. "Legal Formulations of a Human Right to Information: Defining a Global Consensus." *Journal of Information Ethics* 25 (1): 101.

Khamis, Sahar, and Katherine Vaughn. 2012. "'We Are All Khaled Said': The Potentials and Limitations of Cyberactivism in Triggering Public Mobilization and Promoting Political Change." *Journal of Arab and Muslim Media Research* 4 (2-3): 145-63.

Krajeski, Jenna. 2014. "The Last Chance to Stop Turkey's Harsh New Internet Law." *New Yorker,* February 15. www.newyorker.com/news/news-desk/the-last-chance-to-stop-turkeys-harsh-new-internet-law.

Linz, Juan José. 2000. *Totalitarian and Authoritarian Regimes.* Boulder, CO: Lynne Rienner Publishers.

Lipset, Seymour M. 1960. *Political Man: The Social Bases of Modern Politics.* Garden City, NY: Doubleday.

Mossberger, Karen, Caroline J. Tolbert, and Allison Hamilton. 2012. "Broadband Adoption| Measuring Digital Citizenship: Mobile Access and Broadband." *International Journal of Communication* 6, 37.

Mouffe, Chantal. 1995. "Feminism, Citizenship, and Radical Democratic Politics." In *Social Postmodernism: Beyond Identity Politics,* edited by Linda Nicholson and Steven Seidman, 315-31. Cambridge University Press.

Norris, Pippa. 2001. *Digital Divide: Civic Engagement, Information Poverty, and the Internet Worldwide.* Cambridge University Press.

Palfrey, John, and Urs Gasser. 2016. *Born Digital: How Children Grow Up in a Digital Age.* Basic Books. E-book.

Parekh, Bhikhu. 2003. "Cosmopolitanism and Global Citizenship." *Review of International Studies* 29 (1): 3–17.

Peled, Roy, and Yoram Rabin. 2011. "The Constitutional Right to Information." *Columbia Human Rights Law Review* 42 (2): 357–401.

Proenza, Francisco J., and Bruce Girard. 2015. *Public Access ICT across Cultures: Diversifying Participation in the Network Society.* Cambridge, MA: MIT Press.

Reporters Without Borders. 2017. *2017 World Press Freedom Index,* Washington, DC. https://rsf.org/en/ranking.

Samek, Toni, and Lynette Shultz. 2016. "Guest Editorial: Information Ethics and Global Citizenship." *Journal of Information Ethics* 25 (1): 13.

Schattle, Hans. *The Practices of Global Citizenship.* Rowman and Littlefield, 2008.

Searson, Michael, Marsali Hancock, Nusrat Soheil, and Gregory Shepherd. 2015. "Digital Citizenship within Global Contexts." *Education and Information Technologies* 20 (4): 729–41.

Shaban, A. 2017. "Cameroon Restores Internet in 2 Anglophone Regions after 93 Days Offline" *Africa News.* YouTube video. www.youtube.com/watch?v=LwRx5ssUacE.

So, Peter. 2009. "Hundreds of Websites Shut Down As Censors Order 'Server Maintenance'." *South China Morning Post,* June 4, 2009.

Sutter, J. 2011. "Libya Faces Internet Blackouts amid Protests." *CNN Online* (2011).

Taylor, Richard. 1990. "Interpretation of the Correlation Coefficient: A Basic Review." *Journal of Diagnostic Medical Sonography* 6 (1): 35–39.

Toyama, Kentaro. 2011. "Technology as Amplifier in International Development." In *Proceedings of the 2011 iConference,* 75–82. Association for Computing Machinery.

United Nations Development Programme. 2017. *Human Development Index and Its Components,* Washington, DC, 2017. http://hdr.undp.org/en/composite/HDI.

United Nations General Assembly. 1948. *Universal Declaration of Human Rights.*

United States Department of Homeland Security. 2017. *Notice of Modified Privacy Act System of Records.* DHS-2017-0038. Washington, DC. www.federalregister.gov/documents/2017/09/18/2017-19365/privacy-act-of-1974-system-of-records.

University of Alberta. Invited Call for Proposals: Information Ethics Roundtable 2014: Information Ethics and Global Citizenship. https://sites.google.com/a/ualberta.ca/ier2014/home/call-for-proposals-1.

Unsworth, Kristene. 2016. "The Social Contract and Big Data." *Journal of Information Ethics* 25 (1): 83–97.

Varol, Onur, Emilio Ferrara, Christine L. Ogan, Filippo Menczer, and Alessandro Flammini. 2014. "Evolution of Online User Behavior During a Social Upheaval." In *Proceedings of the 2014 ACM Conference on Web Science,* 81–90. Association for Computing Machinery.

Walters, Gregory J. 2002 *Human Rights in an Information Age: A Philosophical Analysis.* University of Toronto Press, 2002.

Waters, Nick. 2016 "Finding Bana—Proving the Existence of a 7-Year-Old Girl in Eastern Aleppo." *Bellingcat,* December 14. www.bellingcat.com/news/mena/2016/12/14/bana-alabed-verification-using-open-source-information/.

Wellman, Barry, Anabel Quan-Haase, Jeffrey Boase, Wenhong Chen, Keith Hampton, Isabel Díaz, and Kakuko Miyata. 2003. "The Social Affordances of the Internet for Networked Individualism." *Journal of Computer-Mediated Communication* 8 (3).

World Bank. 2017. *GDP Ranking,* Washington, DC, 2017. https://data.worldbank.org/data-catalog/GDP-ranking-table.

Xin, Xin. 2010. "The Impact of 'Citizen Journalism' on Chinese Media and Society." *Journalism Practice* 4 (3): 333–44.

Yardley, Jim. 2008 "Violence in Tibet as Monks Clash with the Police." *New York Times,* March 14. www.nytimes.com/2008/03/15/world/asia/15tibet.html?mcubz=0.

ADDITIONAL RESOURCES

Miladi, Noureddine. 2011. "New Media and the Arab Revolution: Citizen Reporters and Social Activism." *Journal of Arab and Muslim Media Research* 4 (2/3): 3-5.

"The Right to Information—Good Law and Practice." The Right to Information—Good Law and Practice— Right2Info.org. www.right2info.org/.

CHAPTER 12

Emerging Issues

Amelia Gibson

Our current social and technological moment has brought with it an array of ethical dilemmas related to information and has repackaged old ones in new formats. This chapter outlines just a few of the emerging ethical issues in information that have arisen over the past few years. Although it is tempting to propose that newer, more ubiquitous technology, bigger data, more expansive social and information networks, and increased capacities have created entirely new ethical quandaries, many of the emerging issues described in this chapter are new permutations of old social problems and ethical conflicts.

The issues and cases discussed in this chapter are multifaceted and thus could be described from a number of perspectives. This chapter is split into two categories: Information and Technology at Social Margins, and Intersections and Managing Expanding Capacity. Each subsection contains a brief description of the topic and a short list of resources for further reading; these include news articles describing cases, academic articles describing issues, and white papers from nonprofit organizations focusing on ethical issues related to information.

INFORMATION AND TECHNOLOGY AT SOCIAL MARGINS AND INTERSECTIONS

Researchers have long shown interest in relationships among identity, sociopolitical power, and information and technology use. Information and technology access and accessibility, literacy, behavior, use, and policy all have moral and ethical implications and influence. They are influenced by identity, privilege, and power. Critical theory and praxis have begun to make their way slowly into information ethics (e.g., Stahl et al. 2014). Critical frameworks that examine race, ability, sexuality, and gender are useful tools for explicitly examining information systems as structural systems of power that impact different groups in different ways. This section addresses a small sample of the broad range of emerging issues related to information, race, gender, sexuality, and other facets of identity and privilege.

Algorithmic Bias

Algorithms are sets of rules or instructions that tell a computer how to parse information in order to complete a task. Because algorithms standardize machine operations and, ideally, enable perfect replication, they have been lauded as a way to reduce human bias and support more "objective" decision-making. Out-of-the-box applications developed by private companies (many of which are based on opaque and proprietary "black box" algorithms) have become popular commercial options for cash- and expertise-strapped organizations and governments (Diakopoulos 2016). Because many are proprietary, there is often no way to know exactly how these algorithms function. In reality, algorithms (including machine learning algorithms) are embedded with the worldview, assumptions, moral codes, and biases of their developers. Although they standardize decision-making processes, they also institutionalize (rather than eliminate) human biases while presenting a misleading veneer of objectivity and fairness.

Further Reading

- Noble, Safiya Umoja. 2016. *Algorithms of Oppression: Race, Gender, and Power in the Digital Age.* New York: NYU Press.
- O'Neil, Cathy. 2017. *Weapons of Math Destruction: How Big Data Increases Inequality and Threatens Democracy.* New York: Broadway Books.
- *ProPublica.* 2017. "Machine Bias: Investigating Algorithmic Injustice." www.propublica.org/series/machine-bias.

The Ethics of Social Media and Social Movements

Social media, messaging, and chat technology have proven to be useful tools for organizing social movements and for providing information "on the ground" during protests and other events. Some have credited the increase in camera-phone use and live-streaming for increased awareness about police violence and the rise of the Black Lives Matter movement. This use of ground trothing and image management is not a new phenomenon. As Tufekci writes, "Images of police brutality have coalescing power for protests" (Tufekci 2017, 233), and have since the invention of the camera. The use of smartphones and social media within movements of resistance, however, have sparked ethical debates about authoritarianism and whether companies should adopt blanket policies about providing anonymity to their users, comply with requests for information from governments or law enforcement agencies, or whether they should exercise judgment on a case-by-case basis. Live video streaming services, such as Facebook Live and Periscope, have been criticized for interrupting live feeds of interactions between police and citizens.

The debate around facial recognition software is an extension of old debates about public surveillance. This software has been advertised as allowing for the identifying of individuals who have their faces covered and for determining sexuality. This has clear benefits in terms of preventing terrorism, but also has implications for authoritarian abuses. This is the next logical step in the debate about public surveillance and authoritarianism. Now we must contend with private companies offering services that often transgress privacy lines with EULA and have more access to information about users than ever before; recording devices are pervasive; eroding of privacy expectations; and additional reliance on company willingness and ability to fight court battle against an increasingly authoritarian federal government.

Further Reading

- Coldewey, Devin. 2017. "Moscow Officially Turns on Facial Recognition for Its City-Wide Camera Network." *TechCrunch,* September 28. http://social .techcrunch.com/2017/09/28/moscow-officiallyturns-on-facial-recognition -for-its-city-wide-camera-network/.
- Fuchs, Christian. 2017. *Social Media: A Critical Introduction.* Thousand Oaks, CA: SAGE, 2017.
- Singh, A., D. Patil, G. M. Reddy, and S. N. Omkar. 2017. "Disguised Face Identification (DFI) with Facial KeyPoints Using Spatial Fusion Convolutional Network." arXiv preprint arXiv: 1708.09317.
- Tufekci, Zeynep. 2017. *Twitter and Tear Gas: The Power and Fragility of Networked Protest.* Camden, NJ: Yale University Press.

Precision Marketing, and Social Responsibility

Surveillance capitalism (Zuboff 2015) describes the monetization of the massive sets of personal, demographic, behavioral, and other data collected by social media companies through "free" platforms such as Facebook and Google. This business model enables companies to capitalize on large sets of extremely granular user data by offering advertisers the option to select very specific target populations, organized by user information behaviors (e.g., search queries, purchases, and articles viewed). Whereas advertisers have previously relied on informed guesses and inferences about the purchasing or voting habits of certain groups of people, social media and data analytics companies are able to "micro-target" (Tett 2017) very finely-tuned segments of populations. For example, Facebook has faced intense criticism for selling Russian advertisers ad space intended to explicitly discourage African Americans from voting in the 2016 election (Entous, Timberg, and Dwoskin 2017) and for selling ad space for guns aimed at people who expressed hatred for Muslims (Oremus and Carey 2017). When combined with psychological and purchasing data, these analyses and advertising strategies have proven very effective at influencing behavior and have prompted questions about the culpability of social media companies when data is used for "evil." Ethical questions include whether companies should be permitted to sell this type of data, whether there should be limits on what types of search activities or identifiers should be made available to advertisers, and whether companies should restrict access to certain types of ads for certain types of people.

Further Reading

- Ahlgren, J., A. Nordgren, M. Perrudin, A. Ronteltap, J. Savigny, H. van Trijp, K. Nordström, and U. Görman. 2013. "Consumers on the Internet: Ethical and Legal Aspects of Commercialization of Personalized Nutrition." *Genes and Nutrition* 8 (4), 349–55.
- Angwin, J., and T. Parris. 2016. "Facebook Lets Advertisers Exclude Users by Race." *ProPublica.* https://www.propublica.org/article/facebook-lets -advertisers-exclude-users-by-race.

- Levin, Sam. 2017. "Facebook Told Advertisers It Can Identify Teens Feeling 'Insecure' and 'Worthless.'" *The Guardian,* May 1. www.theguardian.com/technology/2017/may/01/facebookadvertising-data-insecure-teens.
- Zuiderveen Borgesius, Frederik J. 2016. "Singling Out People without Knowing Their Names—Behavioural Targeting, Pseudonymous Data, and the New Data Protection Regulation." *Computer Law and Security Review* 32 (2): 256–71. doi: 10.1016/j.clsr.2015.12.013.

Technological Unemployment

Whenever a work function is automated, human employment is threatened. Throughout the last century, economists and technologists have sounded warnings about technology-fueled mass unemployment (Keynes 1930; Frey and Osbourne 2017), and information and data-centered automation are no exception. Recent estimations of the threat posed by artificial intelligence (AI) vary, but it is clear that negative employment and income impacts fall along familiar lines, with the most vulnerable suffering the worst consequences. Researchers predict that AI's impacts on employment will be uneven in different countries across the globe, with emerging markets and low- and entry-level workers more susceptible to unemployment (Chui, Manyika, and Miremadi 2017). Initiatives that explicitly seek to automate jobs typically held by people who are members of vulnerable populations (e.g., recent immigrants or people with lower levels of education) have drawn criticism as being morally dubious. Critics have raised questions about the meaning of life without employment (Danaher 2017), the morality of eliminating sources of income for those who can least afford the loss, and the negative effects of the technology itself on human communities. Others contend that the threat of technological unemployment has always been vastly overstated.

Further Reading

- Camps, R. 2017. "Technological Unemployment. A Brief History of an Idea." *ISA e-Symposium for Sociology.* 7, 1–16.
- Hsu, Jeremy. 2016. "Rise of the Ag-Bots Will Not Sow Seeds of Unemployment." *Scientific American,* July 20. www.scientificamerican.com/article/rise-of-the-ag-bots-will-not-sow-seeds-of-unemployment/.
- Segran, Elizabeth. 2017. "Two Ex-Googlers Want to Make Bodegas and Mom-and-Pop Corner Stores Obsolete." *Fast Money*, September 13. www.fastcompany.com/40466047/two-ex-googlers-want-to-make-bodegas-and-mom-and-pop-corner-stores-obsolete.

Misinformation, Disinformation, and Fake News

Fake news, propaganda, hoaxes, misinformation, and disinformation are not new phenomena. The study of political propaganda is broad and well-established, but recent increases in the use of bots to spread disinformation and "fake news" has prompted a range of ethical questions about regulation of online spaces and search engines, as well as clarifying the responsibility of companies that broker and manage information to ensure the quality of the information they promote. As bots become more human-like (Aamoth 2014), they can wield enormous influence on digital platforms.

Because of the general belief that a higher position on a list of Google results indicates higher quality or relevance, Google has been criticized for allowing sites to purchase top result spots. Facebook has been broadly disparaged for its part in posting fake news and misinformation campaigns disseminated by Russian entities (Angwin, Varner, and Tobin 2017) that influenced the 2016 election. But should these companies be responsible for ensuring good information? It may not be possible for a social media company to ensure that the information on their systems are "perfect" or "right." Where is the line? Is it intentionally spreading gross disinformation? Should satire sites be somehow clearly marked? Is the problem about judging content or about providing stronger metadata to help users differentiate among sources? Is this a war of attrition against fake news? If a platform takes a more aggressive position against misinformation, what are the implications for abuse? Does this make platforms arbiters of truth?

Further Reading

- Biddle, Sam. 2017. "Stop Expecting Facebook and Google to Curb Misinformation—It's Great for Business." *The Intercept.* https://theintercept .com/2017/10/03/facebook-twitter-google-internet-fake-news/.
- Emerging Technology from the arXiv. 2017. "First Evidence That Social Bots Play a Major Role in Spreading Fake News." *MIT Technology Review,* August 7, 2017. www.technologyreview.com/s/608561/first-evidence-that -social-bots-play-a-major-role-in-spreading-fake-news/.
- Ferrara, E., O. Varol, C. Davis, F. Menczer, and A. Flammini. 2016. "The Rise of Social Bots." *Communications of the ACM* 51 (7): 96–104.
- Tufekci, Zeynep. 2017. "Facebook's Ad Scandal Isn't a 'Fail,' It's a Feature." *New York Times,* August 23. www.nytimes.com/2017/09/23/opinion/ sunday/facebook-ad-scandal.html.

Open Data, Data Return, and Open Data Ethics

Open data is data that is, ostensibly, available for use by anyone. Open data and open access movements seek to make different types of data publicly accessible (usually via the internet). While this seems like a simple call for equality of access, the bulk of digital divide research makes it clear that data that is said to be available to anyone on the internet is not, in fact, open to everyone. Open science and open government are two well-established areas of research, practice, and advocacy that have enjoyed a great deal of ethical debate in the past two decades (Kitchin 2014). One emerging ethical debate about open data involves the morality of aggregating and publishing data that is publicly available without user consent. The use of bots to scrape publicly available data quickly has made the collection and use of such data easier and more efficient for researchers and companies interested in studying openly accessible data. When Danish researchers published aggregated user profile data for tens of thousands of OKCupid users, there was public outcry about the ethicality of publishing the data without permission and without anonymizing the data (Zimmer 2016). There are currently few ethical guidelines for conducting research using publicly available social media data, outside of those provided by social media companies themselves.

Further Reading

- Kitchin, Rob. 2014. *The Data Revolution: Big Data, Open Data, Data Infrastructures and Their Consequences.* Santa Barbara, CA: SAGE.
- Mittelstadt, B. D., and L. Floridi. 2016. The "Ethics of Big Data: Current and Foreseeable Issues in Biomedical Contexts." In *Ethics of Biomedical Big Data,* 445–80. Springer International Publishing.
- Zimmer, M., 2016. "OkCupid Study Reveals the Perils of Big-Data Science." *Wired,* May 14.

MANAGING EXPANDING CAPACITIES

Development of information technology and expansion of capacities enjoy a cyclical relationship. Expanded capacity of information technology takes many forms, including the availability of information, and a new shift toward or away from democratization of information or technology. These changes often result in the emergence of new ethical conflicts. Social media, search engines, and software-as-service applications (e.g., word processing, collaborative research, and chat applications) have become so intertwined and pervasive that it is difficult for individuals to participate in formal education or to do business without them. They have become gatekeepers to much of everyday communication. This gives rise to ethical and policy questions about whether private companies that operate in information economies should have so much power, or whether they should be more heavily regulated or treated more like utilities. Critics question whether the imbalance of power inherent in the relationship between large corporations that collect and manage personal data (with and without the consent of individuals) demands greater government oversight.

3-D Printing and Regulated Items

Maker movements have capitalized on the boom in DIY culture, improving 3-D printing and other maker technology, and developing and expanding platforms for sharing patterns, templates, and designs. Although 3-D printing is still relatively expensive, costs are dropping rapidly. Many school and public library makerspaces support 3-D printing, and it is conceivable that individual ownership of 3-D printers will increase in coming years. An increase in 3-D printing brings with it ethical questions about the morality and legality of printing items that are currently regulated or prohibited, if companies should assume legal liability for their pattern-sharing platforms, and how to determine age-appropriate use of 3-D printers. There is some concern that 3-D printing will allow people to sidestep regulation completely, and many recent discussions around the ethics of 3-D printing have centered on limiting access to plans for guns.

Further Reading

- Kopfstein, Janus. 2013. "Guns Want to Be Free: What Happens When 3D Printing and Crypto-Anarchy Collide?" *The Verge,* April 12, 2013.
- Ratto, Matt, and Megan Boler, eds. 2014. *DIY Citizenship: Critical Making and Social Media.* MIT Press.

- Thierer, A., and A. Marcus., 2016. "Guns, Limbs, and Toys: What Future for 3D Printing?" *Minnesota Journal of Law, Science, and Technology* 17, 805.

Predictive Analytics

Big data allows for the construction of predictive analytical models in health, law, social networking, and information retrieval. These models may prove to be harmless, but as they become more and more accepted over time (and have the perception of validation through use), there is the temptation to use them in ways that could prove detrimental to users, for example, to set insurance rates, decide who to hire, and to predict social connections among people for law enforcement purposes. This raises questions about when these types of analytics should be used. Should human judgment always supersede algorithmic predictions? Why? Who is to say human judgment is superior to analytical models? Is there a responsibility to use or share outcomes of predictive analysis when doing so increases efficiency (e.g., improving use and allocation of funds, and allowing for greater effectiveness of government programs)? Is there a responsibility not to share data when doing so could harm an individual or group? These questions have been asked in educational contexts where negative predictions can lead to discouraged students or underfunded initiatives (Jaschik 2017). Jaschick asks if technology should be anchored in a "do no harm" ethic. It is unclear if such a guiding principle can even be applied to predictive technology. Perhaps a utilitarian, "least harm" approach is necessary, but it comes with complications. The least harm for whom?

Further Reading

- Church, Christopher E., and Amanda J. Fairchild. 2017. "In Search of a Silver Bullet: Child Welfare's Embrace of Predictive Analytics." *Juvenile and Family Court Journal* 68 (1): 67–81. doi: 10.1111/jfcj.12086.
- Cohen, I. Glenn, Ruben Amarasingham, Anand Shah, Bin Xie, and Bernard Lo. 2014. "The Legal and Ethical Concerns That Arise from Using Complex Predictive Analytics in Health Care." *Health Affairs* 33 (7): 1139–47.
- Paulson, Shirley S., and Elizabeth Scruth. 2017. "Legal and Ethical Concerns of Big Data: Predictive Analytics." *Clinical Nurse Specialist* 31 (5): 237–39. doi: 10.1097/NUR.0000000000000315.

Bots and AI Decision-Making

Bots are pieces of software that are designed to automate processes. Although they are not considered "intelligent," bots have become so intertwined with small, everyday tasks that they have an enormous cumulative influence on our lives. They do things like help complete voice requests, find music, order products online, and use online maps. They also hold great potential for automating processes for people with disabilities and medical conditions who have difficulty interacting with technology. Their use has prompted ethical questions about ownership, "loyalty," priorities, and culpability for problems. It is unclear whether bots should prioritize the desires and needs of the users to whom they are licensed, protect the interests of the companies that provide them, or operate according to some other broadly imposed set of rules. Imagine a bot tasked with ordering toilet paper. Should it prioritize the cheapest toilet paper? Should it prioritize the toilet paper that offers the best financial value? Should it prioritize the toilet paper that is offered by the company that pays advertising costs to the licensing company? Should the user have a choice? Should the bot consider geographic location? The distance from the closest competitor? Other questions involve priorities of greater import—should self-driving cars prioritize general public safety, or the safety of their operators and passengers? Should machine systems be used for policy decision-making? If so, how should they balance competing interests among stakeholder groups?

Further Reading

- Coglianese, Cary, and David Lehr. 2017. "Regulating by Robot: Administrative Decision Making in the Machine Learning Era." *Georgetown Law Journal* 106 (5): 1147.
- Gunkel, David J. 2012. *The Machine Question: Critical Perspectives on AI, Robots, and Ethics.* MIT Press.
- Park, Enno. 2014. "Ethical Issues in Cyborg Technology: Diversity and Inclusion." *NanoEthics* 8 (3): 303–06. doi: 10.1007/s11569-014-0206-x.
- Robertson, Jennifer. 2014. "Human Rights vs. Robot Rights: Forecasts from Japan." *Critical Asian Studies* 46 (4): 571–98. doi: 10.1080/14672715.2014.960707.

Ownership of Health Data

While great strides have been made in resolving ethical issues around patient information in medical settings such as hospitals and clinics (Caine and Tierney 2015), there is less consensus on the ethics of health-related information in the public domain and the responsibility of search engine and social media companies to put controls on the collection and sharing of personal health data when it intersects with issues of public interest (e.g., crimes or outbreaks of disease). There is also little consensus on the rights of individuals to restrict the collection, aggregation, sale, and use of health data generated and collected by mobile health devices.

Further Reading

- Kaplan, B. 2016. "How Should Health Data Be Used?" *Cambridge Quarterly of Healthcare Ethics* 25 (2): 312–29.
- Mikk, Katherine A., Harry A. Sleeper, and Eric J. Topol. 2017. "The Pathway to Patient Data Ownership and Better Health." *JAMA* 318 (15): 1433–34.
- Sutherland, Tonia. 2017. "'Making A Killing': On Race, Ritual, and (Re) Membering in Digital Culture," *Preservation, Digital Technology and Culture* 46, no. 1 (2017): 32–40.

REFERENCES

Aamoth, Doug. 2014. "Interview with Eugene Goostman, the Fake Kid Who Passed the Turing Test." *Time,* June 9.

Angwin, Julia, Madeline Varner, and Ariana Tobin. 2017. "Facebook Enabled Advertisers to Reach 'Jew Haters.'" *ProPublica,* September 24.

Caine, K. and W. M. Tierney. 2015. "Point and Counterpoint: Patient Control of Access to Data in Their Electronic Health Records." *Journal of General Internal Medicine* 30 (1): 38–41.

Chui, M., J. Manyika, J. and M. Miremadi. 2017. "The Countries Most (and Least) Likely to Be Affected by Automation." *Harvard Business Review,* April 2.

Danaher, J., 2017. "Will Life Be Worth Living in a World Without Work? Technological Unemployment and the Meaning of Life." *Science and Engineering Ethics* 23 (1), 41–64.

Diakopolous, Nick. 2016. "Accountability in Algorithmic Decision Making." *Communications of the ACM* 59 (2), 56–62.

Entous, Adam, Craig Timberg, and Elizabeth Dwoskin. 2017. "Russian Operatives Used Facebook Ads to Exploit America's Racial and Religious Divisions." *Washington Post,* September 25.

Frey, Carl Benedikt and Michael A. Osborne. 2017. "The Future of Employment: How Susceptible Are Jobs to Computerisation?" *Technological Forecasting and Social Change* 114, 254–80.

Greenwood, Shannon, Andrew Perrin, and Maeve Duggan. 2016. "Social Media Update 2016." *Pew Research Center.*

Jaschik, Scott. 2017. "The Ethics of Sharing Predictive Analytics." *Inside Higher Ed,* February 27. www.insidehighered.com/digital-learning/article/2017/02/22/corporate-leaders-consider-ethics -sharing-predictive-analytics.

Keynes, John Maynard. 2010. "Economic Possibilities for our Grandchildren." In *Essays in Persuasion,* 321–32. Palgrave Macmillan UK.

Kitchin, Rob. 2014. *The Data Revolution: Big Data, Open Data, Data Infrastructures and Their Consequences.* Santa Barbara, CA: SAGE.

Lipschultz, Jeremy Harris. 2015. *Social Media Communication: Concepts, Practices, Data, Law and Ethics.* New York: Routledge.

Oremus, Will, and Bill Carey. 2017. "Facebook's Offensive Ad Targeting Options Go Far Beyond 'Jew Haters.'" *Slate,* September 14.

Stahl, Bernd Carsten, Neil F. Doherty, Mark Shaw, and Helge Janicke. 2014. "Critical Theory as an Approach to the Ethics of Information Security." *Science and Engineering Ethics* 20 (3): 675–99.

Tett, Gillian. 2017. "Trump, Cambridge Analytica and How Big Data Is Reshaping Politics." *Financial Times,* September 29.

Tufekci, Zeynep. 2017. *Twitter and Tear Gas: The Power and Fragility of Networked Protest.* New Haven, CT: Yale University Press.

Zimmer, M., 2016. "OkCupid Study Reveals the Perils of Big-Data Science." *Wired,* May 14.

Zuboff, Shoshana. 2015. "Big Other: Surveillance Capitalism and the Prospects of an Information Civilization." *Journal of Information Society* 30 (1): 75-89.

ABOUT THE EDITORS AND CONTRIBUTORS

JOHN T. F. BURGESS is an assistant professor and the distance education coordinator at the University of Alabama's School of Library and Information Studies, where he designed and teaches a course on information ethics. He also teaches courses on research methods, the organization of information, data visualization, and reference and instruction. Building on his background in virtue ethics, Burgess's research is on LIS professional ethics as character ethic, the ethics of sustainability, and questions of intergenerational justice in LIS practice. As a member of the IEEE Subcommittee on Classical Ethics in ICT, Dr. Burgess is participating in the broader IEEE Ethically Aligned Design initiative, an initiative designed to raise awareness of ethical issues surrounding the development of artificially intelligent and autonomous systems and to develop best practices for creating those systems ethically. He is the chair of the ASIS&T Information Ethics and Policy Special Interest Group and has served as the co-convener for the ALISE Information Ethics Special Interest Group. He holds an MLIS and PhD from the University of Alabama's College of Communication and Information Sciences, a master's degree in Theological Studies from Weston Jesuit School of Theology, and a master's degree of Sacred Theology in Pastoral Care and Counseling from Boston University.

EMILY J. M. KNOX is an associate professor in the School of Information Sciences at the University of Illinois at Urbana-Champaign. Her book, *Book Banning in 21st Century America,* was published by Rowman and Littlefield and is the first monograph in the Beta Phi Mu Scholars Series. She also recently edited *Trigger Warnings: History, Theory Context,* also published by Rowman and Littlefield. Her articles have been published in the *Library Quarterly, Library and Information Science Research,* and the *Journal of Intellectual Freedom and Privacy.* Dr. Knox serves on the boards of the Association for Information Science and Technology, Freedom to Read Foundation, and the National Coalition Against Censorship. Her research interests include information access, intellectual freedom and censorship, information ethics, information policy, and the intersection of print culture and reading practices. She is also a member of the Mapping Information Access research team. Emily received her PhD from the Rutgers University School of Communication and Information. Her master's degree in Library and Information Science is from the iSchool at Illinois. She also holds a BA in Religious Studies from Smith College and an AM in the same field from the University of Chicago Divinity School.

■■■

Masooda Bashir holds degrees in mathematics, computer science, and psychology and earned her PhD in psychology from Purdue University. She worked for several years as a systems analyst, technical trainer, manager, and global manager for a number of corporations in Silicon Valley, including Lotus and IBM. Most recently, she was the assistant director for social trust initiatives in the Information Trust Institute (ITI) at the University of Illinois. In addition, Dr. Bashir has led multiple ITI educational initiatives, including the Summer Research Experiences for Undergraduates internship program and the Illinois Cyber Security Scholars Program. She teaches courses in privacy in the internet age, information assurance, ethics of cybersecurity, and digital forensics.

Jane Blanken-Webb is an assistant professor in the School of Education at Wilkes University in Pennsylvania. Prior to this appointment, she was a postdoctoral research associate at the both the University of Eastern Finland and the Information Trust Institute at the University of Illinois at Urbana-Champaign, where she was coprincipal investigator on a grant funded initiative, Ethical Thinking in Cyber Space (EThiCS), supported by the National Security Agency. She was the lead instructor for a graduate-level cybersecurity ethics course piloted during the spring of 2018. Dr. Blanken-Webb holds a PhD in Philosophy of Education from the University of Illinois at Urbana-Champaign. Her research draws broadly on the philosophy of John Dewey and aims for the realization of a more just society through educational means. Her work engages with diverse disciplinary perspectives including cybersecurity ethics and education, technology and education, citizenship education, social justice education, and aesthetic education.

John M. Budd is Professor Emeritus at the School of Information Science and Learning Technologies of the University of Missouri. He has also served on the faculties at Louisiana State University and the University of Arizona. He has been president of the Association for Library and Information Science Education and currently is coeditor of the *Journal of Education for Library and Information Science*. He is the author of nearly 150 publications and approximately 125 conference presentations. He has taught and written about ethics and information for much of his career.

Nicholas C. Burbules is the Gutgsell Professor in the Department of Educational Policy, Organization and Leadership at the University of Illinois at Urbana-Champaign. His primary research areas are philosophy of education, teaching through dialogue, and technology and education. He has authored or edited 16 books and over 200 journal articles and book chapters, many of them dealing with technology issues. He is frequently invited to lecture at universities around the world, and a number of his publications have been translated into other languages. He is currently the education director for the National Center on Professional and Research Ethics at the University of Illinois at Urbana-Champaign.

Roy H. Campbell is the associate dean for information technology of the College of Engineering at the University of Illinois at Urbana-Champaign (UIUC), where he is also the Sohaib and Sara Abbasi Professor in the department of Computer Science and director of the NSA-designated Center for Academic Excellence in Information Assurance Education and Research. Previously, he was the director of the Air Force-funded Assured Cloud Computing Center in the Information Trust Institute at UIUC from 2011 to 2017. He received his honors BS degree in Mathematics, with a minor in Physics, from the University of Sussex, and his MS and PhD degrees in Computer Science from the University of Newcastle upon Tyne. Dr. Campbell's research interests are the problems, engineering, and construction techniques of complex system software. His past research includes path expressions as declarative specifications of process synchronization, real-time deadline recovery mechanisms, error recovery in asynchronous systems, streaming video for the web, real-time internet video distribution systems, object-oriented parallel processing operating systems, CORBA security architectures, and active spaces in ubiquitous and pervasive computing. He is a fellow of IEEE.

Peter Darch is an assistant professor in the School of Information Sciences at the University of Illinois at Urbana-Champaign. Prior to joining the iSchool at Illinois, he worked as a postdoctoral researcher in the UCLA Department of Information Studies and Center for Knowledge Infrastructures, with which he continues to collaborate on studies of the building, running, and effects of information infrastructures that support scientific collaboration. His dissertation for the DPhil in Computer Science from the University of Oxford addressed how scientists and software engineers in online citizen science projects manage members of the public to process and generate large datasets. Dr. Darch holds an MA in the History and Philosophy of Science and Medicine from Durham and an MMath in mathematics from the University of Oxford. He is particularly interested in the profound changes in the organization and conduct of contemporary scientific research that result from the interaction of technologies that afford collection of increasing quantities and types of scientific data with broader sociotechnical factors.

Rachel Fischer is a certified ethics officer and research officer at the African Centre of Excellence for Information Ethics at the Information Science Department, University of Pretoria. She comanages the communication and activities for this hub, which is central to the African Network on Information Ethics. She is also the cochair for the International Centre for Information Ethics, an academic community dedicated to the advancement of the field of information ethics. She completed her master's in Political Philosophy with the main focus on Greek Theater as a space for public and private political participation. Her research interests include information ethics, multilingualism, and exploring the spaces for intercultural dialogue.

Amelia Gibson studies health, wellness, and information practices and access in local communities and on the internet. She is particularly interested in the effects of place, space, power, and community on information worlds, information behavior, information needs, and information access. Her current work focuses on information poverty and marginalization, and how intersections of identity, place, space, and social and economic power/privilege influence information access and information behavior among young women of color and people with disabilities. Dr. Gibson is an assistant professor in the UNC School of Information and Library Science (SILS). She earned her PhD and MLIS from Florida State University in Tallahassee, and her AB from Dartmouth College in Hanover, New Hampshire. Prior to joining the SILS faculty, she was a research associate at the Information Use Management and Policy Institute, where she studied issues related to rural communities and e-government, and broadband adoption through community anchor institutions.

Ursula Gorham, PhD, JD, is a lecturer and codirector of the Master of Library and Information Science program in the College of Information Studies at the University of Maryland. She is admitted to practice law in Maryland and previously served as a law clerk in Maryland appellate and federal bankruptcy courts. Dr. Gorham's research spans the role of libraries in public policy and political processes; access to legal information and government information; and, collaborative efforts among libraries, community organizations, and government agencies to meet the information needs of underserved populations. Her research has been published in *Law Library Journal, Government Information Quarterly, Public Library Quarterly, Journal of Education for Library and Information Science, Journal of Open Access to Law, Information Polity,* and *First Monday.* Her first solo authored book—*Access to Information, Technology, and Justice: A Critical Intersection*—was published during the summer of 2017. In addition, she is an editor of *Library Quarterly.*

Kathrine Andrews Henderson was recently appointed as the business intelligence manager for Tech Launch Arizona at the University of Arizona. Prior to this January 2019 appointment, Kat served as a research analyst for LAC-Group. Her areas of expertise include legal and business research, intellectual property, and information ethics. She is a published author who, among other things, coauthored a chapter on hate speech in the Library Juice Press's *Handbook of Intellectual Freedom,* which was awarded the 2016 Eli M. Oboler Award for intellectual freedom from the American Library Association. Previously, Henderson, along with Elizabeth Buchanan, coauthored *Case Studies in Library and Information Ethics.* Henderson holds an undergraduate degree in Management from Arizona State University and a master's degree in Library and Information Science from the University of Wisconsin-Milwaukee (UWN). In 2017, Ms. Henderson was honored as one of 50 Distinguished Alumni from the School of Information Studies at UWM for her contributions to the field of library and information science.

Paul T. Jaeger, PhD, JD, is a professor, diversity and inclusion officer, and codirector of the Master of Library and Information Science program of the College of Information Studies and codirector of the Information Policy and Access Center at the University of Maryland (UMD). He is the author of more than 170 journal articles and book chapters, as well as 17 books. His research has been funded by the Institute of Museum and Library Services, the National Science Foundation, the American Library Association, the Smithsonian Institution, and the Bill and Melinda Gates Foundation, among others. Dr. Jaeger is an editor of *Library Quarterly,* the editor of *Advances in Librarianship,* and an associate editor of the *International Journal of Information, Diversity, and Inclusion.* He is founder and chair of the Conference on Inclusion and Diversity in Library and Information Science, and cofounder and cochair of the UMD Disability Summit. In 2014, he received the Library Journal/ALISE Excellence in Teaching Award.

Erin Klazar a freelance investigative researcher and certified ethics practitioner, focusing on corporate governance and ethical business practices in South Africa. She also works closely with academia in Information Ethics and Information Science, and is a part-time lecturer for the University of Pretoria in knowledge management and information ethics. The main focus of her master's degree in Information Technology was on the management of information systems in academic libraries in developing nations. She has completed multiple research papers on information ethical issues related to privacy and surveillance and the need for education in information ethics throughout all sectors. Her research interests include social justice and responsibility, ethics awareness, as well as educational programs supporting community engagement and development.

Imani Palmer is a recent PhD graduate in Computer Science from the University of Illinois at Urbana-Champaign. She has a profound passion for security and privacy research. Her key research focuses on science of security, applied hacking, and security education.

Dr. Palmer's current research focuses on improving the digital forensic analysis process through the application of artificial intelligence, data mining, and graph theory. She is also passionate about educating the future security workforce and conducts research in building effective security curriculums for K–12 and community college, undergraduate, and graduate programs.

Natalie Greene Taylor, PhD, is an assistant professor at the University of South Florida. Her research focuses on young people's access to information. More specifically, she studies youth information behavior, information intermediaries, and information policy as it affects youth information access. She is an editor of *Library Quarterly* and has published articles in *Government Information Quarterly, Information Polity, Information Retrieval Journal, International Journal of Public Administration in the Digital Age, Journal of Documentation, Journal of Information Science,* and *Public Library Quarterly,* among others. She has also coauthored two books: *Digital Literacy and Digital Inclusion: Information Policy and the Public Library* and *Libraries, Human Rights, and Social Justice: Enabling Access and Promoting Inclusion,* and coedited the book *Perspectives on Libraries as Institutions of Human Rights and Social Justice.*

Michael Zimmer, PhD, is a privacy and internet ethics scholar whose work focuses on digital privacy, internet research ethics, the ethical dimensions of social, mobile, and internet technologies, and libraries and privacy. He is an associate professor in the School of Information Studies at the University of Wisconsin-Milwaukee, where he also serves as director of the Center for Information Policy Research. Dr. Zimmer has published in numerous international academic journals and books, and has delivered talks across North America, Europe, and Asia. He has written for *Wired,* the *Washington Post,* and the *Huffington Post,* and has been a guest on National Public Radio's *All Things Considered, Morning Edition, Science Friday,* and *Here and Now* news programs. Dr. Zimmer has been featured in news articles in the *New York Times,* the *Wall Street Journal,* the *Associated Press,* the *Atlantic,* the *Chronicle of Higher Education,* and *GQ,* as well as MSNBC.com, CNN.com, and various other national and local media outlets. His research has been supported by the National Science Foundation, the Institute of Museum and Library Services, and the American Library Association.

Margaret Zimmerman completed a doctorate in Library and Information Science from the University of South Carolina. She also holds a master's degree in Information Systems and an MLIS with a concentration in digital libraries, both from Drexel University. She is currently an assistant professor with the Department of Library and Information Science at the University of Iowa. Her research areas of interest focus on the impact that information access, information literacy, and health literacy have in affecting the health and well-being of immigrant and refugee women currently residing in the United States. Dr. Zimmerman's recent research includes a comparative study between the health-seeking behaviors of women in Uganda and immigrant women in the United States, a literature review of work that examines the relationship between female literacy and maternal health outcomes, and a study on the reproductive health-related patterns of women who live in poverty. Currently, she is exploring the health information needs of immigrant and refugee women and working on creating measures to assess the health literacy of foreign-born women.

INDEX